The Russian art historian **Natalya Semenova** is author of *The Collector: The Story of Sergei Shchukin and His Lost Masterpieces*, co-author of *Collecting Matisse* and co-editor of *Selling Russia's Treasures*. The award-winning **Arch Tait** has translated over 30 books by leading Russian authors.

Further praise for *Mozorov*:

'What is clear to me . . . is the need we now have of that harmony, that tranquillity and joy, that Ivan Morozov sought and found in the paintings that, one way or another, he bequeathed to posterity.' Simon Wilson, *Royal Academy Magazine*

'This book is a tribute to the commitment of a patron of the arts and a timely warning about the arbitrary power of the state to destroy and mishandle material.' Alexander Adams, *Alexander Adams Art*

'The art historian Natalya Semenova, who told the story of Shchukin and his collection three years ago, now brings her expertise and narrative verve to the less well-known Morozov.' Lesley Chamberlain, *Times Literary Supplement*

'Semenova has performed a valuable service in telling us this entertaining story of how Morozov first brought [his collection] together . . . Something that all art lovers should be grateful for.' Martin Bentham, *Evening Standard*

# MOROZOV

## The Story of a Family
## and a Lost Collection

### NATALYA SEMENOVA

Translated by Arch Tait

YALE UNIVERSITY PRESS
NEW HAVEN AND LONDON

For information about this and other Yale University Press publications, please contact:
U.S. Office: sales.press@yale.edu      yalebooks.com
Europe Office: sales@yaleup.co.uk      yalebooks.co.uk

Set in Adobe Garamond Pro by IDSUK (DataConnection) Ltd
Printed in Great Britain by Clays Ltd, Elcograf S.p.A

Library of Congress Control Number: 2020941220

ISBN 978-0-300-24982-8 (hbk)
ISBN 978-0-300-26703-7 (pbk)

A catalogue record for this book is available from the British Library.

10 9 8 7 6 5 4 3 2 1

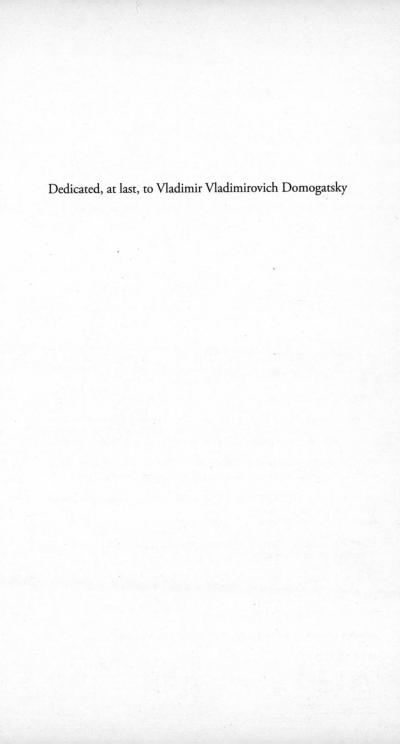

Dedicated, at last, to Vladimir Vladimirovich Domogatsky

Every sound man has, aside from his work, something else to which he devotes himself with a will. Let us call that something his avocation. Sometimes it takes over his life.

Vladimir Ryabushinsky

# CONTENTS

# CONTENTS

# ILLUSTRATIONS

## In text

### Plates

19. A bill received by Ivan Morozov from the Salon of the Golden Rune for the *Night Café* by van Gogh, 23 June 1908. Manuscript Department of the Pushkin Museum of Fine Arts.

20. Pablo Picasso, *Two Acrobats (Harlequin and his Companion)*, 1901. The Pushkin State Museum of Fine Arts, Moscow. © Succession Picasso/DACS, London 2020.

21. The Picasso wall at the State Museum of New Western Art, early 1930s. Courtesy of Collection Chtchoukine.

22. Works of European artists donated by Mikhail and Margarita Morozov on display in room 36 of the Tretyakov Gallery. Manuscript Department of the Tretyakov Gallery.

23. Pierre-Auguste Renoir, *Portrait of Jeanne Samary in a Low-Necked Dress*, 1877. The Pushkin State Museum of Fine Arts, Moscow.

24. Interior of GMNZI (the State Museum of New Western Art), 1932. Courtesy of Collection Chtchoukine.

25. Interior of GMNZI (the State Museum of New Western Art), 1932. Courtesy of Collection Chtchoukine.

26. The Bonnard and Vuillard room at the State Museum of New Western Art, 1933. Courtesy of Collection Chtchoukine.

27. Edouard Vuillard, *In the Room*, 1904. The Pushkin State Museum of Fine Arts, Moscow.

28. The former Music Salon (Denis Room) of Ivan Morozov's mansion, 1940s. Courtesy of Collection Chtchoukine.

29. A library of the USSR Academy of Arts in the former mansion of Ivan Morzov, late 1940s. Courtesy of Collection Chtchoukine.

# A NOTE ON THE TEXT

In the main part of the book, the system of transliteration is based on the Permanent Committee on Geographical Names (PCGN) system, with some simplifications made for the sake of readability. In the Notes and Bibliography, where Russian sources are cited, the Library of congress system for romanization of Russian without diacritics is followed. Throughout the book, names more familiar to readers in a different spelling have not been changed.

Dates in the book are complicated by the switch in calendars in Russia in the early twentieth century. In the nineteenth century there were twelve days' difference between the Orthodox Julian calendar used in Russia, and the Gregorian calendar that had been used in Europe and the rest of the world ever since Pope Gregory XIII's reforms in 1582. This increased to thirteen days in the twentieth century. The Gregorian calendar was adopted by Lenin's government on 31 January 1918, at which point the following day officially became 14 February. In this book, therefore, unless otherwise specified, dates regarding matters in Russia before 1918 are given in the Old Style, and thereafter and elsewhere in the New (Gregorian) Style.

# FOREWORD

Ivan Abramovich Morozov, one of the world's great art collectors, lived in Moscow at the beginning of the twentieth century. With works by Monet and Renoir, Cézanne and Picasso adorning its walls, his private home was a veritable museum of early masterpieces of modern French art. But, despite the astonishing grandeur of the collection Ivan Morozov carefully built up during his life, he was, for a long time, eclipsed by his friend and rival, Sergei Shchukin.

In the 1960s, paintings from the collections of the famous tandem of Shchukin and Morozov – by Monet, Renoir, Gauguin, Cézanne, van Gogh, Bonnard, Derain, Matisse and Picasso – began to be exhibited around the world. In the listings, seniority was prioritized over alphabetic order, and the name of Morozov, seventeen years Shchukin's junior, always came second. So they have remained. If someone says 'Shchukin', the reflex is to add 'and Morozov'. This has come about because their collections – so similar, yet at the same time very different – were both lost during the Russian Revolution. They were then merged, shuffled like a pack of cards, and split between two museums, one batch going to the Pushkin Museum of Fine Arts in Moscow and the other despatched to the State Hermitage Museum in Leningrad. In the process, the names of two of the greatest collectors of modernist art that graced the twentieth century were, for several decades, expunged.

Shchukin's name was, to a spectacular degree, restored with the 2016–17 exhibition of his collection at the Fondation Louis Vuitton in Paris, which attracted a record-breaking 1.25 million visitors – a triumphant success, which reinstated the collector with the unpronounceable Russian name in the history of twentieth-century culture. But Ivan Morozov, like his elder brother Mikhail, has remained in the shadows, with few in the West able to tell the brothers apart or distinguish them from their more famous uncle, Savva.

Fifteen years ago, Pierre Konowaloff, the great-grandson of Ivan Morozov, read my book about the life and collection of Sergei Shchukin and asked me to write about his great-grandfather. Leaving Pierre's tiny Parisian apartment on rue Boucicaut, I could not forget Morozov's tragic face looking out from a last photograph taken when he was already in exile. The sepia tones of the faded image made him appear terminally ill, and the disconsolate look in his eyes haunted me.

But how was the story of someone of whom all that remained was a sun-bleached photograph, two portraits and a single interview to be told? Mikhail, born barely a year before Ivan, had at least left behind books and reviews and featured in the fairly scathing memoirs of his contemporaries. For Ivan there was not a single letter which might have afforded a clue to his personality. There remained nothing but invoices, business documentation, and the catalogues of Parisian salons with laconic pencilled comments: 'not bad', 'unimportant', 'passable'. Even his correspondence with Henri Matisse and Maurice Denis read more like business memoranda, almost all of it mediated by the copperplate handwriting of the secretary of the director of the Tver Textile Mill Company.

Neither do we know what the rooms of the mansion-cum-museum on Prechistenka Street looked like. Apart from the Music Salon, decorated by

Maurice Denis, they were off limits to outsiders. Nor have any photographic portraits of Ivan Morozov survived. All we have are photos in which he appears in the midst of a throng of relatives. The precise date of his birth has only recently been established. Even the whereabouts of his grave was, for a long time, unknown. Happily, a birth certificate was found in an archive and, after many years of searching, his grave was discovered in a local cemetery. Over the years the marble had darkened. Today it is even difficult to decipher the Cyrillic lettering.

I nonetheless managed to produce two books about Morozov, but there still remained a great deal I did not know about his life and times. The challenge ensued, I returned once more to the history of my protagonist and, in the following pages, I have produced what I hope is the definitive life of this great collector.

Moscow, 2020

**Vasiliy Morozov**
serf peasant
(ancestor)

**Elisei Savvich Morozov**
(1798–1868)
merchant of the First Guild,
founder of the textile mill
later to become Nikolskoye
factory (1837)

**Zakhar Savvich Morozov**
(1802–57)
merchant of the First Guild
in Bogorodsk, founder of
the Bogorodsk-Glukhovo
Textile Mill Company (1855)

**Vikul Eliseevich Morozov**
(1829–94)
founder of the
Vikul Morozov and Sons
Company (1882)

**Ivan Zakharovich Morozov**
(1823–88)

**Abram Abramovich Morozov**
(1839–82)
co-owner of
the Tver Textile
Mill Company

=

**Varvara Alexeevna Morozova**
(*née* Khludova)
(1848–1917) later the civil
wife of Vasiliy Mikhailovich
Sobolevsky (1846–1913)

**Alexei Vikulovich Morozov**
(1857–1934)
co-owner of the
Vikul Morozov and
Sons Company,
art collector

**Ivan Vikulovich Morozov**
(1865–1933)
co-owner of
the Vikul
Morozov and
Sons Company

**Mikhail Abramovich Morozov**
(1870–1903)
co-owner of the Tver
Textile Mill Company,
art collector

=

**Margarita Kirillovna Morozova**
(*née* Mamontova)
(1873–1958)

**Yury Mikhailovich Morozov**
(1892–1918)

**Elena Mikhailovna Morozova**
(Klochkova, Yafimovich)
(1895–1951)

**Mikhail (Mika) Mikhailovich Morozov**
(1897–1952)
translator of Shakespeare

**Maria Mikhailovna Morozova**
(Fiedler)
(1904–64)
pianist

**Savva Vasilevich Morozov**
(Savva the First)
(1770–1860)
merchant of the First Guild,
founder of the textile
mills and dye-works

=

**Ulyana Afanasievna Morozova**
(1778–1861)

**Abram Savvich Morozov**
(1806–56)
owner of the Tver
Textile Mill Company

=

**Dariya Davidovna Morozova**
(*née* Shirokova)
(1812–88)

**Ivan Savvich Morozov**
(1812–64)
merchant of the
First Guild

**Timofei Savvich Morozov**
(1823–89)
owner of the Nikolskoye
Textile Mill Company

**David Abramovich Morozov**
(1843–93)
co-owner of the Tver
Textile Mill
Company

**Sergei Timofeevich Morozov**
(1860–1944)
director of the Nikolskoye
Textile Mill Company,
patron of the arts, founder of
the Moscow Crafts Museum

**Savva Timofeevich Morozov**
(Savva the Second)
(1862–1905)
co-owner of the Nikolskoye
Textile Mill Company,
patron of arts, shareholder
and director of the
Moscow Art Theatre

**Arseny Abramovich Morozov**
(1874–1908)
co-owner of the
Tver Textile
Mill Company

=

**Vera Sergeevna Morozova**
(*née* Fedotova,
later Naval)
(1883–1944)

**Ivan Abramovich Morozov**
(1871–1921)
co-owner of the Tver
Textile Mill Company,
art collector

=

**Evdokiya (Dosya) Sergeevna Morozova**
(*née* Kladovshchikova)
(1885–1959)

**Evdokiya (Little Dosya) Ivanovna Morozova**
(Konowaloff, Lesca)
(1903–74)

**Pierre Konowaloff**
(b. 1953)

**Jean (Ivan Sergeevich) Konowaloff**
(1922–2002)

# CHAPTER I

## Sketches for a Portrait

In the spring of 1920, a year before his death, Ivan Morozov gave an interview to the French art critic, Félix Fénéon.[1] It was a year since the famous collector had left Soviet Russia and he had only recently arrived in Switzerland, where Fénéon, the former art director of the Parisian Bernheim-Jeune Gallery, met his old acquaintance. As Fénéon writes:

Last June [1919], together with his wife, daughter and a niece, Ivan Morozov left Russia (where he had resided without respite for five and a half years) to settle in Switzerland – Interlaken, Ouchy, Lausanne . . . We are finally to learn the fate of his collection. With his very first words he reassures us:

'The collection is unharmed. None of the 430 Russian works, none of the 240 French paintings have suffered.[2] The collection is still in the palace where I assembled it and whose walls are decorated with Bonnard's *Spring* and *Autumn* and the *Story of Psyche* by Maurice Denis. It has been nationalized, however, just like my factories, and is now called the Second Museum of Western Art.'

'The second? . . . What is the first?'

'It is the French collection of our mutual friend, Sergei Shchukin, and is now being looked after by his daughter, Ekaterina Keller.'

'And what about you? Do you still have control over the Second Museum?'

'The state has appointed as its – how do you translate *zaveduiushchii*? – as its manager (you would say, "director" or "curator") the sculptor Boris Ternovets, who studied with Bourdelle, and it appointed me assistant manager, allocating me three rooms to live in. The rest of the accommodation is open to the public. The government has just extended my own system. During the Tsarist period I gave open access on Sunday mornings to anyone who was curious and, with a minimum of formalities, artists and critics could visit me on the other days, except Mondays.[3]

'As assistant manager I was required to help compile a catalogue raisonné, and even talked a little to visitors about the paintings. Ekaterina Sergeevna [Shchukin's daughter] performed the same function in her father's museum. We were pleased to be able to celebrate your country's art: the paintings were there as confirmation of what we were saying, and the audience listened attentively.'

'As you have been in such direct contact with these people, Ivan Abramovich, can you tell me which of our painters most appealed to your compatriots?'

'Cézanne. I was able to provide eight pieces of testimony to his genius:[4] two of his paintings of Mont Sainte-Victoire, the *Jeune fille au piano*, a *Jas de Bouffan*, a portrait of his wife, and so on. You know them all, or nearly all. Van Gogh was also much admired. Derain also, and Picasso, but I owned only three of his canvases. That Spaniard and Henri Matisse are much more fully represented in Sergei Shchukin's collection.'

'You have mentioned the names of several French painters in your museum. Could you kindly complete the list?'

'Degas, Camille Pissarro, Gauguin (a dozen works, mostly of Polynesia), Lebourg, Simon, Henri-Edmond Cross, Maillol (four statues and seven statuettes), K.-X. Roussel, Vuillard, Louis Valtat, Lebasque, Marquet, Puy, Guérin, Espagnat, Vlaminck, Flandrin, Friesz, Chabaud, Herbin, I am omitting some which are far from negligible, but if I do not mention Seurat it is not because of a lapse of memory: there is that lacuna in my collection.'

'And in the Russian section of the collection, whom do you have?'

'Whom? Well, to start with those who are dead: Vrubel, Levitan, Serov, Sapunov; then Malyavin, Korovin, Vinogradov, Golovin, Somov, Benois, Igor Grabar, Kuznetsov, Larionov, Natalya Goncharova, Mashkov, Kuprin, Konchalovsky, Chagall, and others.'

'Obviously in this era of the dictatorship of the proletariat your artist compatriots must be unable to function.'

'The government views them as workers who are meeting a positive need, and for the artists it is a means of subsistence. An association has been formed under the chairmanship of Tatlin, and the far-left artists cluster around that. Among its most active members I would name Mashkov and the painter Dymshits-Tolstaya.[5] This committee is in some ways analogous to your Société des Artistes Indépendants: it has no admissions panel, gives no awards, but it enjoys generous government subsidies to pay for exhibitions and acquisitions. In Moscow, during the winter of 1918–19 – my last in the capital – at least ten exhibitions of left-wing artists were organized, each showcasing artists of related trends. The most interesting among them, in addition to Mashkov and Tatlin, seemed to me to be Kuprin, Kuznetsov, Konchalovsky, Krymov, Chagall and Falk. Artists on the right have set up a committee of their own, but it is stagnating because the public authorities are wholly indifferent to it. Many avant-garde painters – and again I instance Tatlin and Mashkov – have got themselves appointed as academics. The old professors continue their apostolic work in parallel and, my goodness, their lectures are absolutely packed because students are entirely free to choose their teachers. In Russia, as elsewhere, the mass of the students gravitate towards academic routine.

'Some adventurous young artists have decamped to the provinces – Saratov, Vyatka, and so on – in order to create centres of artistic propaganda. This has sometimes represented a risk for Museum No. 2. I encountered one emissary from the provinces who, arguing that his town did not have a single Cézanne or Derain, had come to Moscow to requisition one, on the grounds that we had a surplus. To defend the integrity of the museum against his claim I had to appeal, successfully, to the authority of Igor Grabar, the artist and art historian and right-hand man of Madame Trotskaya.'[6]

'Trotsky's wife? Is she actually involved?'

'She is in charge of a committee whose preoccupations can best be explained by an example. In more than one location in the Republic there were grounds to fear that rioting or troop movements might compromise the security of paintings, statues, or religious or secular items of historical, documentary or aesthetic value. At the request of the owner, or officially, if the owner was negligent or had abandoned his residence, Madame Trotskaya's committee brought them, with the assistance of competent commissions, to Moscow, where they were professionally assessed by scholars and officially exhibited. Completely unexpected treasures came to light.'

'Is all this activity due to the initiative of the citizen or of the state?'

'Let us say that it is done, if you will, on private initiative, but often prompted, and always facilitated, by Lunacharsky and his acolytes.'

'Lunacharsky the minister?'

'Yes, the People's Commissar for Enlightenment and the Arts.'

'He failed, at the very least, to stop the muzhiks in Petrograd fashioning themselves boots out of the Rembrandts in the Hermitage.'

'The muzhiks are not so impractical. No, nothing so unfortunate took place in any museum, either in Petrograd or anywhere else. The main works in the Hermitage had already been sent to Moscow at that time, now long past, when Petrograd was expected to be captured. They are waiting in the Kremlin to be sent back.[7] Similar precautions were taken by the Louvre in 1914 and 1918.'

'But in Moscow . . . what about the Tretyakov Museum?'

'It has nothing to complain about. Its catalogue was sketchy and incomplete. Its new director, Igor Grabar, whose name I have already mentioned, has significantly improved it. It includes comprehensive details of the size of the paintings, the surface, the media; the signatures have been scrutinized and, in an undoubted excess of zeal, their length is being registered. Archival research and examination of the originals has made it possible to correct attributions, to identify many subjects, and to establish dates reliably. All this was difficult because of the diversity of the elements which make up the Tretyakov Gallery.'

'Please explain.'

'They come from two brothers of that name, flax spinners. One, Sergei,[8] collected Russian paintings, while the other, Pavel, collected Western art, primarily landscapes by your great painters of the 1830s (Corot, Rousseau, Dupré, et al.). These were supplemented in 1910 by the legacy of Mikhail Morozov, which included a Manet (the sketch for the *Cabaret de Reichshoffen*, which Manet painted twice),[9] a Renoir (the full-length portrait of Jeanne Samary which the *Bulletin de la vie artistique* of 1 January reproduced but attributed to my collection), a Monet, two Gauguins, a Carrière, a Van Gogh, a Bonnard and a Denis.'

'Were you and Mikhail Morozov related?'

'Closely. He was my brother, one year older than me. I was born in 1871. He died in 1904[10] at the age of thirty-three. He wrote a number of books, including *The Life of Charles V*, and published art criticism and letters from Egypt in journals. When we were growing up we took lessons together from Korovin, once a week for two years.'

'So you are a painter!'

'Oh, hardly. In 1892, 1893 and 1894 I was a student at the Polytechnic in Zurich, and when I got tired of drawing plans I painted landscapes on Sundays in oils. I haven't held a paintbrush since. I know too much about painting to attempt it.'

'But now that you have more free time and are not troubled by rheumatism . . .?'

'Perhaps I'll think about it,' Ivan Abramovich says with a smile. 'You'll need to give me the address of someone who sells oil paints.'

It is no easy matter to sketch a portrait of Ivan Morozov. As Abram Efros, an art critic who knew him well, put it, he seemed to walk 'surrounded by silence', unlike his fellow art collector Sergei Shchukin who walked 'surrounded by commotion'.[11] Very few memoirists have reminisced about our hero: he was just too private and shunned the limelight. It is understandable that he wanted to screen his private life from prying eyes, concealing the fact of his marriage to a cabaret singer and pretending his illegitimate daughter was his niece.

The desire to obscure the truth of relations somewhat ran in the family. The Morozovs' spectacular ascent to the summit of Moscow's mercantile Olympus as founders of what would become the magnificent Tver Textile Mill Company had, by the end of the nineteenth century, become so encrusted with myth and legend that it is now all but impossible to separate truth from fiction. The family lived in fashionable mansions, and spent vast amounts of money on all manner of caprices. The most famous representative of the family name today, Savva Timofeevich Morozov – Savva the Second, in our tale – graduated in natural science from Moscow University, went to study chemistry at Cambridge University, donated money to the Bolsheviks, and later became famous for granting 300,000 rubles to Konstantin Stanislavsky to fund the Moscow Art Theatre. But our story concerns his nephew, Ivan, the second of the three sons of Abram Abramovich Morozov and his wife Varvara Khludova. Ivan's elder brother, Mikhail, was much talked about for his palatial residence on Smolensk Boulevard, his very beautiful wife, and his marked eccentricity. The younger brother, Arseny, had a passion for hunting and owned a Moorish-style castle on Vozdvizhenka Street, at the sight of which his mother exclaimed crossly that now it would be clear to anyone who was anyone in Moscow that her son was an idiot. Many were inclined, however, to see the roots of the Morozov brothers' quirkiness in the personality of Varvara herself: the Khludov traits in her sons seem clearly to have prevailed over those of their father and the Morozovs.

The members of this powerful family had no inclination to dwell on the ancestral origins of their clan, and firmly refused to talk about their founding father. For the last thing they wanted was to be reminded that the patriarch of the glorious Morozov dynasty, their great-grandfather Vasily Morozov, had been sold like a domestic animal by his owner. Mr Vsevolozhsky, landowner, had sold to Mr Ryumin, collegiate counsellor and gentleman, land, together with the structures thereon, and also a few dozen serfs, including Vasily Morozov and his entire family. Vasily was a peasant from the village of Zuyevo, a fisherman; but his son, Savva the First, rather than fish alongside him, went into business.

At that time, sons of peasants faced twenty-five years of compulsory army service – not a prospect twenty-year-old Savva particularly relished. The owner of the factory where Savva worked as a weaver, Fedor Kononov, lent his industrious worker 1,500 rubles to buy himself out; fortunately, Peter the Great's decree allowing payment in lieu of recruitment extended to all classes, including serfs. Many a serf who had thus escaped the soldier's lot would just have drunk himself silly in celebration and there his story would have ended. Savva Morozov, however, was made of sterner stuff. His wife Ulyana, a peasant from a neighbouring village, brought her husband a modest dowry but, more importantly, her family's secrets for dyeing fabrics. These enabled Savva to pay back his debt in a matter of two years.

Why, then, should he not start a business himself? Plucking up courage, Savva began producing silk lace, with which peasant women were delighted to trim their traditional sarafan dresses. In 1798 the first child of Savva and Ulyana, Elisei, was born, and, by the time their fourth son appeared, Morozov's workshop, employing twenty workers, was annually producing silk goods worth over 1,000 rubles. The 1812 war against Napoleon contributed not only to the beautification of a rebuilt Moscow but also to the prosperity of the Morozov business. Thanks to the inhabitants of the old capital and their desire to look elegant and fashionable, Savva Morozov was able to earn sufficient money to liberate his entire family, including his aged father. He paid the landowner the colossal sum of 17,000 rubles in cash.[12]

The Morozovs were Old Believers, and lived according to Holy Scripture. 'Except the Lord build the house, they labour in vain that build it' (Psalm 126). The Lord did, no doubt, lend a hand, but shortages after the war with Napoleon also helped. There was a great demand for fabrics, and especially for linen and the cotton Savva Morozov was still producing at his first factory. The legend that the nimble merchant left his village at dawn and was in Moscow by dusk is just that: the most fleet-footed walker would have taken at least two days to put those 60 miles behind him, assuming he carried no baggage. What we do know is that, year by year, the enterprising Savva grew richer, not only arousing envy, but also gaining the respect of his entire neighbourhood, which was a rare achievement. His fellow villagers entrusted to him for safekeeping the rubles they had earned by the sweat of their brow, knowing he would look after the money well.[13] Savva did not, however, merely store the peasants' money, but invested it, without taking a single kopeck for himself in commission. If the Morozovs had been

1 Representatives of four branches of the Morozov clan. From left to right, Abram Abramovich, Timofei Savvich, Ivan Zakharovich (?) and Vikul Eliseevich, mid-1860s.

ennobled, their family motto could justly have been 'Honesty and Diligence'. It is said that Timofei, the youngest son of Savva the First, born in 1823 and a merchant of the First Guild, travelled the expanses of Russia quite without cash, concluding his deals on the basis of the Morozov word of honour.

By the start of Alexander II's reign in 1855, Savva the First was considered the largest producer of high-quality cotton yarn in Russia. His sons too were enjoying success in the textile industry. When the elder sons,

Elisei and Zakhar,[14] split off and began running their own business, the youngest, Timofei, became the main force driving his father's enterprise. The middle brothers, Ivan and Abram, were also involved in the company, but showed no great aptitude for commerce and remained in secondary positions.

The Morozovs had by then been living in Moscow for some time, and had settled in the Rogozha quarter, today the district of Nikoloyamsky Street. As early as 1825 the head of the family had established a manual weaving mill, modest for the times, with only 200 looms. Savva went on to acquire the adjacent two-storey stone-built house and garden, and over the next thirty years tirelessly increased his Moscow property holdings: today's Shelaputin Lane should in all justice be renamed Morozov Lane. At the same time Savva was buying up plots of land in Vladimir province, where the main Morozov enterprise, the Nikolskoye factory, would shortly be built. On his father's instructions, Timofei, Savva's right-hand man, began buying land for a new factory in the neighbouring Tver province.

The statute of the Tver factory was to be approved in 1859, when Timofei's brother, Abram, was no longer alive. Abram's sons, twenty-year-old Abram Abramovich and his younger brother, David Abramovich, became full directors of the Savva Morozov and Sons Trading Company, established in 1860. Timofei signed the minutes of the first general meeting of shareholders on behalf of his father because Savva, the founder of a vast textile empire, could neither read nor write.

The second generation of the Morozov clan was also less than brilliantly educated, but all the brothers studied the Bible. This was particularly true of Abram. Like most of the Morozovs, he and his wife, Dariya, belonged to the Old Believer sect, and gave their sons Old Testament names. Son David inherited his mother's piety. He married the daughter of an extremely wealthy Moscow furrier, and built an almshouse and refuge bearing his own name on the site of the factory his grandfather had founded in Shelaputin Lane. When his father,

## 4) Т-во Тверской м-ры бумажныхъ издѣлій.

Оживленіе промышленнаго движенія въ Россіи вслѣдъ за окончаніемъ Крымской войны, а съ другой стороны—по случаю открытой между Мо-

Абрамъ Абрамовичъ
Морозовъ.

Варвара Алексѣевна
Морозова урож. Хлудова.

сквою и Петербургомъ, нынѣ Петроградомъ, Николаевской жел. дор., вызвало въ концѣ пятидесятыхъ годѣ москов фактурныхъ никовъ потре удобныхъ мѣ постройки выхъ хлопча фабрикъ на ленномъ ра сквы, съ бо вымъ топли чими людьми, Москвой.

Иванъ Абрамовичъ
Морозовъ.

годахъ, когда ло построено нашихъ ману

довъ въ срескихъ манупромышленбность искать стностей для своихъ паротобумажныхъ болѣе отдадіусѣ отъ Молѣе дешевомъ и рабочемъ подъ Въ 1856—8 именно и большинство фактурныхъ

фабрикъ и по нынѣ существующихъ, небольшой группой московскихъ мануф. промышленниковъ и торговцевъ въ лицѣ С.-М. Шибаева,

2  Owners of the Tver Textile Mill Company: Abram Abramovich, Varvara Alexeevna and Ivan Abramovich Morozov, 1915.

Abram Savvich, died, David's mother, Dariya, became a nun and ended her days on earth in a nunnery under the name of Deborah.

David's brother, Abram Abramovich, was less devout and not particularly enterprising, but did become chairman of the board of directors of the Tver Textile Mill Company.[15] The brothers came into full possession of the Tver factory only in 1871, when their grandfather's legacy was finally shared out. Their Uncle Timofei ceased involving himself in managing it and concentrated solely on the Nikolskoye factory.[16] That same year Abram and his young wife Varvara had a second son, Ivan.

# CHAPTER II

# Varvara Khludova

The life of Varvara Morozova, née Khludova, has all the elements of the plot of a play: a setting of the scene, a complication, peripeteias, a climax, a dénouement and an epilogue. A young girl from Moscow's merchant district of Zamoskvorechiye, kind-hearted by nature albeit independent and emphatic, has dreams of dedicating herself to a noble cause. 'I often have a sense that I am not altogether an ordinary being and that I absolutely must distinguish myself in some extraordinary manner, by saving my fatherland, for example, and so on,' she notes in her diary.[1]

One of Moscow's foremost beauties, young Varvara goes to balls and flirts with would-be suitors, but to her diary she confides: 'How ridiculous it is to pay attention to every young man, to show off to him, to try to please and even to fall in love with him. That is what every woman does nowadays, but it is not only out of pride and vanity that I want to be different: there is something in my head. Would it not be better to live my life the way I dream of living it now? That is, to remain a maid, because marriage seems simply dire. I know I could never be happy in marriage, unable to fulfil my desires independently, to do good . . . By

13

willpower and using my intelligence I can realize my plans . . . I would like to pay no attention to men, and yet it is so tempting to look at them and to be liked, first by one, then by another.'[2]

'If I were in good hands I could become a good human being . . . I want to live decently, if not really well . . . to help the poor to the best of my ability, not to squander money.' Such is the aspiration of Varvara Khludova, wealthy debutante. She wants to do something useful with her life. 'This is how I would like to spend it: firstly, never to get married, to give music and French lessons to children, and help the poor with those earnings because I will have no need of them.'[3]

Varvara Khludova had no one to share her feelings with and could confide them only to her diary. 'I don't even have a friend . . . I'm too hot-headed and, over the years, I fear that will probably become more pronounced,' Varvara writes, as if foreseeing her future.

Her mother died, and from the age of six the little girl was brought up by a nanny and a governess. For all that, she considered she had had a happy childhood. Her father adored her and her older brothers thought she was wonderful. Young Varvara might have gone on to live her life much like other girls, but when she was sixteen or so the merchant's daughter noticed injustice being done all around her and became pensive. She began reading books, often without her father's knowledge. By chance she came upon *Sovremennik*,[4] a journal popular in those years, and reading it she 'developed a hatred of evil and attraction to what was honourable, noble and exalted'. It awakened 'a desire to endure suffering and ordeals'. Instead of reading novels for entertainment, the merchant's daughter secretly studied critical articles of 'the incomparable Belinsky'. 'We really must progress, at least a little. You cannot just read Belinsky and leave it at that. I have fallen in love with him, although I have only ever seen his portrait, in which he is not at all handsome. That is how important his intelligence is!'[5]

Her first disillusionment was with her beloved father, for whom his loving daughter's admiration gradually ebbed away: 'I consider Papa almost perfect, and if he were just a little more educated I would consider him perfect.' A much more severe assessment appears a few months later: 'I too am becoming a hero. I advance my little self to rebuff what is bad, which for me is personified by my father. These domestic squabbles drive me to distraction. They are just frightful.'[6]

This overweening tyrant, her father Alexei Khludov, was the son of a humble weaver and co-owner of A. and G., Sons of Ivan Khludov. Varvara's grandfather, Ivan Khludov, wove belts and silk sashes for coachmen on a handloom in his village in Ryazan province before, just like Savva Morozov the First, becoming a merchant and moving in 1817 to Moscow. In 1845 his sons, merchants of the First Guild, built a factory in the city of Egorievsk on the banks of the River Guslyanka, and there 300 workers on 15,000 spindles produced 2,200 pounds of yarn per day. Alexei Khludov travelled to Liverpool, and the brothers brought back with them machinery and specialists in the trade. He firmly told his wife, who was urging him not to get involved in such a risky enterprise, 'Our decision is irrevocable: we shall either be rich men or we will go a-begging.'[7] The Khludov brothers were soon rich men. In the early 1870s the Egorievsk Cotton-Spinning Mill, one of the first in Russia, was producing some 36,000 pounds of yarn every day.

Alexei Khludov built his Yartsevo factory near Smolensk, equipping it with the latest machinery. He married young, at the age of eighteen, and just eighteen years later became a widower. He was left with seven children in a huge, three-storey house in Khomutovka Close, later renamed Khludov Close. The ideal successor for the family business was Alexei's eldest and favourite son, Ivan. He studied at the College of Saints Peter and Paul in St Petersburg, where he learned German, and went to study for a time in Bremen. After graduating, Ivan travelled to England, and then set off to study cotton production across the Atlantic. The timing of his trip was unfortunate, because the American Civil War had broken out. Ivan returned from North America unscathed, but without managing to get a deal with the Americans to supply cotton directly, cutting out intermediaries. At this time the Khludovs became interested in Central Asia, and Ivan, eager to stay ahead of the competition, travelled to Turkestan, only to die of a fever in Samarkand.

Having lost his prime candidate, Alexei Khludov was in a quandary over who should inherit the millions he had built up. He decided to bet on Mikhail. This was not an easy decision to make: this son was a daredevil and hell-raiser. The adjutant of General Skobelev, he participated in the capture of Tashkent and Kokand. Mikhail Khludov liked to throw his money about and led a fairly eccentric life. Another son, Vasily, was the exact opposite. He graduated from the natural science and medical faculties of Moscow University, attended a course of lectures in chemistry at Heidelberg University, spoke three foreign languages, travelled the length and breadth of Europe, played the piano admirably, and improvised on an organ ordered from Germany (which was subsequently donated to the Moscow Conservatory). Vasily had broad interests, and studied metallurgy, experimental medicine, biology, endocrinology, horticulture, theoretical mechanics and astronomy. And yet, despite his dazzling education, he was hopeless at business. This enraged his successful father, who considered him wholly unsuitable to inherit his business empire. Eventually, however, no longer able to condone the drunken revelry and general misconduct of Mikhail, Alexei Khludov changed his will in favour of the hapless Vasily, cursed Mikhail and threw him out of the family home.

At this point Mikhail Khludov's sister decided to intercede for her favourite brother, promising her father that, if he forgave Mikhail, she would marry Abram Morozov, who had long been vainly seeking her hand in marriage. It is far from clear that Mikhail was deserving of such a sacrifice. He forged his father's signature on promissory notes, but that was the least of it: he killed his beautiful wife, admittedly by accident, when she drank the poisoned coffee he had readied for his brother Vasily. The blustering Khlynov in Ostrovsky's *The Ardent Heart* is Khludov down to a tee, and he was indeed the prototype for the wheeler-dealer in the play: 'Khlynov has a lot of money and he finds life boring, because he hasn't a clue how to spend it enjoyably . . . He lives in a country dacha now, out in his woods, and has just about everything anyone could have! He's put numerous arbours and fountains in the park and spends his time sitting on the balcony. He's drinking champagne from first thing in the morning. There are throngs of people around the house, all of them just gawping at him. And when he gives orders for them to be allowed into the park to see all the weird things he's been up to there, he has the paths watered with champagne. It's not life on this earth, it's paradise!'[8]

One of Mikhail's relatives gave this description of him: 'Mikhail Khludov was a pathological individual. No matter where he lived, he left behind legends of derring-do on an epic scale. In spite of his insane drinking sprees and the outrages he perpetrated, something gleamed through that people found attractive . . . His limitless courage and immoderate physical strength, which he employed solely for his own gratification, astounded everyone.'[9] Mikhail was quite likely to appear in front of his guests 'blacked up', or as a semi-naked Roman gladiator. He did possess a tiger. At night he would tether the animal to an iron ring in an arbour because, when the worse for wear, he liked to sleep in the open. The Khludovs had an extensive garden, so they did not even have to retreat to the countryside in the summer.

In the hope that her Papa, despite his manifest arbitrariness, might nevertheless give in to her request, Varvara Khludova became engaged to Abram Morozov. 'I have resolved to sacrifice myself, but will I have sufficient strength of will and stamina to endure the dreadful fate awaiting me? . . . Farewell to my youth, farewell to my happiness! Soon I shall cease to live for myself and will embark on a life for others . . . Papa wants this marriage. Well, I consent. Shall I be happy with A.A.? Hardly, I think! I shall try, nevertheless, to be a good and honest woman,' she writes in her diary.[10]

Very soon, however, she began to repent her high-mindedness. 'When everyone had departed, I became quite despondent. I saw clearly that the sacrifice was more than I could bear, and indeed I doubt if anyone is possessed of the strength it would call for . . . There have been times when I have been tempted to fling myself out of the window.' Varvara hurriedly wrote to her fiancé to say she had changed her mind. Somebody witnessed Abram Morozov reading the letter twice over and turning as white as a sheet: he truly was head over heels in love with her. Varvara, for her part, had few illusions about Abram Morozov: compared with her, he was a complete dunce. She did her best to be charitable. 'A.A. said this time that he sympathizes with the poor, and that he has read something. That cheered me.' She herself was reading a lot, playing the piano, studying French, going to the theatre, and visiting exhibitions. The only redeeming feature she could find in Morozov was his wealth. 'Does it really make any difference whom you marry? This one is at least rich, so I won't have to plead to get some sad little house for myself, or tremble for the fate of my children,' she reflects.

Behind all her agonizing and sacrifices, her consents and refusals, loomed the figure of her ruthless Papa who was eager, in the furtherance of his business interests, to intermarry at all costs with the Morozovs. Money to money. One of his relatives said bluntly, 'They want to get a good price for the girl.' After her father, Varvara's uncle started trying to talk her round, but she told him she would prefer to become a nun than to marry. 'I have found this saga morally beneficial . . . I have seen that I am a better fighter than I had supposed. I have seen clearly that I behave with greater courage and nobility than others,' she notes proudly in her diary. Her displeased father, meanwhile, sought to humiliate his recalcitrant daughter in every way possible, forbidding her to order dresses, or indeed to buy anything at all without his permission. 'He has sometimes been on the verge of striking me, and I have decided that if he continues in this way, or if he does hit me, then I shall leave his house and earn a living by my own efforts,' Varvara wrote, noting that she had cried at dinner, then gone up to her room and read a book on public education by Laboulaye.[11] She wondered how she could earn a livelihood and was attracted by the notion of becoming an actress, as she seemed to be unqualified for anything else.

After several months of being locked up, however, Varvara was assailed by doubts and wondered if she was making a mistake. 'Sitting locked in here with a father whose primary ambition is to sell his daughter as profitably as he possibly can, while spending as little time as possible at home – or to live . . . with a brother who, they say, captures cities and then cries about how servile and shameful everything is, while not lifting a finger to bring about change?' Perhaps marriage would be a better option than living such a life.

At the theatre she encountered Abram Morozov who was a shadow of his former self and who went pale at the mere sight of her. 'From the looks he kept giving me I could tell that he has not yet completely ceased to care about me.' At a dance party Morozov was constantly gazing passionately at the beautiful Mademoiselle Khludova. 'While I was dancing, A.A. was following me about like a shadow and kept watching and looking at me.' Three days later, at a ball at her uncle's, the same thing occurred. 'A.A. kept ogling me. He is repulsive . . . he stood in the doorway the whole time devouring me with his eyes. I made a point of flirting . . .'

Varvara Khludova chose the lesser of two evils. 'I even think it would be better to be married to A.A. than to continue leading such an abominable existence . . . I think I am going to do it!! Well, so be it!' She did decide to do it but then, three days before the wedding, locked herself in her room and cried and cried. She agonized up to the last minute. On the way to the ceremony she flung her engagement ring from the carriage, overlooking the detail that a wedding ring awaited her at the church.

What conditions did twenty-one-year-old Varvara Khludova impose on her husband-to-be? We know that because, in her diary, she ponders the role of woman. 'I shall give him my consent, but warn him about my views, about which I care a great deal . . . No, a woman can do a lot of things besides being married. She can support the poor not only materially, but also morally. She is better able to give them guidance, help them to see reason. Men are too crass for that. A woman is much gentler and more patient!!!! But will I be able to do all that while fulfilling the duties of a woman? It is hard to know that. At present I am not yet living. My present life is no more than a prelude to real life.'[12]

In 1869 Varvara Khludova married Abram Morozov. Next year she gave birth to a son, who was named in honour of the brother who had been cursed by her father and whose nephew, the newborn Mikhail Abramovich Morozov, was, incidentally, to resemble him remarkably in character. In 1871 a second son, Ivan, was born, and Abram Abramovich became chairman of the board of directors of the Tver Textile Mill Company. In 1874 Arseny was born, and her husband gave Varvara shares in the company. For the moment she had only five shares, but within ten years she had 594. In 1881 Varvara's husband was taken seriously ill and, at his wife's request, was certified as having dementia and diagnosed as 'suffering from progressive paralysis'.

Abram had an agonizing death. His brain was affected (as a result of syphilis) and he completely lost his mental faculties. One person claims that he had been ill for five years, another says the illness lasted for two. He had a difficult personality, possibly owing to the onset of disease, but he idolized his wife and wrote her touching, tender letters, albeit with atrocious spelling. Mindful of how important her charitable work was to his wife, he left her a full half million rubles in his will. Varvara never was able to truly love her husband, but stayed with him to his last breath because she regarded marriage as a sacrament. 'My husband has a fixed abode in Moscow and that is where he presently resides and will reside, surrounded by his family, with me and in my care,' Varvara Morozova wrote in a submission to the Moscow Family Court.[13] Abram Morozov died on 25 February 1882, in the forty-third year of his life.

'Matrimony', the first act of her drama, ends on a tragic note. The second, main act begins: the real life of Varvara Morozova, owner of the factories of the Tver Textile Mill Company, where thousands of workers weave muslin, chintz and velvet.

Abram Morozov had been treated by Sergei Korsakov, a doctor at the Preobrazhensky Psychiatric Hospital who was later to found the Moscow school of psychiatry. Korsakov was opposed to the contemporary harsh regime of psychiatric hospitals and supported non-compulsion in the treatment of the mentally ill. He advocated that people unfortunate enough to suffer from mental illness should be kept under supervision at home. Varvara Morozova wholly concurred with his approach and, upon the death of her husband, notified the rector of

3 Abram Abramovich Morozov, 1870.

Moscow University that she proposed to build a clinic for the mentally ill. She allocated 150,000 rubles for the purpose from the half million bequeathed by her husband, 'for the welfare of the poor, the arrangement and maintenance of schools, almshouses and care institutions and for donations to the church'. The A.A. Morozov Psychiatric Clinic for the Mentally Ill opened in 1887. Needless to say, when the Bolsheviks came to power it was renamed, like everything that had been built with the Morozovs' money, and became the Korsakov Clinic.

Half a million rubles for charitable purposes proved not to go all that far: there was the 150,000 rubles for the psychiatric clinic on Malaya Pirogov Street, the same amount for a vocational school for the poor, and the rest went on minor works. Ten thousand was donated to the Rogozha Primary School for Girls, 50,000 to the Ivan Turgenev Reading Room, to Zemstvo and village schools, an asylum for those suffering from nervous ailments and, finally, the Morozov Cancer Institute on Devichie Field, charitable institutions in Tver, and a tuberculosis sanatorium for workers. 'She was a good woman. She helped people suffering hardship and tried to do good. She was the richest person in the parish and everyone turned to her for help, either directly or . . . through the priest. She would give money, or cloth for a dowry for poor girls. Or a cow if there was an outbreak of cattle disease,' a peasant from the village next to her estate at Popovka recalled. People looked forward to the mistress's visits, hastening to open the village gate for the landowner's horse and trap in return for a coin or a sweet from the hands of her ladyship.[14]

Varvara Morozova was every inch the liberal philanthropist and, in accordance with long-standing merchant tradition, donated solely to the healing or instruction of the common people. She belonged to every conceivable society, and was a member of various institutions, from the Association of Governesses and Schoolmistresses to the Society for the Relief of Minors Released from Places of Detention. Elementary education classes and vocational schools, hospitals, charitable maternity units and almshouses were named after her. 'Madame V.A. Morozova' was incised on the pediment of one of the buildings of the Shanyavsky People's University, and she gave 50,000 rubles to the Institute of Chemistry. She also donated 2,000 rubles to the three-storey building of the Prechistenka Workers' Courses in Kursovoy Lane, which opened in 1897. The philanthropic millionairess can hardly have been aware that the college her funds were paying for (and which in 1919 was renamed the Nikolai Bukharin Workers' Faculty) was an illegal Bolshevik headquarters.[15]

The Craft Museum was awarded 3,000 rubles.[16] A substantial sum was donated to assist the emigration to Canada of the Dukhobor Christians. Leo Tolstoy was a sympathizer and Varvara visited him in his house in Moscow. People seeking financial assistance for purely cultural initiatives remote from the needs of the common people were invariably disappointed. For example, 'with a cold, amiable smile' she refused Stanislavsky point blank when he came seeking money for his new theatre. The founders of the Moscow Art Theatre held that against her for many years. The situation was saved by her late husband's uncle, Savva Morozov the Second. Varvara Morozova did, however, offer the City Duma a public reading room in Moscow in honour of Ivan Turgenev. Turgenev was not only the author of fashionable novels, but also drew up the programme of the Society for the Advancement of Literacy and Education. Varvara initially financed the building of the first free library and reading room in Russia, and then paid for it to be stocked with books. It opened its doors on Myasnitsky Gate Square in 1885.[17]

Varvara realized the dreams of her youth in full measure. The final chord was her will. Factory-owning Madame Morozova, who was represented in Soviet history books as the epitome of a money-grubbing capitalist, gave instructions that all her assets were to be converted into securities, deposited in the bank, and that the income from the operation was to be distributed among the workers of her factory. The new owners of the Tver Textile Mill Company were unable to benefit from her act of unprecedented generosity. Varvara Morozova died just one month before the Bolshevik coup in October 1917, and their legacy was turned into the nationalized Proletarian Labour factory.

Back at the time of her husband's death, however, the wealthy young widow had not been focused solely on the advancement of public education. His demise did not strip her of her feminine charm or her desire to be thought attractive. She wanted to be a socialite, to receive guests, to travel: in a word, to enjoy all the blessings that came with being an unattached, thirty-five-year-old millionairess.

Varvara's first priority was to shake off the memories of twelve years of forced marriage, spent in a merchant quarter on the wrong side of the River Yauza. For all its elegant six-pillar portico, Varvara felt no regrets about leaving the villa she had inherited from her husband. She would have wanted to leave if only because of the name of the nearby street: Durnoy [Evil] Lane. Before that it had even been known as Devil's Lane.[18] She moved well away from Taganka, to the other side of the Moscow River. A widow with three children, she bought a property previously owned by the princely Dolgoruky family on Vozdvizhenka Street, a stone's throw from the Kremlin, and began building. The fashionable architect Roman Klein, famed for his design of the Museum of Fine Arts on Volkhonka Street, built her a classical mansion with pillars, gryphons, stylized lilies and a fountain in the garden. It was a capacious house, with twenty-three rooms with marble fireplaces and a further nineteen rooms in the socle storey, which the commonality might have called a basement. The proprietress clearly had large-scale receptions in mind: an enormous hall, with frescoes in the style of Pompeii, could accommodate 300 guests with ease.

Every woman, not only the heroines of American soap operas, has an image of the man of her dreams. The embodiment of Varvara Morozova's ideal was Professor Vasily Sobolevsky. Varvara was the widow of a merchant, Sobolevsky was a highly educated nobleman. He fell in love with her just as Abram Morozov had all those years before and, just like

4  Vasily Mikhailovich Sobolevsky, a prominent Russian economist and journalist, and Varvara's civil husband, 1890s.

Morozov, was to adore her until the day he died. Except that now all the money was hers. Everything she dreamed of in her youth had come true. 'A majestic, beautiful wife, a sharp-witted factory owner and yet, at the same time, the elegant, educated hostess of one of the most intellectual salons in Moscow; in the morning she is clicking away at the office abacus keeping the accounts in order, yet in the evening those same fingers are eliciting the magnificent melodies of Chopin, she is discussing the theory of Karl Marx, and reading her fill of the most up-to-the-minute philosophers and journalists.'[19] Such is one characterization of Varvara Morozova, to whose cultural oasis on Vozdvizhenka Street the elite of the literary and art worlds flocked. It attracted also the academic elite, and those whom Petr Boborykin felicitously dubbed 'the intelligentsia'. She hosted Ilya Mechnikov, who in 1908 was to win the Nobel Prize for Medicine; the writers Vladimir Korolenko, and Gleb Uspensky after whom she named her son by Sobolevsky. Varvara effortlessly met up in Nice with Chekhov, and wrote to Tolstoy. Sobolevsky was on friendly terms with the writers Dmitry Mamin-Sibiryak and Mikhail Saltykov-Shchedrin, and was a celebrity in his own right as the editor of the 'professorial' *Russkie vedomosti* [the Russian Gazette], a widely read newspaper to which leading academics gladly contributed.[20]

The liberal spirit of *Russkie vedomosti* suited Varvara down to the ground, and she lived her life in accordance with its noble aspirations. Indeed, she proved more radical in her liberalism than many of those who assembled at her gatherings. She had so much in common with Sobolevsky, and did her utmost to fit into his unfamiliar circle. Her wealth enabled her to propagate all that was good, rational and eternal, while he advocated a renewal of Russia, believing that widespread dissemination of education and culture would save the country. 'Education for all!' – such was their joint motto. There were persistent rumours that Varvara was the newspaper's financial mainstay, so that Sobolevsky was not only the editor-in-chief but also co-owner of the printing press. Vladimir Nemirovich-Danchenko in his play *The Price of Life* was clearly alluding to the couple: his protagonist, the writer Solonchakov, is presented with a publishing house by Klavdiya Rybnitsyna in return for the bonds of marriage.

This was all a complete fantasy. *Russkie vedomosti* was a joint stock company and Varvara paid only for the sustenance of its family-based editorial office. V.N. Aseev has meticulously researched the accounts in the Morozov archive and discovered that the 'marriage partners' hardly lived in the same house at all.[21] Fifteen years after they met, Sobolevsky, by then the father of Varvara Morozova's son and daughter, was still residing in the nearby publishing house. Then, for a full ten years, he rented an apartment, and it was only in the four years before his death that he moved to a house Varvara bought in his name adjacent to her own mansion. Their children, Gleb and Natalya, bore the Morozov surname, but their patronymic was Vasilevich/Vasilevna, indicating that Sobolevsky was their father. They were considered illegitimate. Gleb was legally adopted by his father only many years later. In the next generation Varvara's middle son, Ivan, was to adopt and give his surname to a daughter born out of wedlock. This situation created, to say the least, many difficulties. To be known as illegitimate was unimaginably humiliating in those times, and few people with such a blemish in their birth certificate would have been able to free themselves of a shaming inferiority complex.

By persisting in this lifestyle, Morozova and Sobolevsky demonstrated to those around them that they were above such prejudices. On the other hand, the couple would almost certainly have solemnized their relation with a church wedding had it not been for a harsh stipulation in Abram Morozov's will that, in the event of her remarrying, his widow would forfeit the name of Morozov, and with it her vast inheritance. Knowing what we do of her husband's personality and his passionate love for his wife, we need not, perhaps, be too surprised by this imposition from beyond the grave. The upshot was that this staunch upholder of equality for women and founder of the first club for women was also virtually the only public figure who had the audacity to cohabit openly. Under the morality of the time such behaviour represented overt defiance of public opinion and was little short of scandalous.

We have no information about how Varvara's elder sons related to Sobolevsky, or what her younger children thought of having a father who was little more than a gentleman visitor. Sympathizing wholeheartedly with penniless students, male and female, and with humble teachers who could lodge for long periods in her house, Varvara seems to have been all but incapable of showing affection to her own family. 'She was neither a loving mother nor wife, and indeed there was never any indication that she felt warmly towards any of those in her immediate family circle,' her daughter-in-law Margarita Morozova admitted, after trying in vain to get closer to her mother-in-law. 'We had been brought up differently, and had very different personalities.'[22] The brusqueness and intransigence of this generous philanthropist were legendary. It was said she broke off all contact with her sister Tatiana when the latter left her husband for Vladimir Snegirev, a famous gynaecologist. Varvara considered the bonds of holy matrimony to be sacrosanct. Although Tatiana broke with Snegirev and lived as a recluse, it was said that Varvara would not even agree to walk behind her sister's coffin when she died.

Day after day Varvara put her ideas into practice and constantly engaged in self-improvement. At the age of fifty, she started learning German and was soon reading classics in the original. She took lessons in Russian literature. Every day without fail she spent an hour at the piano, learning new pieces. Her daughter Natalya recalled that Varvara was an excellent teacher. Before she entered seventh grade of secondary school, her mother herself helped her with many subjects. Natalya Morozova is the only one of her children to have left even brief reminiscences.[23] She wrote them in the Soviet Union in 1958, so makes a point of talking about her mother's socialist views, of how she worked to have revolutionaries released from prison, and of searches of their mansion by the tsarist secret police. Natalya expresses the conviction that Varvara Morozova would have sided with the revolution if she had lived to see it, and 'would have become an important worker in the field of education, because she could not live without working for the benefit of society'.

Natalya writes almost nothing about her elder brothers. As far as one can tell, relations with her mother were very strained, but again, we can only speculate. The ambiguous situation in the family, with a brother and sister 'born in sin', their mother's brusqueness, her startlingly generous acts of charity and her despotic personality, can only have aggravated her elder sons. Their friend, the painter Sergei Vinogradov, claims that all three of them, Mikhail, Ivan and Arseny, detested their mother's liberal views and, indeed, their mother herself, and that those feelings rankled with them to the end of their days. Were they the reason why one built a Moorish castle, another gambled away an entire fortune, and the third collected decadent paintings? All these Morozov quirks and obsessions did not just materialize out of thin air.

# CHAPTER III

# Mikhail Morozov

Mikhail and Ivan were born within a year of each other and had a close physical resemblance (we shall come shortly to Arseny, the youngest), but they were very different in character. A family business is traditionally inherited by the eldest son, but this was not so in the case of the Morozovs. Ivan, whom his mother saw as assisting with the business and in the future becoming its owner, was sent to a vocational school, while Mikhail, whose ability and interest in art and science had been evident since childhood, was sent to the more academic lycée. Ivan, calm and reasonable, posed no problems, but coping with Mikhail and his antics was another matter.

In 1887 Varvara gave birth to Natalya, and just four years later her eldest son got married. Mikhail Morozov was twenty-one and he married no ordinary bride. The Mamontov sisters, Margarita and Elena, were considered the most beautiful young women in Moscow. If Elena's was primarily 'a beauty of line coupled with a certain dullness of colour', Margarita, in the words of Tatiana Aksakova-Sivers, 'had attractive colouration and resembled the muses of Titian'.[1] Margarita and Elena, both of whom bore the enviable surname of Mamontov, were classic

5 & 6  Mikhail Abramovich Morozov and Margarita Kirillovna Morozova
(*née* Mamontova), late 1890s.

maidens without a dowry. Both, however, almost as soon as they were presented to society, were snapped up, and by Moscow millionaires. Alas, their family idylls came to an end almost simultaneously, when Rodion Vostryakov abandoned Elena and Margarita was widowed.

There were no other beauties in the Mamontov family who could compare with them, which is hardly surprising because only these sisters had that amazing mix of German, English and Armenian blood on their maternal side. They had no typically Russian features, and were more akin to exquisitely refined foreign princesses. Their German grandfather, Otto Löwenstein, a fervent Catholic, was the warden (*starosta*) of the Roman Catholic Church of Saints Peter and Paul in Milyutin Lane, which he built together with his future father-in-law, Agapit Elarov, an

31

Armenian. For the Löwenstein-Elarovs the name 'Margarita' ran in the family, one grandmother being Margarita Agapitovna and their mother being Margarita Ottovna Löwenstein. Although the latter married Kirill Mamontov, she never converted to Russian Orthodoxy, but she did have her daughters baptized in the Orthodox Church. Kirill Mamontov had been left a useful legacy by his father, but his ambition was to triple it and he embarked on a succession of enterprises, buying and selling, buying again and selling again. He rushed about, unable to decide what to focus on, and ended up in such a muddle that all his property was inventorized and sold to pay off his debts. By then he was on the run. He would turn up in France, or be spotted in Crimea trying to charter vessels. The Russo-Turkish campaign was in full swing, and there was good money to be made transporting troops, but again he was a failure. Kirill, the cousin of Savva Mamontov, the brother-in-law of Pavel Tretyakov, had again to flee his creditors. He was last seen playing roulette in Monte Carlo where, needless to say, he lost money, and resolved all his problems with a single gunshot. In Marseille, the family believed.

Margarita Ottovna Mamontova accordingly found herself widowed at the age of twenty-five. As her daughter, Margarita the Younger, later related, her mother had spent her childhood in the lap of luxury, surrounded by grandmothers and grandfathers, only now, like a hapless Dickensian or Dostoevskian heroine, to find herself facing the option either of falling at her mother's feet and begging her to shelter her and her two little daughters, or of turning for protection to the family of her feckless husband. Margarita, however, had her pride: she had no intention of scrounging off her mother and having to endure her despotism, and the Mamontovs seemed in no hurry to help out the young widow either. Varvara Khludova would surely have been full of admiration for the course chosen by the mother of her future daughter-in-law. Finding herself in dire straits, Margarita Mamontova opened a small workshop and set to work sewing lingerie and dresses. It was the kind of thing only foreign women could have brought themselves to do. This was, after all, Moscow in the 1880s, and for a woman to be called 'emancipated' was a term of abuse.

'Mama rose early in the morning and was busy until evening . . . I remember her busy at work throughout her life, until the day she died,' Margarita the Younger recalled. The three of them lived in a tiny apartment 'furnished, despite the modesty of our means, very elegantly . . . Mama still had a few items of her dowry, some embroideries and knick-knacks brought back from Italy and Spain.'[2] Every day their nanny would take the girls out to walk on Tver Boulevard, even in the summer, because to go to a dacha in the country was beyond the means of this branch of the Mamontov family. At home Margarita the Elder spoke to her daughters in French and they had a Russian language teacher. They could also read German and were soon enrolled in the German Academy of Saints Peter and Paul.

But to return to Margarita the Elder. The widow of Kirill Mamontov had almost no contact with the family of her late husband (and there may have been reasons for that), but when her daughters grew up they began to be received by their father's relatives. 'Most often we visited Aunt Vera, and my godfather, Uncle Ivan Mamontov,'[3] Margarita the Younger recalled. They went on trips to Lavrushinsky Lane, where Vera's husband, Pavel Tretyakov, founded the renowned art museum. 'We sometimes visited the Tretyakovs on Sundays, and in winter we went every Thursday for lunch and dancing lessons . . . After lunch Aunt Vera would usually play a duet on the piano, or symphonies with three other pianists . . . There was a door leading directly from the dining room to the main, great hall of the art gallery . . . Of course, we absolutely loved going in there. We stood for ages in front of our favourite paintings, talking among ourselves and imagining entire stories.'[4] Most of all, the girls admired Pukirev's *The Unequal Marriage*, Flavitsky's *Princess Tarakanova*, Repin's *The Unexpected Return*, and Kramskoy's *Inconsolable Grief*. The tearful woman seemed to the sisters very much to resemble their mother.

Margarita the Elder, meanwhile, continued to clothe the fashion-conscious ladies of the old capital. She opened an atelier of ladies' fashions, and followed up with a school to teach patterning and cutting. Madame Mamontova led a very private life. There were almost no visitors to her house – other than Dmitry and Sofiya Botkin (Margarita the Younger was actually born in the Botkins' house on Pokrovka Street); the Old Believer industrialist and art collector, Kozma Soldatenkov; and Moscow's Chief of Police, Alexander Kozlov. Kozlov was a bachelor and had every right to adore Margarita the Elder. His visits to the fashionable, high-society dressmaker were much gossiped about. The humorous magazine *Budilnik* [The Alarm Clock] even allowed itself a cartoon with an insinuating caption: 'In the past the goat [*kozyol*] marched down the boulevard but now he crosses it', alluding to the fact that his heart's desire had moved house.

The widow Mamontov and her daughters had indeed moved from Polyakov House on Tver Boulevard, which had an enormous garden opening on to Bronnaya Street, to the corner of Leontiev Lane and Bolshaya Nikita Street. Naturally, the girls very soon met up with their cousins, the daughters of Anatoly Mamontov, whose family home was nearby. It was thanks to the Mamontovs, who kept open house, that Margarita and Elena were welcomed into the beau monde. Two years later, Margarita was courted by Mikhail Morozov. Upon reaching the age of majority, he had acquired the right to the Morozov millions, a considerable change from the wretched allowance of seventy-five rubles a month his strict mama had been providing. Overnight the student in the Faculty of History and Philology of Moscow University became a man of means. He promptly married eighteen-year-old Margarita Mamontova the Younger in the university church, transforming her from Cinderella into a fairy-tale princess dressed in finery, bejewelled, and residing in a sumptuous palace.

There was a lavish wedding, a reception at the Hermitage restaurant, prime venue of Moscow's high society, and then a fairy-tale honeymoon which lasted half a year. As Mikhail's brother Ivan went off to study in Switzerland, the young newly-weds sped to St Petersburg, where a suite in the Grand Hotel Europe awaited them, along with the opera, the theatres and, of course, the Imperial Hermitage. From the northern capital they travelled by the Orient Express to Paris, then south to Nice and the casinos in Monte Carlo.

Their honeymoon was highly cultural and educational: in the afternoon, museums; in the evening, theatres. There was, however, time also for plenty of entertainment. They regularly travelled from Nice to Monte Carlo where, in 1879, Margarita's father had lost what remained of his fortune. 'What has stayed in my mind from Monte Carlo is the figure of Princess E. M. Yurievskaya, the widow of Emperor Alexander II, seated at the gambling table.[5] She was a very plump, red-haired blonde . . . playing roulette with great concentration.'

The young couple returned to Moscow in early spring, and in the autumn moved into their own house, or rather, palace, with a snowy white colonnade and a winter garden.[6] In this luxurious mansion, with lackeys, a housekeeper, maids, cooks, a kitchen maid and a butler, the new mistress who, until recently, had been leading a decidedly modest life, felt ill at ease. Her husband, on the other hand, who had manifestly decided to outdo his mother with his palace, was proud and happy.

Margarita did not abandon her self-improvement. Her attitude was something she had in common with her mother-in-law, Varvara Morozova, and her husband was fully supportive. After graduating from the Faculty of History and Philology, he enrolled in the Faculty of Natural Science (but can hardly have been a serious student). His wife, in addition to studying French, which she knew from childhood, took lessons in history and Russian literature, and also practised the piano every day.

The previous owner of the house on Smolensk Boulevard had been Konstantin Popov, a merchant who inherited tea plantations in China and several dozen tea shops. Even as K. and S. Popov Brothers Ltd,

Russia's largest company trading in tea, was setting about growing tea on the Black Sea, the novice millionaire set about building himself a palace in Moscow. That Konstantin Popov had been keenly aware of his exalted status is evident from the fact that he commissioned Alexander Rezanov, the architect of Grand Duke Vladimir Alexandrovich's magnificent mansion on Palace Embankment in St Petersburg, adjacent to that of the tsar himself. Professor Rezanov was a master of working 'in styles', as people said at the time. This was otherwise known as eclecticism, or 'the architecture of rational choice'. Rezanov was adept at combining the styles of different periods, as he demonstrated in the palazzo he designed on the corner of Smolensk Boulevard and

7 Mikhail and Margarita's mansion, late 1890s.

Glazov Lane, of which, in 1891, Mikhail Abramovich Morozov took possession.[7]

'The house had a semicircular facade with a protruding terrace and white marble columns in the middle. Its foundation was faced with dark red granite. Inside, the house was eccentrically and, in my opinion, very unattractively designed. There was a mixture of every style: the vestibule was Egyptian, the hall a kind of *style Empire*, the anteroom to the hall was Pompeian, the dining room Russian, and another room was Moorish. The whole time I lived there I longed to redesign it all,' Margarita the Younger confesses.[8] She found her palace overlarge, and the ostentatious luxury and innumerable staff merely an irritant. 'There was even a horologist who came each week, since there were beautiful clocks to be wound up in absolutely every room.'

Mikhail ran his house and his household on the grand scale. Electricity was just beginning to be installed in Moscow, but young Morozov did not feel like waiting his turn and engaged an electrical engineer to set up his own generator. Neither did he stint on transportation. The family had two coachmen and two equipages: Mikhail's was *à la russe* with a bearded Russian coachman, and Margarita's was *à l'anglaise* with a liveried coachman.

Every aspect of life in the mansion seemed to be for show. Margarita describes it: 'My husband liked fine cuisine and engaged a good chef. He loved to invite people for dinner. He required an excellent table setting, and a butler, who needed assistants. Our life was from the outset very grand, and only became grander as the years passed.'[9] There was also a chambermaid, a valet, a laundress and a liveried porter, who doubled as a footman because it was de rigueur to go to the theatre in a carriage with an attendant footman to watch over the master and mistress's fur coats during the performance.

Two hundred people at a time were invited to the Morozovs' balls, the ladies in evening dress, the gentlemen in tails. The artist Vasily Perepletchikov[10] has left us a description of one in his diary:

The season of 1901 opened with a ball given by Mikhail Morozov. A lot of people, Varvara Morozova, the mother of Mikhail, is present. On the outside at least, she is a liberal, and surrounded by a coterie of more liberals. She does not by nature 'approve', but 'condones'. Balls of this kind are not, after all, something liberals do approve of. Ilya Ostroukhov is here with his wife, also people you would really not expect to find at a ball. Here is Sergei Shchukin, collector of the last word in Western art. Here is Petr Shchukin,[11] collector of antiquities, who has his own museum. Here are the artists Apollinary Vasnetsov and Sergei Vinogradov.

Mikhail Abramovich is looking preoccupied. He must stand by the staircase and receive his guests. The gathering began at ten in the evening. The guests spread out evenly through the rooms. The art gallery is locked because that is where supper will be served. Hippolyte Labadie, a composer of waltzes and celebrated pianist at balls in Moscow, hammers away. Count Ignatiev is harassing some officers huddled in a corner who are reluctant to dance. That will never do! What do they think they are here for? He gives them no respite. He has eaten three soft-boiled eggs to clear his throat. But why is he so pale and exhausted? It's a hard life for the master of ceremonies at a dance. The artists, in view of their humble station but also of their independent position, are not dancing. They slink from room to room, drinking tea. The evening is not exactly tedious, but fun in a slightly tedious way. There are so many diamonds they no longer amaze. What people are wearing, so meticulously thought about, commands little attention: there is just so much of everything. One last dance and everybody heads for supper.

Everything is in accord with the latest gastronomy, and there is an ocean of champagne. After supper, a mazurka and carriages. It is seven in the morning. Only close friends remain. Mikhail Abramovich is having something to eat: the poor man had no time to eat his supper properly. His wife Margarita is surrounded by diamonds: not only the ones she is wearing but also the ones she has in front of her which have been lost by guests and kindly handed to the hostess for return to their owners. Rigaud's strings are still playing away. The ball has been a great success, everyone enjoyed themselves. Everyone who was invited came. The supper was excellent. The electricity did not fail (which does happen). Well, thank heavens for that.

'Everything was fine, everything was just fine,' Mikhail Abramovich pronounces, despatching the fish. 'The ball was a success.'

'To find something pleasant to say to everyone, to find just the right tone, well, no, that is not something every hostess manages,' one of the organizers is telling Madame Morozova.

'Even at our respectable table,' says art critic Mikhail Sizov, 'we enjoyed ourselves.'

'A marvellous ball,' says balletomane Chechelyov. 'The masqueraders danced really well, it was ballet . . .'

'The ball was a success,' says Vinogradov. He is pleased. He had his tailcoat specially restyled to the latest fashion, has drunk a very satisfactory amount of champagne, and seen a lot of pretty women. What more could anyone ask for?[12]

Sundays were officially considered 'receiving' days, while Saturdays were for visitors for the children. Mikhail Morozov's son, Mikhail the Second, or Mika, was born in 1897, and remembered the house in which he spent his childhood down to the last detail. First there was the Egyptian front entrance with its sphinxes where, next to a new-fangled telephone, by which a porter was on duty, stood an absolutely genuine Egyptian sarcophagus with a mummy, which scared the children. (In fact, Mika had never seen this sarcophagus, acquired by his father in 1894 in Cairo during his exotic Middle East voyage, because both sarcophagus and mummy were given as a gift to the Rumyantsev Museum one year before Mika's birth.)[13] The other rooms in the mansion were also decorated 'in styles'. The architect had designed a blue sitting room *à la Louis XV*; it faced a Moorish smoking room in pink marble and furnished with low divans. The main dining room was *à la Russe*, and the small dining room was *à la Henri IV*, with stained-glass windows (little Mika particularly liked the knights with their multi-coloured glass mosaic legs). The vast stateroom was in *style Empire*. Adjacent to it was the sizeable Pompeian room, which was faced with marble. For the background of his formal portrait of Mikhail Morozov, Valentin Serov chose the marble fireplace in this room, which established the grey-brown tone of the two-metre canvas.[14]

Recalling the carefree days of her youth, Margarita Morozova wrote, 'At half past one my husband invited everyone to luncheon. At first a relatively small circle of people attended these luncheons and they took place in the small dining room. Gradually, however, the number of people invited increased, and the luncheons were moved to the large dining room. There were always twenty or so guests, but often as many as thirty. The table was very long; I sat at one end and my husband at the other . . . When the luncheon was over, the receiving day began, and quite a lot of people would come. We often organized little games in the hall and had lots of fun.'[15]

Mikhail Morozov's close friend, the artist Sergei Vinogradov, has left a nostalgic and detailed account of those Sundays:

Oh, those marvellous, unforgettable Sunday lunches! How much genuine, interesting conversation there was during them . . . The beautiful Margarita sat at the head of the table, herself a wonderful table decoration. She would be the only lady there, although Elena, her sister, sometimes came. Towards the end of a leisurely lunch which, on winter days went on until dusk, other people would begin to arrive, now specially to see Margarita Kirillovna – gallant officers, illustrious ladies. For the most part the conversation would be conducted in French, and Margarita Kirillovna would majestically withdraw with her visitors to her part of the house. This was her receiving day and Mikhail Abramovich and the rest of us would depart to the gallery, where there would be such conversations, such disputations! There would be endless discussion of all kinds of works of art. The sweetish, aromatic smoke of English tobacco and top quality cigars, the pink champagne poured in abundance into flutes added to the cosiness and delight of these Sundays. It had to be pink champagne, because drinking 'classic' champagne during the day was not the done thing.[16]

We shall have recourse to Vinogradov's memoirs in the pages below, and we will return also to the paintings and the Sunday lunches, at which one would meet the luminaries of the entire Moscow art scene. For the moment, however, let us attempt a portrait of Mikhail Morozov himself. (We must not forget, of course, that for us the protagonist is undoubtedly his brother, Ivan Morozov. Ivan's brothers, his cousins and other family members are essential only for the context they provide.)

A heady mix of Khludov and Morozov blood seethed in the veins of the epic, robust frame of Mikhail Morozov. The Khludov blood line, moreover, clearly had the ascendance. Such heredity did not bode well. In his lack of self-restraint, Mikhail reminded his mother, Varvara, only too startlingly of her own brother, in whose honour he had been named. Margarita the Younger shared the anxieties of her mother-in-law: she had heard plenty about the wild side of the Khludovs.

Sergei Vinogradov gives this description of them in his memoirs: 'The Khludovs had the reputation in Moscow of being highly gifted and intelligent, but eccentric, people. It was as well to keep your distance from them, as people unable to control their passions.' Margarita tells us that Mikhail Khludov, her husband's uncle, had a serious drink problem. 'He would be served a glass of tea and a bottle of brandy. He would sip a spoonful of the tea and wash it down with the brandy, continuing to drink the tea in this manner until the bottle of brandy was empty.'[17] He ended his days in a dreadful fashion. His second wife locked her rampaging husband in a room padded with felt and with bars on the windows. At the age of forty-two, Mikhail Alexeevich died in his own house in Khludov Close from delirium tremens.

Mikhail Morozov also liked to drink, and ate peppered raw meat as an accompanying *zakuska* (literally, 'after-bite'). Many years later, any allusion to this terribly offended his granddaughter, Tatiana Morozova-Fiedler, but it is no exaggeration. Her grandfather really did enjoy behaving eccentrically. One time when he and his pregnant wife were sailing down the Volga from the Tver estate, he suddenly decided to take the helm. The ship hit a rock and sank immediately. 'Everybody somehow fought their way to the surface, but I was wedged by the cabin furniture and for a long time floundered about under it on the riverbed. Everyone started screaming . . . Our engineer dived down and by chance caught hold of my hat. I clutched his hand and he pulled me out,' Margarita recalled.[18] Her husband later bought Isaak Levitan's landscape *On the Volga*. It must have reminded her of that terrifying episode.

Choosing her words with exceptional care, Margarita Morozova remarks tactfully that her husband 'had an exceptionally lively, indeed stormy, personality. All its manifestations, whether of anger or gaiety, were stormy.' Ordinary Muscovites were both annoyed by his antics and admiring of them: the grandson of a former serf, and look at the way he lives now! They familiarly called him Misha Morozov although, far from being a boy, he was portly and looked very solid and established. His brother, on the other hand, was invariably referred to respectfully by his first name and patronymic as 'Ivan Abramovich'. It was said, for example, that when Misha Morozov moved into a hotel, the first thing he did was demand that all the other people on his floor should be moved out, and that he was entirely willing to pay through the nose just for the privilege of not seeing anybody anywhere near him. He loved big-time gambling and once, in the English Club, lost more than a million rubles in a single night to Mikhail Bostanzhoglo, a tobacco manufacturer who was a passionate card-player. It was an epic loss, and perfect fodder for the gutter press. How can one not be reminded of his thrill-seeking uncle, Mikhail Khludov, who, for a dare, during the war made his way into the enemy camp of the Turks, and whose pet tiger prowled freely through his vast mansion?

In her memoirs Margarita does, however, let out of the bag something of the wild scenes her husband perpetrated. Relations between them were, to say the least, difficult, and after six years of living with him her patience snapped. She left him, but her mother-in-law, Varvara, managed to persuade her to return. The son showed no gratitude towards his mother for her intercession. There were many things he could never forgive her for: his 'stepfather', Professor Sobolevsky, the halt and the lame whom she allowed to live for years in their home, and other downsides of her charitable impulses. Childhood grievances have a tendency to rankle, and this was 'Misha' Morozov's way of trying to attract attention. It is common enough behaviour in people who have been deprived in childhood of parental affection. He did, however, make just too much noise, was sometimes downright offensive, and the real problem was, as Sergei Vinogradov puts it, that he was doing it primarily to spite his mother and 'her circle'.

# CHAPTER IV

## 'A Russian Rough Diamond,
## Polished by Civilization'

'I made the acquaintance of Misha and his younger brothers when he was a student, in a dandified uniform, ruddy-faced, cheerful, with amazingly luminous, short-sighted eyes, big and loud,' Vinogradov recalls. 'I remember how often he ranted against his mother's "liberals", somehow spitting the word out with a special charge of hatred, and constantly complained that his mother gave him an allowance of just seventy-five rubles a month, as a result of which he was constantly finding himself in idiotic situations.'[1] Although Vinogradov also writes that when he became a multimillionaire Misha dropped out of university, the truth is that Morozov graduated from the Faculty of History and Philology. A year after his wedding, he sat the exam and was awarded a first-class degree. He published several historical articles at his own expense, clearly with the aim of pleasing his mother, whose hope was that her son would become a university professor. His academic and literary efforts were, however, to work to his disadvantage.

A presentation copy of Morozov's monograph *Charles V and His Time* found its way (and was most likely intentionally sent by its budding author) to the playwright Alexander Sumbatov-Yuzhin.[2] He read the

8 Mikhail in his study in the Smolensk Boulevard mansion, late 1890s.

book and was struck by the author's pretentious style and eagerness to astound the reader with the profundity of his thinking. Just as, a century later, Moscow's intellectuals were desperate, after reading his detective novels, to work out who was concealed behind the pen name of Boris Akunin,[3] Sumbatov was desperate to discover the identity of Mikhail Yuriev (Morozov's pseudonym). One thing was clear: the author was brash, well educated and indubitably rich.

The nouveau-riche author was just asking to be put into a play, and Sumbatov-Yuzhin obliged. He was no Ostrovsky or Chekhov, but his plays on the hot topics of the day were put on in Moscow and the provinces with invariable success. In an intimate setting, over dinner, Sumbatov read the first two acts of the future of *The Gentleman* to Vladimir Nemirovich-Danchenko, who praised them.[4] Instead, however, of being curious to find out how the third act would end, the director began to press him for information about Mikhail Morozov. Sumbatov was taken aback. He was not acquainted with Morozov, and had made no connection between the extravagant millionaire and Larion Rydlov, the hero in his play. Nemirovich, who had cracked the secret of the identity behind the pseudonym, and certainly also the audiences who later saw his play, refused point blank to believe his protestations. Audiences love to recognize the prototypes of characters, especially if they are famous. *The Gentleman* was guaranteed to run to full houses.[5] 'Everyone in Moscow is saying he (Sumbatov) is describing Mikhail Morozov, and now they are all debating whether it is acceptable for an author or a playwright to base a character wholly on the life of an actual person. Wherever you go, that is what everybody is talking about!', a close lady friend wrote, passing on the latest Moscow news, to Chekhov.[6]

Although the comedy was supposedly finished before its author became personally acquainted with his hero's prototype, the resemblance to Morozov is striking. 'I first met M. A. Morozov, not only after the comedy was written, but even after it had first been staged at the Maly Theatre,' Sumbatov later averred.[7] However, no matter how much he later protested that, 'Having no knowledge of the subject, I could not and have not painted a portrait of him', the truth of the matter is that, having learned the identity of 'Mikhail Yuriev', the playwright acted like a typical paparazzo. He added facts from Morozov's life and spiced up the plot even more. The figure of the lovely Cath is added to the play, the daughter of a Russified Englishwoman, whom Rydlov 'buys' as his wife. ('I have sold myself, and sold myself for the rest of my life,' the heroine wails.) This is an obvious allusion to Margarita Mamontova, who married Morozov for his money, and to her half-German mother, whose fashionable atelier is turned in the play into an aunt's glove factory. Use is even made of the rumours that Margarita the Younger had left her husband, only later to return. In the play, Larion's mother persuades Cath to return. 'I'll go right now and send Larik to you. I'll make him kiss your feet to get you to come back to him, because where is an idiot like him going to find another girl as clever and pretty as you? After that you can take him in hand and do whatever you will, just don't abandon him completely.'

Sumbatov probably knew that, in addition to another monograph on *Controversial Issues of Western European Historiography*, Morozov-Yuriev had written an improbably awful novel in which the hero is unfaithful to his wife, hurls himself into the depths of depravity, stumbles around in dark places, clambers out of the abyss, and embarks on the path of righteousness. For some inexplicable reason, the novel was banned by the censor and the printed copies destroyed, although the author had not, in fact, made any transparent allusions to high-ranking personages as was alleged, and there was nothing frivolous about the text. His only erotic scene had already been replaced by *five* rows of dots. The novel truly was terrible, as Morozov himself admitted, laughing at his own work and its auto-da-fé. Like a changeling, Morozov's novel, *In the Darkness*, becomes in Sumbatov's play a psychological novel titled *The Abyss*, and 'Mikhail Yuriev' becomes 'the Marquis Voldyr'. 'He wrote a novel in the psychological genre and published it under the pen name of "the Marquis

Voldyr" – Rydlov backwards. He even has his own portrait and the text in some illustrated magazine. His ugly face is illumined like in a Rembrandt painting but, alas, it all looks very sweaty,' Rydlov's fellow writers comment in Sumbatov's play.

The owner of a mansion with a winter garden, a cognoscente of oysters and champagne, Larion Rydlov so closely resembles his prototype, albeit much caricatured, that there could be no doubt: he was Misha Morozov. It is not easy to work out where the dramatic character ends and the real person who served as his prototype begins. 'Well, some people have everything: Babylonian luxury, the whole world dancing attendance on them,' one of the characters in the play says. 'Railway trains convey their useless bodies from one corner of the earth to another. Telegraphs and telephones communicate their thoughts and desires around the world. For them other people weave, build, plough, sow, think, write, study, invent – all for their convenience, comfort, and pleasure.'

And here is what Perepletchikov wrote in his diary: 'This person has his own style, a trotting horse, rubber tyres, a coachman, a chocolate-box house, an outspoken article about an exhibition with a hint of insolence. It is all very embarrassing and disagreeable.'[8]

The hero of *The Gentleman* delivers a monologue which is literally copied out of Yuriev-Morozov:

'I wish to write a series of essays along the lines of an analysis of modern society. It is, after all, on us, the third estate, that all of Russia is now relying for salvation. Come along now, the people is saying, you millionaires, show us your cultural capital. In the past it was the nobility that provided the writers, but there is no getting away from the fact that now it is your turn.

(*Counting on his fingers.*) By your leave: in the first place we have the benefit of freshness of outlook. We have not degenerated, as has the nobility. Secondly, we are well off, and that too is an important factor: one can create only if one has the freedom to do so. What kind of freedom does a person have if they have pawned even their bootlaces? And finally, I shall bring my book out in such an edition that it will dazzle all who see it. So there you have it: we are now the cream of society. Like it or not, no one is going to keep us down! Nowadays everything is con-cen-trated around capital.

. . . I feel within myself – ambition, far-reaching plans. I have put myself to the test and what have I found? I can be a critic, a musician, an artist, an actor, a journalist. Why? *Because I am a Russian rough diamond, but polished by civilization* (My emphasis. – *N.S.*) The only difficulty is that I am pulled in one direction and then another, because I feel I am bursting with energy.'

Yuriev-Morozov, unlike Rydlov, did show he could be both critic and journalist by publishing a hefty tome of *My Letters*, in which he collected his published and unpublished critical articles and travel notes. 'Whatever people may say, it has to be admitted that our bourgeoisie here in Moscow is a force. It is the bourgeois who applaud at first nights in the theatre, who buy paintings and talk politics. If in the past they were afraid of a police inspector, called a bottle a jar, and said "fill" when they meant "pour", now they do in general speak grammatically – although they still use expressions like "I was right weary" – and they have a university degree. Now the bourgeoisie is afraid of nothing, except perhaps that Princess Hardov-Hearing may not invite them to a ball, or that an aide-de-camp of their acquaintance will not come to their dinner party.'[9]

There is another passage in *My Letters* which reads, 'It is true that education has found its way to the bourgeoisie. Young people of the merchant class have a lot of knowledge (except, perhaps, in respect of their acquaintance with foreign literature and languages), but what does the bourgeoisie have to offer us in the intellectual realm?'[10] It is a question which might more rightly have been asked not by twenty-three-year-old Mikhail Yuriev but by critics of this wealthy graphomaniac so desperate to impose himself on the literary scene, whom he asked for leniency. 'By all that is holy, gentlemen, analyse my letters, decry them, scold me, but be unbiased and assess me as a writer, not as a person.'[11]

Perepletchikov complains to his diary, 'A third article by Morozov has appeared in *Novosti dnia* [the Daily News]. It is so crass when people start writing about art who, in essence, love nothing and nobody so much as their own person ... It really is deplorable when someone whose intended by nature to reach for the scissors and clip dividend coupons, reaches out to finger art, and who, but for his dividends, would be in a very different situation.'[12]

I would like to feel sorry for the young author. It is, of course, not Yuriev-Morozov's fault that he inherited a fortune from his parents. At first sight he is a brawler and a hell-raiser, but in reality he is a sulking boy who wants to assert himself by whatever means he can: through his house and his wife, by his articles, books and positions. Morozov even makes bold to write about art exhibitions and allows himself to be decidedly caustic on the subject of other people's painting. He poses as a controversialist: 'Not a single new hue, not a single new brushstroke; everything is the same as we have already seen time and time again in the paintings of Polenov', which are downright tedious; and 'Ostroukhov's twilight is grimy, and one detects a tentativeness in the strokes of the sky.' He has no compunction about chiding Levitan for his 'unsuccessful' painting *Above Eternal Peace* in which 'the earth seems to have been cut out and pasted on to the water, and the storm cloud is missing its reflection in the water'. His former drawing teacher, Konstantin Korovin, he declares has no understanding whatsoever of drawing. He complains that in his Paris boulevard paintings 'there is far too much imitation of French contemporaries', and the colours are so bizarre that he has completely given up trying to understand the artist.

These venomous philippics put an end to any further excursions into literary and art criticism on the part of Yuriev-Morozov, but that did not make the prospect of sitting in the office on Varvarka Street augmenting his father's capital any more appealing. After two years as a director of the company, he gave up but, remaining a full shareholder, carried on watching his wealth increase. With his millions, any whim was readily realizable. On one occasion he took it into his head to become warden of the Cathedral of the Assumption. He made a succession of incredibly generous dona-tions, and was duly elected warden of the most important church in the Kremlin, in which all the sovereigns of Russia had been crowned. 'Misha was childishly delighted, laughing and constantly repeating, "Now mother and her creepy liberal friends are furious, squirming on their tails with rage,"' Vinogradov writes, recalling that Misha stood in the election only to assert himself. 'At that time he was still little more than a boy and had yet to find his feet. He was all over the place, showing off and making mischief, and soon cooled towards his new position and ceded it to Fedor Plevako,[13] a famous lawyer. He did, though, continue to finance the upkeep of the church.'

In fact, Mikhail was twice elected warden of the cathedral and occu-pied the position from 1897 to 1903, the year in which he died. He even began writing a history of the building. Margarita Morozova related that 'the Morozovs had, since time immemorial, been Old Believers, and were very zealous. Each of the sons . . . of [Savva the First] belonged to a different denomination. One of them, Elisei, even formed a denomina-tion of his own, which was duly called the Elisei Faith.[14] Mikhail's father, Abram, adopted the more conciliatory United Faith denomination, which acknowledged the priests of Russian Orthodoxy, when he married Varvara Alexeevna Khludova . . .[15] so that Mikhail was brought up in a family remote from the customs of the Old Believers. Nevertheless, a love of church art passed from his fathers and grandfathers to my husband. He formed an interesting collection of icons, which combined curiously with his collection of far-left-wing French paintings. Both those trends, although markedly different from each other, struck deep roots in Mikhail's psyche.'[16]

People in the arts were drawn to the wealthy Mr Morozov and he, full of ambition, willingly accepted invitations to join various associations and committees. He thus became a director of the Russian Music Society, and sat on the Committee for the Establishment of a Museum of Fine Arts in Moscow, to which he and his brother Ivan donated a substantial sum of money in the hope of seeing a plaque with their names in one of the halls of the future museum of casts of sculptures. Mikhail Morozov seems not to have turned anybody down: he was elected an honorary magistrate and became a member of the Society of Art Lovers, Writers and Scholars; of the Association for the Advancement of Education; of the Philharmonic Society; and even served as treasurer of the Moscow Conservatory.

Within the ranks of the civil service Mikhail Morozov rose to the position of Titular Counsellor and received the rank of Collegiate Assessor and the Order of St Anne (Second Class) in recognition of the length of his service.[17] Margarita writes of this in her memoirs: 'It ought to be said that he took this area of his life only half seriously, more or less laughing at himself. On the one hand, he really did want to be awarded the Order of St Vladimir and be ennobled, while on the other, if anyone teased him about it, he would laugh loudly and sincerely, albeit he made no apology and did not deny it. He was very proud of his uniform. He loved wearing it with all his orders and his cocked hat, and did then look very distinguished.'[18] If Morozov had lived just a few more years, he would undoubtedly have been awarded the Order of St Vladimir.

'Mikhail Abramovich Morozov was a major industrialist and businessman only on high days and holidays: what he was really fervent about was art.'[19] The word 'fervent' was well chosen. Mikhail put his heart and soul into everything he did, as if afraid of not having enough time in his life. His books were derided, the comments about his critical articles were unkind, but Morozov was indefatigable; in a word – true to his Khludov pedigree. Sometimes he did throw his money about but, unlike Khlynov-Khludov in Sumbatov's play, he did not complain of being bored. Mikhail had many enthusiasms: he was a passionate theatregoer, never missing a premiere at the Maly Theatre, and was very pleased if his review appeared in print. Sumbatov in *The Gentleman* did not deny himself the satisfaction of sounding off about this too:

> 'Who on earth will want to read his articles? He may have attended several questionable universities, but it has had no impact on his lofty intellect. He does not laugh at what is comical: he is not saddened by what is sad.'

> 'Oh, put him in charge of the theatre section then.'

A balletomane and music lover, Mikhail Morozov retained a box at the Bolshoy Theatre and, in his wife's words, reacted only too heatedly to everything that occurred in artistic life. His sudden decision to start painting and 'get daubing', as Vinogradov put it, did not surprise anyone. The Morozov boys had been taught drawing far more seriously than was usually considered appropriate in merchant families. They first studied in the studio of Nikolai Martynov, who later taught classes in the visual arts at the Prechistenka College which Varvara Morozova was to finance.[20] After that, Konstantin Korovin, then a young student at the School of Painting, Sculpture and Architecture, came to teach the brothers once a week for a couple of years. Korovin went on to become an academician of painting, but was reluctant to remember this part of his biography, or, indeed, that his grandfather's house was very close to the Morozov mansion in the Taganka quarter.[21] Korovin's successor was the venerable Egor Khruslov, a landscape painter of the *Peredvizhnik* [Itinerant] school who was to become the curator of the Tretyakov brothers' gallery. This put an end to Khruslov's painting career. In the summer the brothers painted studies in Popovka, the Morozov estate in Tver, under the guidance of their new teacher. Khruslov took the adolescent boys on a trip down the Volga to the Caucasus, where, of course, they were supposed to work on their painting. Alas, their mentor found the trip far from satisfactory. 'I parted company with the Morozovs in Sevastopol and they returned to Moscow. We undertook an enormously long journey and spent 2,000 rubles to no purpose whatsoever. If we had been travelling together for another week I should have had a nervous breakdown. The whole trip was idiotic! We saw plenty but did nothing, absolutely nothing because "if the team doesn't pull together . . ."[22]

Despite Khruslov's exasperation with his wards, he did manage to stimulate the brothers' interest in art. At the age of nineteen Ivan Morozov made his first acquisition at the nineteenth exhibition of the Itinerants – *Winter*, a landscape by Petr Levchenko.[23] The bill for 200 rubles is signed by his teacher, E. M. Khruslov, on behalf of the Itinerant Art Exhibition Company. The Morozov and Khludov families had an undoubted penchant for fine art. The boys' uncle, Sergei Morozov, enjoyed landscape painting and was an admirer of Levitan's paintings. He even provided him with a studio he had equipped for his own painting endeavours in a wing of their town house in Bolshoy Trekhsvyatitel Lane.

Mikhail Morozov's paintings have not survived, but we have Margarita Morozova's word for it that her husband was really quite good. Vinogradov, however, who tried to teach him, told his friend it would be better for him to try something else, and Mikhail readily concurred. It was clear he was not going to distinguish himself in the fields of literature or art criticism either. His decision to collect works of art was a last effort. Mikhail was a gambler, a thrill-seeker, and the acquisition of paintings, a high-risk activity, gave him an opportunity to prove himself. This, given his pathological Morozov ambition, was no small matter. It also afforded an excellent opportunity to flaunt his wealth. 'This was real. He threw himself passionately into art collecting,' Vinogradov, who became his consultant, writes with genuine satisfaction.

Mikhail Morozov had a sumptuous mansion on Smolensk Boulevard, plenty of room in it for works of art, and collecting paintings was stylish and prestigious. Having moved into his palace, the new millionaire could afford to buy anything his heart desired, but took every opportunity to haggle:

'The price?'

'Eight hundred.'

'Come now, that's ridiculous!'

'Write to the artist yourself about the price you are prepared to offer, Mikhail Abramovich. I am not going to do it for you, and I really don't advise you to,' says the organizer of the exhibition. 'And if you are writing, you might as well offer fifty rather than 150, because the result will be the same. The artist is not going to be impressed either way,' the manager responds. His manner is jocular, but underneath it one detects a degree of disdain for Morozov and his wealth.

Mikhail Abramovich expostulates, 'It's unbelievable the prices Russian painters are trying on. This is ridiculous, for that amount I can buy any number of paintings abroad! The exhibitions are weak, there are no decent paintings,' he says, attempting to goad the organizer. 'What d'you say? Are you not going to concede? Well, all right, 175, but that's my last word.' The organizer shrugs. 'Well, in that case, goodbye.'

'Goodbye,' the organizer says, shaking his hand with a display of courtesy. They know each other well and the exchange has been light-hearted. 'Will you be back, perhaps?'

'I will, but I won't be paying any more.'[24]

As a result of his new hobby, the young millionaire's entourage began to change. At first those around him had been nattily dressed, 'white-lining' former fellow university students.[25] He 'seemed barely to be registering their presence, not noticing them, looking myopically through their heads to somewhere behind them, and talking about something strange, often absurdly paradoxical, but invariably interesting'.[26] His white-lining friends were gradually displaced by painters. At the famous Sunday lunches one might encounter gloomy Serov and carefree, artistic Korovin, the Vasnetsov brothers and merchant's son Vasily Perepletchikov, who systematically entered in his diary every impression from his visits.

Mikhail Morozov's first 'coups' as a collector were, as related by Perepletchikov, something of a joke. Like many an aspiring collector he decided to begin with old masters. Hearing of his new hobby, some enterprising traders arranged an auction just for him. They found a respectable-looking location and invited some fake buyers, instructing them to dress as classily as possible. For the organizers the auction was a brilliant success, and it provided Perepletchikov with another opportunity to ridicule Morozov, who bought Raphael, Rembrandt and Ribera at knock-down prices:

> The paintings were obligingly delivered after the auction to his home. He wiped the 'dust of centuries' from his 'genuine' (signed) Rembrandt with a damp cloth and, to his horror, erased the signature, which was now no more than a grubby mark on a towel. Rembrandt had undoubtedly painted the picture, but added his signature so much later that it had not had time to dry and could just be wiped off. Such accidents do happen. How long, however, do the signatures of great masters take to dry? It is extraordinary, and no doubt that is part of the reason why they are such great masters. Where is that collection now? Not with Mikhail Abramovich. He soon became disillusioned with it.
>
> He travels abroad now and buys his paintings there, but only new ones. For some time now he's been steering clear of old masters.[27]

Perhaps some such mystification really did occur, and once and for all put Mikhail Morozov off buying old Italian and Dutch masters. The fact of the matter is, however, that Mikhail had everything a true collector needs: not only flair, a paradoxical approach and penchant for risk-taking, but also education. Margarita writes that her husband read widely, and not only the literature on art. The Morozov library, nationalized in 1918, comprised over 40,000 volumes. Vinogradov recalls a number of long tables littered with art magazines in several languages. Also, of course,

Morozov had disposable income. He had access to numerous museums and exhibitions, and benefited greatly from Vinogradov's masterclasses. Accordingly, the rich young man from Moscow became a discerning connoisseur of art in a surprisingly short time: he assembled his collection in a matter of just five years.[28]

Mikhail Morozov acquired roughly equal numbers of works by Russian and foreign artists. It is not entirely clear whether he had a preference for his compatriots or, as later his brother Ivan had, for foreigners. His collection was eclectic, because Mikhail bought anything he liked, from paintings of the 1870s 'everyday life' genre to the Russian version of Art Nouveau, from Vasily Perov's *The Dovecote* and *Botany* to *The Vision of the Youth Bartholomew* by Mikhail Nesterov. (The sketch was in no way inferior to the painting itself, which hung in the halls of the Tretyakov brothers' gallery.) Morozov managed to acquire Viktor Vasnetsov's *Three Princesses of the Underground Kingdom*, commissioned by Savva Mamontov for the board of the Donetsk Railway, and put up for auction after it went bankrupt. The melancholy landscapes of the newly fashionable Isaak Levitan hung side by side with the impressionistic paintings of Konstantin Korovin. Mikhail Morozov's collection included works by members of the World of Art group, by Konstantin Somov, an aficionado of the Age of Chivalry, and of Alexander Benois, the 'rhapsodist of Versailles'. He bought ten studies and sketches for Surikov's major epic paintings: *Boyarina Morozova*, *The Capture of Snow Town*, *The Conquest of Siberia by Yermak*, and *Suvorov Crossing the Alps*. Mikhail and Margarita Morozov became good friends of this leading figure of the Itinerants, entertained him at home, attended concerts, and listened to Skryabin with him. Historical paintings were the favourite genre of Pavel Tretyakov, who created an amazing gallery of Russian art. Surikov's sketches, however, with the fabric of their painting, the blending of colours, tone values and textures, occupy a different dimension. Collectors of sketches are unquestionably the most percipient of art lovers.

57

Mikhail Morozov also became one of the first collectors of Mikhail Vrubel. To take the decision to buy the foremost Russian decadent undoubtedly called for courage, indeed daring. And, of course, a nose for quality. In Morozov's collection at Smolensk Boulevard there were several of Vrubel's works, including *The Fortune Teller*, painted after a trip by Vrubel to Spain, the panel *Faust and Margarita in the Garden* (painted for the Gothic study of Mikhail's cousin, Alexei Vikulovich Morozov, but rejected by the client), and several drawings. Vrubel was one of those invited to a famous lunch on the occasion of the purchase of Besnard's *Féerie intime*, which had caused such a sensation in Paris. After spotting Vrubel among the guests, Vinogradov never forgot that day, nor indeed the scandalous painting itself.

Vrubel's *The Swan Princess*, bought by Mikhail Morozov from the artist a year previously, was no less spectacular. It depicts a bird-maiden sailing out to an expanse of stormy sea. So beautiful and enigmatic was Vrubel's princess that people could not tear their eyes away from her. It is not surprising that the theme proved popular. 'Mikhail . . . has painted another *Swan Princess*, but it is not, in my opinion, as good as the one that horrid man Morozov got his hands on . . . He is thinking of doing a repeat of *The Swan Princess* for another customer, and to spite Morozov for paying so little,' wrote the offended opera singer Nadezhda Zabella-Vrubel, the artist's wife, whose performance of the role had inspired him.[29] For a 1.5 metre canvas Vrubel had asked 500 rubles, but let it go for 300, which would have converted into less than 1,000 francs. Morozov paid fifteen times that amount for Besnard's painting! After seeing it at the Salon, he was so fired by it he brought back a photograph, and then dithered for a long time over whether or not to buy it. It has to be said, the painting was no bargain. In the end he made up his mind and telegraphed Durand-Ruel in Paris to buy it without delay.[30]

Absolutely everyone who was anyone came together to view *Féerie intime*, ceremoniously installed on an easel in Mikhail Morozov's large dining room: writers and artists, decadents and 'old men', headed by Mikhail's stepfather Sobolevsky. It was a scene straight out of *The Gentleman*:

'They print reports in St Petersburg nowadays of all the routs, balls and weddings. In Paris never a fashionable wedding takes place without a newspaper report. Describe the house, the electric lighting, the car they own.'

'Should we say how many guests there were?'

'Absolutely essential. Did you notice all of them? There were eight officers from St Petersburg. Here is the supper menu. Oh, let's go the whole hog and include all their names.'

Paul-Albert Besnard was a fashionable Parisian portraitist of the Belle Époque[31] and painted only duchesses and baronesses. The 'sugar king' Pavel Kharitonenko commissioned portraits of his daughters from him. Kharitonenko lived in grand style in his mansion on Sofiya Embankment (where today the British ambassador holds his receptions). He held concerts and balls no less notable than those of Mikhail Morozov. Not wishing to be outdone by his rival in any respect, Morozov doubtless toyed with the idea of commissioning a portrait of his wife from Besnard, which he would have done very well. Sofiya Giatsintova, an actress, recalled, 'Tall, slender, with a broad-brimmed hat above her lovely face, she had only to appear for a wave of admiration to ripple through an audience.'[32]

Margarita Morozova had her portrait painted by several artists, and the best was undoubtedly the one unfinished by Serov. Besnard was not among her favourite painters, and the ornamental fantasy of *Féerie intime* always irritated her. After her husband's death she got rid of the painting, sending it back to Paris to be resold.[33]

According to the insurance inventory, *Féerie intime*, together with the landscapes of Corot and Jongkind, was one of the most valuable works in the collection, with the exception, of course, of the collection's principal masterpiece – the grand, full-length *Portrait of the Actress Jeanne Samary* by Renoir.[34] It is a pity Vinogradov did not describe the society rout organized to celebrate the arrival of the portrait, whose purchase he had witnessed:

> And then the negotiations began for acquiring Madame Samary. How interesting it was, positively poetical, to view this wonderful work several times each day in the celebrated rue Laffitte in a commercial gallery. Samary, a bewitching blonde, a Parisienne to the marrow of her bones, in a pale pink dress in the comical style of the 1870s, bathed in light, devoid of shadows, is painted so perfectly that even the French can boast few works of such artistic distinction. The bargaining began. [Ambroise] Vollard wanted 24,000 francs, we offered less, and finally bought the item for 20,000 francs.[35]

Vinogradov's memory rather failed him. The portrait of Samary, an actress at the Comédie-Française, was exhibited by Renoir at the Salon of 1879. They managed to bargain the price down to 19,000 francs, and the scene he describes took place not at rue Laffitte, but in the Bernheim Gallery in rue Richepanse.

We should allow ourselves a digression on the role of Vinogradov, who described himself as an adviser in the buying of paintings. The son of a village priest, Sergei Vinogradov had a European demeanour and aristocratic appearance. He was much respected by the sugar producer, Pavel Kharitonenko, who patronized his painting, and was a welcome guest in the family of Savva Mamontov. He was a connoisseur of the Impressionists and a familiar figure in the studios of Paris. At ease conversing at any level of society, in his paintings he combined with the same ease a freely impressionist manner with the traditions of the Itinerants. Vinogradov's landscapes were in demand among the cognoscenti. He was formidably knowledgeable about contemporary painting in the late 1890s, and no less so in the mid-1920s when, together with Igor Grabar, he organized an exhibition of Russian painting in America. From there he never returned to Soviet Russia, preferring bourgeois Riga to Bolshevik Moscow. Grabar, rarely lavish with his praise, spoke highly of Vinogradov, noting his ability to distinguish the genuinely talented from run-of-the-mill painting. He found it entirely credible that all of Mikhail Morozov's collection, and a substantial portion of that of his brother, Ivan, had been acquired solely on the recommendation of Vinogradov.

Vinogradov himself says as much, recalling that his 'friend Misha' trusted him implicitly when they visited Durand-Ruel and Vollard, the principal Parisian *marchands*. Not always, however. For example, no matter how much he urged Morozov to buy a still life by Cézanne, his friend flatly refused. Vollard was apparently asking a mere 150 francs for the Cézanne, a name completely unknown to them, and that was far less than Vinogradov's own landscapes were fetching. To the end of his days he could not forgive himself for lacking the courage of his convictions and buying the painting himself.

They missed out on Cézanne but, to Vinogradov's amazement, Morozov was greatly taken by Gauguin:

> The paintings were very interesting in their colouration, but so untraditional, with such a primitive moulding of form, that it took a lot of courage to acquire such a thing at that time. Even so, after recovering from the initial bewildering impression, I sensed that this was genuinely art, and considerable art at that. I set about trying to persuade M.M. to buy one painting which had particularly wonderful colouring. They were going for a song. Misha hooted with laughter and wanted nothing to do with it. I decided I would buy it for myself, at which point Misha gave in and the painting was bought for 500 francs.[36]

Vinogradov performed what he described as 'the same trick' with a van Gogh. With his own money he bought *The Sea at Les Saintes-Maries-*

*de-la-Mer* from Bernheim, later persuading Morozov to take the picture himself.

It transpires that van Gogh was first to be seen in Moscow thanks to Mikhail Morozov, who until a short time previously had not been ready to understand and appreciate even the impressionist experiments of Korovin. It was Mikhail Morozov, not Sergei Shchukin, who brought the Tahitian canvases of Gauguin to Russia. Other than Mikhail, no one bought the paintings of Edvard Munch. *The Girls on the Bridge* remained the Norwegian Symbolist's only painting in Russian collections. 'We sent back a whole transport of outstanding items to Russia, to Moscow. The purchases included Degas, de la Gandara, Forain . . . the Norwegian, Munch . . . but, of course, ruling the roost over all of them was brilliant Renoir,' Vinogradov recalled, proudly.

But let us come back to Gauguin. The first purchase was *Landscape with Two Goats*, followed the next year by *Canoe*, also known as *Tahitian Family*. That painting was slightly larger, and it cost three times as much. The price was almost twice that paid for *The Swan Princess*! A few years later, when prices for Gauguin had crept up, Vollard is said to have suggested to his Russian client's widow that she might sell *Canoe* for 10,000 francs. That seems entirely realistic, unlike the fantasies spun by Konstantin Korovin, who erroneously claims that Mikhail Morozov had not two but four Gauguin paintings which he managed to sell at vast profit. As portrayed by Korovin, Morozov appears even more of a madcap than in Sumbatov's play. Here is how, according to Korovin, Morozov described his purchases of Gauguin:

'I went to Paris one time, read in the newspapers about this posthumous exhibition of Gauguin. He went to the islands of Tahiti, God only knows where that is. Amazing women, built like Venuses, skin the colour of bronze. Pink sky, blue trees, pineapples, white oranges . . . And he turned into a savage, and began painting like a savage. Of course he did, seeing all that sort of stuff. The exhibition opened and I was in there like a shot. Good God, it was amazing! I thought, this I like! I'll buy some paintings and hang them in the dining room. I chose four large ones, checked the price. They were going cheap. Five hundred francs a pop. I bought them. Not the kind of pictures you're going to understand straight away. I thought, never mind, I'll take a proper look at 'em later.'

Morozov brings the paintings back to Moscow, throws a grand dinner party, invites nearly all the big-name merchants. There are Gauguin's paintings, hanging on the wall in the dining room. The owner, beaming, shows them off to his guests. 'Here,' he says, 'you've got a real artist. Went to the ends of the earth in the cause of art. Fire-breathing mountains everywhere, people walking around naked . . . Heat . . . This is not your job lot of birch trees! The people there look like bronze . . .'

'As you will,' one of the guests remarked. 'It is certainly curious, but you shouldn't talk down our birch trees. You'd have to go far to find anything to rival our birch liqueur. To tell the truth, after looking at these paintings – I don't know about anybody else, but I'm ready for a birch brandy!'

'Well, how about that!' Morozov retorted. 'Well, Olympovich, my butler, tells me, "After you hung these pictures up, we've been getting through three times the amount of wine." How do you like that! Who says art can't change anything?'[37]

It tells us something about Korovin's reliability that he claims the paintings were bought at the posthumous exhibition of Gauguin held in 1906. That was three years after Mikhail Morozov's death. It casts doubt on his oft-repeated story of the tripling of wine consumption after four Gauguins were hung in the dining room, and suggests that the reminiscences of Korovin, whose charm and artistic temperament Margarita Morozova had admired, are the product of an overactive imagination.[38] Vinogradov, on the other hand, almost always gets his details right. He recalls that Mikhail Morozov loved spending time in Paris, where he kept an apartment with a maid. 'In Paris,' Mikhail declared, 'I cease to be a tourist and become just a human being. That is why I love the city.' His apartment, we have discovered, was at 72 rue Jouffroy d'Abbans. That is the address at which Paul Durand-Ruel wrote to Morozov when he was in Paris.[39] Ivan Shchukin, another of Durand-Ruel's Russian clients, resided permanently in Paris at 91 Avenue de Wagram, and it is entirely possible he may have introduced Mikhail to Durand-Ruel.

Mikhail Morozov began visiting Paris regularly in 1898, as did Ivan Shchukin's brother, Sergei. Among those seriously collecting contemporary art in the late 1890s, Mikhail Morozov could well claim pride of place. There is no telling what the order of preeminence might have been if he had not passed away at the early age of thirty-three. Morozov rushed ahead and was in no way lagging behind Sergei Shchukin, except that his modus operandi was less orderly. Both of them, the solid, forty-five-year-old merchant and the headstrong young collector, vied with each other to buy the genre paintings of Charles Cottet, the landscapes of Frits Thaulow, and paintings by Eugène Carrière and Maurice Denis. Sergei Shchukin was a brilliant art collector and such a powerful personality that for a century no one doubted that he, not Mikhail Morozov, had been the first owner of Édouard Manet's *In the Bar 'Le Bouchon'*. This came about because of an annoying slip in the first monograph on Manet, whose author erroneously gave Shchukin as the owner.[40] It is hard to believe that a quick sketch of the life of a Parisian bar could have been chosen by Mikhail Morozov without any outside guidance. But for an entry, noticed by chance, in the gallery's accounts indicating that Paul Durand-Ruel purchased *In the Bar* at the sale of the Tavernier Collection at the request of Morozov personally, nobody would have questioned the view that Sergei Shchukin had lost interest in the picture and resold it to Morozov. It is noteworthy that there were only two works by Édouard Manet in Russian collections: his *Portrait of Antonin Proust*, sold by Ivan Shchukin to Ilya Ostroukhov; and a sketch for the painting *Corner of a Café-Concert*, which found its way into the collection of Mikhail Morozov.

Sergei Shchukin used to get completely carried away by an artist, falling head over heels in love with the painting of his latest god. In all probability, Mikhail Morozov simply did not live long enough to become fixated on the work of any one artist. Or was he perhaps attracted to collecting precisely because of the diversity? May this account for the eclecticism of his collection and the constant shifting this way and that, which most people saw as evidence of his dilettantism? How could he buy Claude Monet's *Poppy Field (Argenteuil)* from the collection of the famous writer of farces, Georges Feydeau, and at the same time be seduced by the genre paintings of that epigone of Romantic painting, Gabriel Cornelius von Max? How could he hang Charles Cottet's *Stormy Evening*, a painting redolent of the style of the Itinerants, next to *Violet Cliffs* by Louis Valtat, painted before the birth of Fauvism but in no way inferior to the works of the 'wild beasts'? How could he reconcile the refined ladies in crinolines of Charles Guérin and the amazing pastel *Woman Drying Herself* by Degas with the extravagant *Spanish Dance* of Hermenegildo Anglada Camarasa and the aesthetically unappealing bodies of the *Women Wrestling in Devonshire* by Jean Veber? It was the kind of behaviour one could expect only from the young Morozov. He stood out even among the famously eccentric merchants of Moscow.

Here is Vasily Perepletchikov's description of the Morozov mansion: 'I visited him at home. Everything was very expensive and opulent but, heavens above, there was just the same lack of unity as in his book. A good painting was hanging next to a bad one; the loud bittiness of the floor clashed with the drapery.'[41] By 'bad paintings' the artist plainly had in mind Veber's naked *Women Wrestling in Devonshire* for the entertainment of some admiring spectators, which did verge on indecency. Needless to say, when Margarita Morozova was left a widow, she sold it.

The collection grew apace. The winter garden had to be sacrificed to make way for an art gallery. 'What a treasury of art Mikhail Morozov would have created if only he had lived,' Vinogradov lamented. He had, however, little time left. His last acquisition, a portrait of the singer Yvette Guilbert by Toulouse-Lautrec, was bought for its Russian client by the Bernheim-Jeune Gallery at the sale of Arsène Alexandre's collection in the spring of 1903.[42] There were hugely ambitious plans for new acquisitions. In the summer Morozov was intending to buy another Corot, and was prepared to spend a vast sum of over 40,000 francs to acquire a painting by Millet. He also asked Durand-Ruel to reserve him a painting by 'the Russian Alma-Tadema', Stefan Bakałowicz.[43]

For all his foibles, Mikhail was a colourful person who loved life. He was huge and had limitless energy; he ate and drank beyond all reason, knowing full well that he was destroying himself. 'Mikhail Morozov has put on even more weight and continues to cavort through life regardless. There are already disturbing signs of a reckoning to come, but these subtle warnings seem to have no effect on him. Wine, women and paintings, the preoccupations of the environment in which he has his being, are how he passes his time,'[44] Perepletchikov noted censoriously. Margarita lamented that, 'As a boy of ten he had scarlet fever, with complications in the heart and kidneys . . . It was essential that he should go easy on them throughout his life and take care of himself. Of course, he wanted none of it and did exactly what was most damaging for his heart and kidneys . . . Even after the doctors had diagnosed inflammation of the kidneys he carried on drinking vodka every day, accompanying it with raw meat and pepper. It was terrible to behold!'[45] The pleading of his wife and recommendations of his doctors were to no avail.

The Morozovs had a genetic predisposition to obesity, and Mikhail Morozov, because he was so overweight, looked much older than his years. 'Mikhail Abramovich sits in a chair, breathing heavily. It is not easy for him to breathe, especially when, God forbid, he is agitated. He is very fat: from behind you cannot tell where his head ends and his neck begins. There are folds of fat. He has a redoubtable paunch, which looks like it belongs to a big Cochin-China cockerel,' Perepletchikov

9  Margarita (seated, far left) with her children (from left to right) Yury, Yelena and Mikhail
(Mika) sitting before her on the floor, with the portrait of Mikhail Morozov
by Valentin Serov behind them, late 1903.

tells us. 'Yet despite all these burdens, Mikhail Abramovich is radiant. His pink, ruddy face shines; his great bald spot, which occupies the whole of his head, shines; his gold chain and half boots shine; the buttons on his frock coat shine; his cufflinks shine; indeed Mikhail Abramovich himself shines. Devout people believe that in the olden days the saints had a halo of light around their heads: that is evidently not the source of the radiance of Mikhail Abramovich.'[46]

As a chronicler, Perepletchikov is fairly unforgiving in his diary towards his protagonist: 'He is conscious that all of Moscow society knows him; that is, the people who go to exhibitions, to the theatre, to the stock exchange, in the city. Everyone's eyes are on him and that gives him pleasure. He progresses around an art exhibition like a king, and indeed he is a king of sorts, only a chintz king. His Tver factory produces chintz worth many millions every year.' Our diarist waxes vitriolic on the subject of Morozov's enthusiasm for art, considering his love to be feigned and his understanding of painting to be superficial and 'chintzy': 'Mikhail Abramovich loves art, but does he understand it? Well, of course he does, after a fashion, but it is a chintzy fashion. Nothing wrong with chintz, of course: it is a very fine fabric. But velvet it is not!'[47] Perepletchikov was not alone in that judgement.

But young Mikhail Morozov was just beginning to grow up and mellow. 'In the last three years, life with my husband changed a great deal; it took on a quite different character,' Margarita insists in her memoirs. 'The life of partying we led for several years was over. A period of greater maturity was coming. It was just at that moment that my husband died.'[48]

# CHAPTER V

# To Moscow! To Prechistenka!

The view in the family had been that young Mikhail was good at science and the arts, and accordingly should go to the lycée and on to university. What was certain was that business was not his forte: Mikhail Morozov lasted just two years as chairman of the board of directors.

The youngest son, Arseniy, although he had practical training in England (from the end of the 1860s the Trading Company of Savva Morozov and Sons had an office in Liverpool), never put in an appearance at the factory, preferring to go hunting and fuss over his beloved dogs.

As for Ivan, he was serious-minded and conscientious. He was accordingly despatched to Zurich to learn to be a chemist, a profession highly relevant to the textile industry just then. His grandfather, 'owing to his inability to read and write', could not even put his signature to business papers, but here was his grandson graduating from the Faculty of Natural Science of the Zurich Polytechnic in the very year that Albert Einstein matriculated there.[1] If the founder of the theory of relativity had been born a few years earlier, they might have been attending lectures in the same lecture theatre.

10  Ivan as a student at the Zurich Polytechnic, early 1890s.

Ivan, however, lost no time in leaving Zurich, and went directly from Switzerland back to Tver to engage seriously in running the factories. Nothing particularly formative seems to have occurred during his years in Tver. He improved the production process, increased capacities, developed sales, and grew richer. His brothers, shareholders in the company, grew richer too.

Ivan Morozov appeared to have turned into a typical factory owner. His sister-in-law, Margarita, wrote that he was born to take charge of the business. His personality was not, however, quite as simple and straightforward as might have appeared at first sight. Ivan Morozov was a gentle, reflective, sensitive person, averse to trouble of any sort. Sergei Vinogradov described him as having 'the friendly eyes of a calf', and Yury Bakhrushin saw him as 'idle, but a good sort'. Nikolai Varentsov recalled that he 'was one of those people who are greatly discouraged if the even flow of their life is disrupted'.[2]

What Ivan Morozov wanted was not to be a factory manager at all: he wanted to paint. Even when he was studying chemistry in Zurich, he would go sketching. On Sundays he painted landscapes in oils in the open air. 'Morozov . . . painted landscapes really quite well, and the two of us would sometimes go of a Sunday off round Lake Zurich to paint. He studied chemistry diligently . . . attended seminars reluctantly, and did not at all enjoy drafting designs for factories. He would appeal to me for help,' recalls architect Ilya Bondarenko, who was on friendly terms with Ivan in Switzerland:

Konstantin Korovin's portrait of Morozov . . . conveys his personality accurately and fairly. He was always lively and cheerful, with kind eyes in a plump, ruddy face, framed by light brown hair and a goatee beard.

Morozov had only the outward appearance of a merchant; by nature, in those years when he was studying in Zurich, he was good-natured and reserved. He had been well brought up, and could clearly discriminate a genuine interest in learning and knowledge from a purely outward, affected iconoclasm. His brother Mikhail had taken it into his head to write a book about Charles the Fifth, needless to say, using some student to do the donkey work! . . . How Ivan laughed, quite without malice, at his brother, who must surely have been more at home with the Gypsy chorus at the notorious Yar restaurant than writing a completely superfluous history of Karl the Fifth!

71

On those days we spent hours together, sketching picturesque nooks of some village like Bendlikon, and would return for a late meal at the first-class Kronenhalle restaurant. Despite the high quality of the food, the prices were modest, and Morozov once complained indignantly that it was impossible to spend more than 100 francs, or 37 rubles, even with champagne.[3]

We have already mentioned that the Morozov brothers studied drawing and painting under the guidance of the outstanding artists their mother, Varvara, employed as tutors for her sons. Little can she have dreamed where her concern that her boys should learn to paint would lead.

'In Zurich, every free minute I would take my box of paints and go into the mountains to paint studies. These are my happiest memories,' Ivan Morozov would say dreamily. He could not, however, allow himself the indulgence of taking up painting as a profession. There was already one writer in the family, Arseny was indolent, and one of the brothers had to take responsibility for the family business. Moreover, Ivan harboured no illusions about his own artistic talent. Yury, the son of art collector Alexei Bakhrushin, would later recall Ivan musing that, 'To become a real artist you have to work very, very hard, to dedicate your whole life to painting. Otherwise it will all come to nothing. You will only get somewhere if you look at everything in life through the eyes of an artist. That is not given to everyone. It has not been given to me, and *I have to settle for delighting in the works of other people* [emphasis added] . . . In art, the most dreadful thing is mediocrity. It is better to be hopelessly bad. That at least deceives no one.'[4]

Ivan Abramovich was probably judging himself too harshly. His efforts at painting have not come down to us, but we can tell he had a subtle sensitivity for painting, since otherwise he would never have been able to assemble such an amazing collection.

Be that as it may, Ivan Morozov gave priority to business over painting. Of the three brothers, he proved to be the most responsible, the Morozov spirit of enterprise counterbalancing the Khludov flightiness. When Mikhail accused his mother of overdoing her enthusiasm for charity, Ivan usually sided with Varvara. Mikhail was indignant when his mother and brother decided to pay compensation for industrial accidents to workers in their factory. It was the indignation of Larion Rydlov in *The Gentleman* when he fulminated, 'The first thing I shall do is abolish all your projects: those tea houses of yours, your theatres, and streetlights, and hostels. Each person should stick with his own party: you are either a capitalist or you are a worker.'

Margarita Morozova did her utmost to shield her husband, insisting that the real conservative was not Mikhail but Ivan, in whom 'there was none of that Slavic dreaminess at all'. Ivan had every justification for constantly repeating that Slavic dreaminess could do nothing but harm in business.

By nature Ivan was reserved and meticulous, and that proved very good for the business. Although Margarita notes that, for the sake of the business, he was prepared to sacrifice a great deal and to subordinate his desires to it, he had not the least intention of staying in the provinces forever. He decided it was perfectly possible to manage a factory in Tver, which he had just spent five years putting in order, from an office in Moscow.

Ivan Morozov saw in the new twentieth century as a homeowner in Moscow. He decided not to chase after fashion, and settled himself in an estate which had originally been owned by a member of the nobility. The mansion on Prechistenka Street, which he bought from the widow of his Uncle David, was in no wise inferior to any of the other Morozov residences in size, sumptuousness or situation, and there remained barely a handful of such properties on the market in Moscow. The old, aristocratic mansion looked remarkably elegant and yet entirely suited to modern life, which left no one in any doubt that the director of the Tver Textile Mill Company was not only rich, but also had good taste.

11 Prechistenka Street in the early 1920s. Ivan Morozov's mansion is adjacent to the palace of the princely Dolgoruky family.

The urban estate on Prechistenka Street, which survived the fire of 1812, had belonged to Major General Alexander Tuchkov, and in 1817 passed into the ownership of Count Sergei Potemkin. Over the course of the nineteenth century it passed from hand to hand and the main house was altered many times. The last time was in the early 1870s, when the architect Petr Campioni was commissioned by its then owner, Anna Martynova. In 1889 she sold the house to David Morozov, and it was subsequently bought by his nephew, Ivan.

The thirty-year-old millionaire now had a house, and it only remained to warm it with visitors. It hardly seems likely that Ivan Morozov would have gone out of his way to lure writers, actors and artists away from

Margarita's salon on Smolensk Boulevard: they would simply have gravitated to him. He was a man of substance, a patron of the arts, who also possessed an excellent wine cellar and was a generous host. It was accordingly not long after the death of Mikhail Morozov that his coterie of artists migrated to Prechistenka Street, where they could continue as before to debate issues of politics and art in agreeable surroundings. Their meetings would have been along the lines of a big bachelor dinner party described by Ilya Ostroukhov. 'A lot of interesting people: that sweet, young, sixty-year-old Sorokoumovsky; Sadovsky, Chaliapin, Vasnetsov . . . a fine meal, candles, wine, and after dinner, until midnight, cards. In the most jovial company. I had hardly played for a year and, to my misfortune, Ivan Abramovich and Chaliapin managed to win a terribly large amount from me . . . It took until eight in the morning for me to reduce my debt by hook or by crook to a respectable level of a few hundred rubles.'[5]

We can see that the pragmatic, business-like manufacturer did not stint himself: he enjoyed convivial gatherings no less than his brothers. He gambled (within reason); he kept up with fashion (as we see from Korovin's portrait of the thirty-year-old Ivan Morozov with a flower in his buttonhole); he was not averse to eating well, and soon turned into a 'stout, pink sybarite'.[6] He gained the reputation of having a soft spot for the Yar restaurant, or rather, for the ladies who sang there, a subject to which we shall return.

The upper floor of his old-world mansion was fully furnished but unoccupied, until Ivan Morozov began collecting paintings. In the latter years of his studies in Switzerland he had given up oil painting, but he did not lose his love of art and, almost as soon as he returned home, began attending exhibitions and acquiring paintings. Initially, he was far more restrained and prudent than his brother, selecting at exhibitions of the Itinerants Society what Igor Grabar would describe as 'docile' canvases. Within a few years Mikhail had become a familiar presence at the Paris Salons and galleries, but Ivan, busy managing the factories, had no time to spend on European trips. He made it to Paris only in spring 1903, in the company of his brother.

Ivan's first visit was Mikhail's last. The Salon of the Société Nationale des Beaux-Arts to which his brother brought him impressed Ivan by its sheer scale: 1,500 paintings, another 500 drawings, pastels and water-colours, to say nothing of the engravings, sculpture and other *objets d'art*. Ivan was still little versed in contemporary French painting, so focused his attention on works in a style he was familiar with. The impressionist canvases of Konstantin Korovin, who had recently painted his portrait, are in no way inferior to the genre paintings of the Spaniard Sorolla y Bastida,[7] and Serov is no worse than Lucien Simon of the so-called *Bande noire*.[8] Sergei Shchukin already had both of them in his collection, which was reassurance that they could safely be acquired. Ivan particularly liked saucy subjects, of a kind nowhere to be found in Moscow. For the first two years, the Yar's regular customer concentrated on aquiring depic-tions of ladies of the demi-monde behind bar counters and elegantly attired beauties languishing at tables in cafés. Over several years he was to assemble a whole gallery of paintings and drawings by artists popular at the beginning of the twentieth century but now long forgotten: Guiguet, Lempereur, Lissac, Minartz, Helleu, O'Conor, Morrice.

The 'Paris strand' in Ivan Morozov's biography begins with his acqui-sition of a pastel by Louis Legrand. For his 'cautious echo of Toulouse-Lautrec and Art Nouveau'[9] Ivan Morozov paid 1,500 francs, and the following year, for a second pastel, a cool 2,500. For Picasso's *Harlequin and his Companion*, which he bought five years later, Morozov paid one-fifth of what he paid for *The Supper of the Apache*. It is painful to contemplate the difference today between the prices paid for the forgotten Legrand and for Picasso.

Ignacio Zuloaga's two-metre canvas *Preparation for a Bullfight* was Ivan's most extravagant acquisition in spring 1903.[10] The Spanish theme, with its typical subject matter, from sultry beauties to bullfighting, was

. 'Konstantin Korovin's 1903] portrait of Morozov . . . conveys his personality ccurately and fairly. He vas always lively and heerful, with kind eyes in a plump, ruddy face, framed by light brown hair and a oatee beard,' recalls Ilya Bondarenko.

. Dosya (Madame Morozova) provoked a lifferent reaction, at least n Valentin Serov who alled her 'a painted doll'. His condescension is isible in his portrait of the newlywed: the plunging neckline, the sumptuous dress, the fingers freighted with rings, the bejewelled gold bracelets, the earrings, the pendant – Serov included every last extravagant detail.

3. Adored both by art critics and the general public, Serov's portrait of Mika, the youngest of Margarita and Mikhail Morozov's children, is sometimes called the best child portrait in modern Russian painting.

4. This engagingly domestic portrait of Dosya by Sergei Vinogradov is dated 1918, one year before the Morozovs left Russia.

. The spectacular Music Salon (or Denis Room) in Ivan Morozov's mansion on Prechistenka Street. Morozov paid Maurice Denis 70,000 francs for the panels. The photographs of this room, published by *Apollon* magazine in 1912, are the only surviving images of the mansion's interior from the period.

. The Music Salon has been recreated in the State Hermitage Museum, evoking the visual impact of the original. 'Elegant roses, delicate greenery, vivid violets and pale, translucent blue hues. What joy, what tranquillity Maurice Denis has brought into this light, wealthy house. It is as if he has managed to capture, in the midst of the Russian winter, a memory of a Greek, or perhaps rather, a French springtime,' wrote Émile Verhaeren.

7. A reconstructed photograph from the early 1930s showing the main staircase of Morozov's mansion as seen from the first-floor landing, with Bonnard's *On the Mediterranean* panels, *Autumn* and *Fruit-Picking*. Looming near the column is Auguste Rodin's *Jean d'Aire, Les Bourgeois de Calais* from Mikhail Ryabushinsky's collection.

8. Morozov had only to open his front door and look up for this southern landscape to appear before his eyes: a blue strip of sea, the sun, golden sand, children playing. *On the Mediterranean* was a kind of trompe l'œil: three separate tall canvases affixed to the wall between semicircular pillars. The Mediterranean world captured here served as a prelude to the classical mythology of Denis's Music Salon.

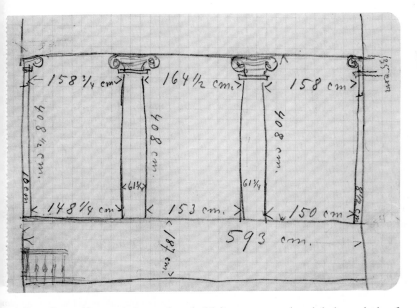

9. As Pierre Bonnard began painting a park on the Mediterranean coast, he only had a rough idea of the Moscow mansion: he was furnished with photographs of the staircase and measurements of the space between the semicircular pillars. This is Bonnard's own sketch of Morozov's staircase.

10. (opposite, top) Valentin Serov's arresting 1910 portrait of Ivan Morozov the collector. Henri Matisse was not one of Morozov's favourite painters, but Serov nevertheless placed *Fruit and Bronze* in the background of his portrait: a vivid red, yellow and blue still life with a carpet, apples, pomegranates, lemons and one of Matisse's bronze statuettes.

11. (opposite, bottom) These three works in the middle of the top row painted by Matisse in Tangier, Morocco, were not initially conceived as a triptych, but Matisse realized that they made a perfect ensemble and added a blue light to link them. In April 1913, Matisse exhibited the Moroccan triptych among other works in Paris, and soon almost the entire Moroccan series of eleven paintings became the property of Russian collectors. While there are no photographs of Matisse's Moroccan triptych in Morozov's mansion, the Matisse Room of the State Museum of New Western Art in 1933 combined the Morozov and Shchukin collections.

12. (above) *The Casbah Gate* is the right-hand image of the triptych.

13. Paul Cézanne was one of Morozov's favourite painters, and the eighteen works he owned by Cézanne were regarded as the jewel of his collection. This is the Cézanne Room in Morozov's old mansion in 1923, after it became the second unit of the State Museum of New Western Art.

14. Cézanne's *Great Pine at Aix*. After falling in love with Cézanne's art, the dealer Ambroise Vollard acquired around 200 of his works. During seven years of passionate collecting, Morozov in turn purchased fifteen Cézannes from Vollard's gallery.

5. Even though it remained unfinished, this portrait of Cézanne's wife is one of the artist's finest works. Morozov acquired it from Vollard's gallery in Paris in 1911.

16. *Night Café* is one of van Gogh's most interesting interiors. An article on Dostoevsky's *Notes from the House of the Dead* had a profoundly disturbing effect on the artist: 'In my picture I have tried to show that a café is a place where you can go mad or commit a crime. In short . . . to reproduce the atmosphere of the flames of hell . . . to convey the demonic power of the tavern-snare.'

17. Van Gogh's paintings on display in the Morozov section of the Sate Museum of New Western Art in 1928, the legendary *Night Café* still among them. However, on 9 May 1933 the directors were ordered to hand over four works to the Antikvariat to be sold abroad. The paintings, including Cézanne's *Madame Cézanne in the Conservatory* and van Gogh's *Night Café*, sold for $260,000 to the American collector Stephen Carlton Clark.

8. Paul Gauguin's *Night Café in Arles*. The two *Cafés*, hanging in the same room in Morozov's collection, were a reminder of the friendship of their painters, who had lived and worked together in Arles in the autumn of 1888. The artists not only depicted the same interior, but gave the paintings the same name.

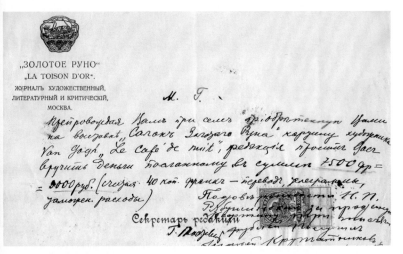

19. This bill shows that Morozov paid 7,500 francs or 3,000 rubles, 'taking the exchange rate as 40 kopecks to the franc, including postal bank fees, telegrams and customs expenses', for van Gogh's *Night Café*.

20. Morozov acquired *Two Acrobats (Harlequin and his Companion)* from Vollard. H[e] took a shine to this work by an unknown artist: the vivid colours, strong, fluent outline[,] a melancholy Harlequin with[a] whitened face and a girlfrien[d] whose face resembled a Japanese mask. It was only when he was preparing for the feature in *Apollon* that Morozov realized he had not even bothered to find out the full name of the artist: one Pablo Picasso.

21. The Picasso wall at the State Museum of New Western Art in the early 1930s shows Picasso's *Two Acrobats* and *Young Acrobat on a Ball*, from Ivan Morozov's collection.

22. The room of Mikhail Morozov's collection of paintings bequeathed to the Tretyakov Gallery in 1910. In 1918, the Bolshevik authorities demanded that his widow surrender everything that was meant to remain in her possession throughout her life. Margarita did not dare to object. In exchange for ten paintings and Rodin's marble Eve, she was promised two rooms in the mansion requisitioned from her in August 1918, to accommodate the few valuable objects that were being left in her safekeeping.

23. As far as collecting paintings was concerned, Ivan felt that he was following in his brother Mikhail's footsteps. Sometimes he did indeed buy the same artists as his brother, even with the same models, like the actress Jeanne Samary. In November 1904, after the Renoir retrospective at the Salon d'Automne, Ivan bought his first Impressionist masterpiece: the *Portrait of Jeanne Samary in a Low-Necked Dress*, which was in no way inferior to the large, formal portrait of the actress which his brother had acquired.

24, 25. In 1928, the contentious decision to form a single museum from the two great original collections was made. This new State Museum of Western Art held nineteen canvasses by Claude Monet, eleven by Renoir, twenty-nine by Gauguin, twenty-six by Cézanne, ten by van Gogh, nine by Degas, fourteen by Bonnard, twenty-two by Derain, fifty-three by Matisse and fifty-three by Picasso. The museum managed to survive for twenty years, even though attempts to destroy it were undertaken virtually from the day it opened its doors. These photographs are from 1932.

6. The Bonnard and Vuillard room at the State Museum of New Western Art in 1933. Bonnard's emblematic five-square-metre (202 x 254 cm) canvas *Summer* from Ivan Morozov's collection hangs in the centre of a display of his and Vuillard's works.

27. Ivan Morozov looked for tranquility and joy in paintings, which is why he loved the Nabis. This interior artwork by Eduard Vuillard, one of the Nabis, was among Ivan's first acquisitions. Intriguingly, Sergei Shchukin's collection of modern French art began in 1899 with the acquisition of a very similar interior painting also by Vuillard.

28. The former Music Salon (Denis Room) of Ivan Morozov's mansion in the 1940s. On 27 June 1941, five days after the outbreak of war, the museum moved onto a war footing. The paintings were removed from their frames and hastily packed into crates and on 15 July a special museum train took most of the collection east to Novosibirsk.

29. Alexander Gerasimov took over as president of the USSR Academy of Arts in the summer of 1947. It was his idea to use the former mansion of Ivan Morozov as the Academy's Moscow headquarters. Gerasimov had a visceral hatred of the State Museum of New Western Art, which continued even after the collections had been combined and he had taken possession of Morozov's study. Indeed, there are tales that the president of the Academy threatened to hang anyone who dared to exhibit Picasso.

all the rage. Zuloaga's dramatic, indeed theatrical, paintings of dancers, bullfighters and dwarfs did not come cheap, but Ivan, like his brother Mikhail, susceptible to fashionable names, was not deterred. Unable to resist the painterly skill of a Spaniard who had conquered the Parisian public, Morozov wrote out a cheque for 15,000 francs having, with some difficulty, bargained the price down by 1,000 francs. In the course of three days in April 1903 he deposited 20,000 francs in the tills of the Salon.

In addition to the Salon there were the galleries, to which he duly repaired with his brother. Mikhail spent his last holiday in Paris with his customary gusto: smart restaurants, theatres, motor car trips. Durand-Ruel was hosting an exhibition of another celebrity of the time, Maxime Dethomas, a master of genre sketches in the spirit of Toulouse-Lautrec, a student of Carrière and a close friend of Zuloaga. Pastels and watercolours were inexpensive, and Ivan bought two illustrations: *The Slanderers* for himself[11] and *The Governess* as a gift for Mikhail. Although this was not the most outstanding of the many exhibitions arranged by Durand-Ruel, it has its place in history because of a rapturous recollection of his visit to it by Marcel Proust, a friend and admirer of the talent of Dethomas, who was very rarely seen in society because of ill health.

A few days later Ivan Morozov was back in rue Laffitte, and luckily the gallery was open without the need for an appointment. He had just acquired an inexpensive river scene by Albert Lebourg, one of the less prominent participants in two exhibitions of the Impressionists, recalling how he had himself once painted similar views from nature in Switzerland.[12] Of all paintings, landscapes were the most popular commodity and there were plenty of them in the Durand-Ruel Gallery. The Russian visitor's eye was caught by a wintry view, a great rarity for French painters. But the price! 'Make me an offer!' the marchand invited him. Morozov named the amount he was willing to pay and asked for the canvas to be reserved for him. He was ready to transfer the money providing his offer was accepted. The letter agreeing to let him have

*Frost in Louveciennes* by Alfred Sisley for 11,500 francs caught up with him only when he was already back in Moscow.[13]

Durand-Ruel did not attempt to drive hard bargains. He was appreciative of Russian customers and had a gut feeling for promising clients. The future Tsar Alexander III had himself visited the gallery in 1874 and acquired a painting of a knacker's yard. The Barbizonians, in whom Durand-Ruel specialized, let alone the Impressionists, were of no interest to the tsarevich. His Royal Highness called them all 'that ugly lot'. In the 1890s, the first Russian names in the gallery's ledgers were those of Alexei Bogolyubov and Sergei Tretyakov. They were followed by 'Botkine', 'Ostroukhoff', 'Stchoukine' and 'Morozoff'. Later there were three Shchukins, and two Morozovs.

The English painter, Alfred Sisley, an admirer of Constable and Turner and a friend of Monet and Renoir, died in 1899 without living to see his paintings become famous. Barely was he in his grave than the prices paid for his lyrical landscapes began creeping up. Morozov agreed with Octave Mirbeau that in Sisley's painting there was 'more charm than strength', and 'an innate grace, something that was alert, bright and easy, a delightful air of devil-may-care; he infused the unfinished with a poetry that was often exquisite.'[14] To anticipate, we might mention that Ivan Morozov was to acquire five landscapes by Sisley, all painted between 1873 and 1885. The artist's late manner, which replaced his calm, harmonious style, appealed neither to the marchand nor to his Russian client.

The Paris voyage left many pleasant memories, and Ivan intended to repeat it in the autumn and to plunge headlong into the whirlpool of the art scene. The brothers may have agreed to travel there together, but in September Mikhail felt unwell. Despite the best endeavours of Dr Zakharin to intimidate him, he carried on drinking and eating as if there were no tomorrow, accepting no restrictions. Professor von Leyden was summoned urgently from Berlin and diagnosed acute nephritis. The German doctor had treated Tsar Alexander III himself, so charged an astronomical fee for his visit but was, alas, unable to do anything to help, and on 12 October 1903 Mikhail died. In August that year he had turned thirty-three.

As far as collecting paintings was concerned, Ivan was to feel until the end of his life that he was following in his brother's footsteps. Sometimes he did indeed buy the same artists as his brother had, even with the same models, like, for example, the actress Jeanne Samary. This has caused bewilderment among journalists, who often attributed purchases by Mikhail to Ivan. The view spread that as a collector Ivan Morozov was his brother's successor, having taken over the baton from him. Few people were aware that Ivan had been buying paintings before his brother's death, or that he never had any intention of merely following Mikhail's artistic predilections. No more was he aiming to compete with Sergei Shchukin, whose example must, of course, have inspired him.

For the first three or four years, Ivan seemed to be gauging his strength. He needed a run-up before he could attempt the mighty leap which would enable him, if not to equal Shchukin, then at least substantially to reduce the gap between them. Sergei Shchukin and Mikhail Morozov had begun to find their bearings in the Paris art market in 1898, which meant Ivan Morozov was a full five years behind them. Beginning only in 1904, he was to visit Paris systematically, in spring and autumn, because the Salon des Indépendants was held in April and the Salon d'Automne in October. In the spring he could also visit the Salon de la Société Nationale des Beaux-Arts and off-season exhibitions in the Paris galleries.

At the end of the 1904 Salon d'Automne, Ivan bought his first Impressionist masterpiece – the *Portrait of Jeanne Samary in a Low-Necked Dress*, which was in no way inferior to the large, formal portrait of the actress which his brother had acquired.

Navigating the Salon in the Grand Palais was no simple matter, and to select paintings was even more difficult. There were over 1,000 of these by exhibitors alone and, in addition, retrospectives of the leading French artists. Passing through the halls of Puvis de Chavannes, Redon and Toulouse-Lautrec, Morozov lingered by Cézanne and Renoir. He was clearly not yet ready to purchase Cézanne, who would shortly become his favourite artist, but could not resist Renoir. 'Who has painted women better, especially young women? (I make no mention of Ingres),' Sergei Vinogradov wrote in the margin of his catalogue, taking it upon himself to oversee the purchases of his new ward. At the same time, he entered a bracketed reservation that he disliked the pink background of Renoir's portraits. Morozov was less wordy, and only marked a cross against No. 25, *Portrait de Samary*.[15]

After furious haggling with Durand-Ruel, Ivan purchased the *Portrait of Jeanne Samary*.[16] Because, in addition to the Renoir, his customer was taking two landscapes by Sisley, the marchand agreed to part with all three paintings as a job lot for 40,000 francs. *The Garden of Hoschedé, Montgeron* had come from the collection of singer Jean-Baptiste Faure, who was a major collector of Impressionism. This painting, the best of Morozov's Sisleys, was to remain in Moscow, while Morozov later returned the second landscape, or rather, exchanged it, for the melancholy *Windy Day at Veneux*, which had been languishing in the rue Laffitte gallery for over twenty years. The rich man from Moscow preferred pastoral paintings. That was a requirement admirably met by the canvases of another impressionist, Camille Pissarro. Like Mikhail, Ivan became a regular visitor to the Vollard Gallery, and was to choose there an early landscape, *Ploughed Land*, in a grey-brown palette, almost like that of the Barbizonians. Three years later he was to acquire, by correspondence, a second, late Pissarro, *Autumn Morning at Eragny*, which was just begging to be paired with Sisley's sunlit *Garden of Hoschedé*.

Industry Councillor Ivan Morozov was a busy man. From his house on Prechistenka Street to the office of the board of directors at 9 Varvarka Street and back: such was his daily commute. The managing director of the Tver Textile Mill Company did not regularly travel the 160 kilometres to Tver to check how things were going at the factories: it was

12 The main office building of the Tver Textile Mill Company at 9 Varvarka Street
at the beginning of the 1900s, since destroyed.

just too far. He took the waters in Carlsbad or Biarritz in the summer, after the Nizhny Novgorod fair; and in spring and autumn there were the Salons in Paris. In the French capital there were art exhibitions and auctions every month. The postal service between Moscow and Paris worked smoothly, and letters, invitations to openings, and catalogues arrived at Varvarka Street precisely three days after being posted. It would be a long time yet before a foreign client could be contacted by telephone, but the world was already using the wireless telegraph, the invention of which was a matter of dispute between the Russian Popov and the Italian Marconi.

Paul Durand-Ruel acted on behalf of his Moscow client only once, in March 1907, when he was organizing a sale of the collection of Georges Viau.[17] The Parisian dental surgeon would assemble a collection of paintings, sell it, and then start all over again. He managed to pull this off three times. From his first auction Morozov was able to acquire Pissarro's *Autumn Morning* cheaply. Renoir's *In the Garden. Under the Trees of Moulin de la Galette*, however, cost him ten times as much. Durand-Ruel took his usual ten per cent commission.

Ivan Morozov had first seen *Under the Trees of Moulin de la Galette* in the Renoir retrospective at the Salon d'Automne of 1904, after which he had bought the wonderful portrait of Samary. He did not, however, award Renoir's painting a cross. Perhaps the scene in the famous Montmartre restaurant struck him as too sketchy. *La Loge* (The Theatre Box) was quite a different matter: he put against it not one, but an exceptional two crosses. The picture was in every respect to his taste: the theatre, a box at the opera, a couple in evening dress. In place of Nina Lopez, a model from Montmartre who posed in the nude, he could imagine his beloved wife Dosya, and the man in the tailcoat could be, not Renoir's brother, Edmond, but himself. However, it was intimidating even to enquire after the price of such masterpieces and, in any case, Ivan initially spent very little on paintings. By 1907, however, every trip to Paris was leaving him the lighter by six-figure sums (in francs).

Aware that his ward was now acting more freely, and beginning to 'acquire items of the very first importance', Vinogradov, who still retained his influence, set about trying to persuade Ivan to buy the Renoir masterpiece:

I was often in Paris, and every Tuesday I would visit Durand-Ruel's apartment (on Tuesdays the family departed to their estate to give art lovers an opportunity to marvel at the wondrous paintings) . . . and always found an empty space where *La Loge* should have been. It was invariably away on its travels. Then, suddenly, on one of the Tuesdays, I saw this prodigy! . . . From then on I tried to persuade Ivan to acquire *La Loge*. He dismissed the idea, saying the picture would cost an incredible amount of money. For some reason I imagined it would be possible to buy it for 150,000 francs. I pointed out that in our money that was only about 50,000 rubles, which he could afford for a treasure like that. He would perpetuate his name for all time if he was the possessor of *La Loge*.

Ivan Abramovich was terribly unsure about it . . . but in the end I succeeded in persuading him and we went to Paris to buy *La Loge*. How extremely ill at ease he was as he stood before the painting, when it was finally time to ask the price! He went bright red, then he turned pale, his brow even a little damp. He stuttered, had trouble breathing, and finally blurted out the question of how much the painting would cost. Durand-Ruel, a cosy little old man in soft boots, speaking somehow very gently, replied, 'I do not know how much this item should cost. Last year in America I was offered 350,000 francs for it. I didn't accept it, and actually I think it should stay in France and be in the Louvre.' Ivan sighed with relief, recovering his breath.[18]

Sergei Shchukin also made a bid to acquire *La Loge*, probably unaware of just how much such a purchase might cost. 'We have not offered the Renoir to anyone. *La Loge* is not for sale,' Durand-Ruel telegraphed him in Berlin.[19] This was in the late autumn of 1904, when Shchukin had gone to see Paul Cassirer about buying Monet's rejoinder to Manet's *Le Déjeuner sur l'herbe*. Durand-Ruel had no problem parting with this rarest canvas of the early Monet, and forwarded it to the Berlin gallery owner to sell on commission. He could not bring himself to part with *La Loge*, however, even though he did in principle sell paintings from his private collection.

Petr Ivanovich, yet another of the art-collecting Shchukin brothers, managed to persuade Durand-Ruel to part with Renoir's *Nude Seated on a Sofa*, which was hanging in his apartment. Petr delegated his already mentioned younger brother, who lived in Paris, to negotiate for the painting. Petr Shchukin hung Renoir's *Nude*, also known as *The Pearl*, also known as *Mademoiselle Anna*, in his bedroom next to another pearl of his small collection, Degas' *Woman Combing Her Hair*. Ivan Morozov was not able to obtain paintings by Degas as beautiful as those which the Shchukin brothers acquired. He had to be content with a sketch of dancers and a large pastel of a nude with a towel. His brother Mikhail had acquired a pastel on a similar theme.

Ivan had better luck with Renoir. In 1908, Vollard sold him *The Frog Pond (La Grenouillère)*, one of three versions of a delightful motif, painted in 1869 by both Renoir and Monet, who placed their easels side by side on one of the Croissy islands. The Paris suburb was famous not so much for its bathing and restaurants as for its ladies of easy virtue. In the time of the Goncourt brothers, Zola, and Maupassant, who came here in search of amusement, the demoiselles were called *grenouilles*, frogs, because they spent their time hopping from one client to the next. Unsurprisingly, in the Soviet period Renoir's *The Frog Pond* was retitled *Bathing in the Seine*. The carefree atmosphere attracted young Pierre-Auguste Renoir and Claude Monet to this welcoming spot, and their paintings depicted young men in white trousers and boaters, ladies in light dresses with full skirts, and couples boating or enjoying an intimate lunch on the grass.

To succeed in buying *The Frog Pond*, painted even before the term 'Impressionism' had been invented, was an incredible success, not least because with every year that passed it became increasingly difficult to find early works by Renoir. Of the entire cohort of Impressionists, Renoir was the most expensive. Paul Durand-Ruel matured paintings like fine vintage wine: the price of *Girl with a Fan* (*La Femme à l'éventail*), featuring Renoir's favourite type of woman, rose year by year. A quarter of a century before selling it to Morozov, Durand-Ruel had bought the painting for 500 francs: he sold it for 40,000, a flat increase of 320 per cent per year!

His six Renoir paintings cost Morozov almost 200,000 francs, including the cost of the frames. Most expensive was *Boy with a Whip*, which he bought from Vollard in 1913. It is the portrait of one of the older children of Senator Étienne Goujon. Morozov could, of course, have continued to buy 'late Renoir', but the maestro's later paintings were less interesting than their predecessors. Severe rheumatism obliged the aged artist to move to Cagnes-sur-Mer on the Côte d'Azur. He died there in 1919, the same year Ivan Morozov emigrated from Russia, leaving behind in Moscow the paintings of Renoir's finest period.

By no means everybody gave Morozov's nous and taste their due, dismissing him as just a rich man buying expensive paintings. There was gossip to the effect that Ivan Abramovich knew nothing about art, enabling the Paris dealers to dump their unsaleable stock on him. In reality, Durand-Ruel, although generally considered a highly skilled salesman, offered Morozov exceptional items of the highest quality. The epithet 'unsaleable goods' might only be credibly applied to *Head of a Woman*. This exquisitely painted but oddly composed painting was sold to him by Vollard.

In his *Recollections of a Picture Dealer*, Ambroise Vollard describes in detail how *Head of a Woman* came to be in his gallery. By coincidence, he was in Renoir's studio at the very moment the portrait of a lady in a blue dress with a plunging neckline was brought back. Many years previously Renoir had given it to Degas, and after the artists quarrelled, the furious Degas sent the painting back. Renoir was enraged by such discourtesy:

In his anger, seizing a palette-knife, he began slashing at the canvas. Having reduced the dress to shreds, he was aiming the knife at the face:

'But, Monsieur Renoir!' I cried.

He paused with his arm in mid-air:

'Well, what's the matter?'

'Monsieur Renoir, you were saying in this very room only the other day that a picture is like a child one has begotten. And now you are going to destroy that face!'

'You're a nuisance with your helpful advice!'

But he lowered his arm, and said suddenly:

'That head was such a lot of trouble to paint! Ma foi! I shall keep it!'

He cut out the upper part of the picture. That fragment, I believe, is now in Russia.

Renoir threw the hacked strips furiously into the fire.[20]

# CHAPTER VI

## Chevalier de la Légion d'honneur

Without exception, people who knew Ivan Morozov well considered him a quiet man, and insisted there was not an iota of the impassioned Morozov-Khludov temperament in him. On the contrary, 'this kind, lazy man was suffused with invariable goodwill and kindliness'.[1] Ivan did not astound Moscow by gambling away millions, like his elder brother Mikhail, or with reckless dares, like the younger Arseny. The managing director of the Tver Textile Mill Company was renowned for different eccentricities. If we discount his *mésalliance* with a chorus girl, his main craziness was paintings or, more precisely, the fact that he spent hundreds of thousands of rubles on them.

Ivan Abramovich was a pedant who meticulously preserved all financial documentation. He did not destroy a single item, whether that was a tiny receipt signed by Yury Bychkov, the permanent secretary of the Union of Russian Artists, or an invoice from a Paris marchand. It was this punctiliousness that allowed Boris Ternovets, into whose hands the collection passed after nationalization, to establish its value.[2] It was not a trifling amount: almost one and a half million French francs. That is exactly how much Morozov spent in the course of eleven years, quietly surpassing Sergei Shchukin – if not in terms of the number of paintings acquired (he was some way behind by that criterion), then in the hundreds of thousands of rubles and francs he spent on them.[3]

Ivan Morozov is considered to have been one of the wealthiest people in Russia at the beginning of the twentieth century. 'We have an abundance of means to live an easy life, but despite that most of us work nine to twelve hours a day. We have very little free time,' he is widely reported as having said. It is indeed from life's routines that people are drawn to beauty in all its manifestations: some to music, some to painting, and some, like Alexei Bakhrushin, to collecting ballet shoes. The younger Bakhrushin believed his father became a friend of Morozov's precisely because they both saw business as only a means to raise money for 'the main mission of their lives'.[4]

Paris, with its exhibitions, auctions, galleries and studios, was different, and made it possible to take a break from the preoccupations and drudgery of everyday life. Another of Moscow's art collectors, the perfumier Henri Brocard, a russified Frenchman, confessed that, 'Crossing the border, you feel as if you have changed into a clean shirt.' Speaking of shirts, it was said that Mikhail Morozov sent his to be laundered in London, while Ivan preferred Paris, and specifically the Grand Hotel where, for many years, he invariably stayed. Unlike Mikhail, who liked to show off, Ivan, as befits a really rich person, did not throw his money around. He declined to take over his brother's apartment in the 16th arrondissement, and saw no reason to buy one of his own. Why incur needless expense?

Collecting paintings proved an absorbing occupation which took Ivan's mind off the routine of the factories, with its eternal pursuit of orders, and workers endlessly demanding higher wages. In the early years of his management there were two strikes: a first in 1897, and a second, much more serious, in 1899. After the second, he decided to move away from Tver, although he continued to visit the factory regularly (though not as frequently as his mother, who went there weekly for many years). Then there came the revolution of 1905. 'Mikhail was dead by this time, and

Ivan was prematurely stout. His obesity earned him offensive, appalling abuse from the workers. It was a bad time, mutinous.'[5] Vinogradov is outraged as he recalls the opprobrium suffered by Ivan. Such rank ingratitude did not deter his mother, Varvara, who valiantly continued her charitable endeavours. Had she survived until October 1917, there is little reason to suppose her own workers would have defended her, for all her good works and everything she had done to ameliorate their lives. The factory 'was a whole township adjacent to the city of Tver. There were some 20,000 workers. The factory estate was astonishingly well endowed. What a huge theatre was built there, with seats for thousands of spectators, what reading rooms, a library, and exemplary apartments for the workers,' Vinogradov wrote admiringly in 1936, having decided not to return to the USSR.[6]

In autumn 1905, factories went on strike, the trains stopped running, the water supply failed, the electricity was cut, and newspapers were not published. The unrest reached the factories in Tver. Ivan Morozov did his best to steer clear of politics, but did not always succeed. Indeed, the Russo-Japanese war brought the Tver factory an exceptionally large order for cloth for the army, which promised vast profits. Work began at six in the morning and latecomers were fined ruthlessly. The working day was twelve hours in stifling conditions amid the roar of the machinery, in return for earnings of 250 rubles a year, which was what you could expect to pay at an exhibition for a painting by an up-and-coming new talent. The factory workers had had enough, and because of riots, in December the owners had to resort to extreme measures to 'pacify' the rebels. Troops were called in from Moscow.

Although Sergei Eisenstein did not film the mass scenes of *Strike* in Tver, he gave an account very close to what took place in the Morozov factories. Eisenstein pointedly made his capitalists caricature fatties, exactly like the Morozov brothers. He deliberately gave them not a single redeeming feature in his film, although there were many among the liberal-minded bourgeoisie and merchants who sympathized with

13  Brand label of the Tver Textile Mill Company, 1910s.

14  The main entrance to the company's site in Tver, 1900s.

the workers. Ivan's mother, Varvara, and his brother's widow, Margarita, for example, both expressed support for the 'proletarians', albeit each in their own way. Almost every evening lectures were held in their homes in Vozdvizhenka Street and Smolensk Boulevard on topical issues: the history of the revolutionary movement, the agrarian question, on political parties, and on how to improve the welfare of the people.

Uncle Savva Morozov went further than anyone else: after mass strikes he demanded that his mother should make over her factories to him to dispose of as he saw fit. He was the managing director of the Nikolskoye factory of Savva Morozov, Son and Company only on paper. In reality his mother, Maria Fedorovna, the principal shareholder and one of the richest women in Russia, was in charge. Savva Timofeevich believed the workers should receive a share of the profits, and intended to put the idea into practice after taking control of the factories. For such seditious intentions, his mother came down on him like a ton of bricks. She declared him all but insane and, threatening to have him placed under guardianship, forced him to resign. Savva was expelled from Moscow by force. Accompanied by his wife and a personal doctor, he departed for treatment on the Côte d'Azur. In the ill-starred year of 1905, in May, at the Royal Hotel in Cannes, he committed suicide.

That same spring, as Savva Morozov was being 'deported' to France, his nephew Ivan was strolling round the Salon des Indépendants where, unlike the other salons, artists could exhibit without being selected by a jury. As a result, the exhibitions of the Indépendants were a positive 'whirlpool of schools, tastes and views, from the extreme right to the extreme left, from ridiculous dilettantism and amateurishness to high quality, important works'.[7] Ivan Morozov's purchases of 1905 merit no special attention. Worthy of mention would have been Renoir's *Portrait of a Young Woman* (1876), but the painting was returned shortly afterwards to the vendor.[8] This is in contrast to the acquisitions of the following year of 1906, when the Morozov collection was enhanced with paintings by Signac, Valtat, Manguin and two works by Maurice Denis.

The owner of the Tver Textile Mill Company, the landscape painter manqué Ivan Morozov, had a real sensibility for painting. He understood not only how patterns were born for Morozov shawls and chintz, but also how the fabric of a painting is woven. Pausing in front of a picture and wondering whether or not to buy it, he would mentally take up his palette and brushes, and ponder where to place a brushstroke, how to mix the paints, which hue to choose. The *Woman Bather* of Manguin, *Spring in Provence* by Signac, *The Boat* by Valtat, *A Corner of Paris* and *Landscape in Dauphine* by Bonnard, marked the dominant tone of the collection from then on.

In spite of the disturbing events of 1905, Morozov missed neither the Salon des Indépendants nor the Salon d'Automne at which Matisse, Derain, Marquet, Vlaminck, Friesz and Manguin exhibited paintings executed in a new manner. They were later to be called Fauvists. The critic Louis Vauxcelles, struck by the contrast between the works of Gustave Moreau's former students and the academic sculptures surrounding them, unintentionally gave the new movement its name, exclaiming, *'C'est Donatello dans la cage aux fauves!'* ('This is Donatello in a cage of wild beasts!')

Cautious Ivan Morozov bought not a single painting at the Salon d'Automne. He was not yet ready for the Fauvists. For the present he was wholly focused on Impressionists. From Durand-Ruel he bought four masterpieces by Claude Monet. Firstly, *The Boulevard des Capucines* in Paris, a painting no less important for the beginnings of Impressionism than Monet's *Impression, Sunrise*, which, with a helping hand from critic Louis Leroy, had given the new trend its name. Secondly, *Haystack at Giverny* and *Corner of the Garden at Montgeron*. And of course, *Waterloo Bridge: Effect of Fog* where Monet 'finally renounces form, seeking in the formless fabric of the subtlest nuances to capture the miracle of light'.[9] The following year Morozov was to find in Vollard's bins a matching painting for *Corner of the Garden*, the two-metre high *Bank of the Pond at Montgeron* – without a stretcher, rolled up, its varnish damaged. Ivan Abramovich decided that five landscapes by Monet, two Pissarros and five paintings by Sisley was enough. He bought no further Impressionists, making an exception only for Renoir, for whose canvases he continued to hunt to the last.

It remains a mystery why it should have been Ivan Morozov, who was not at all inclined to provocative behaviour, who assembled an impressive collection of one of the first scandalous 'isms' of the twentieth century. It is no easier to explain his sudden passion for paintings and his immoderate spending on them. We may speculate that an exalted French title played a part. Monsieur Ivan Morozoff was elected an honorary member of the Salon d'Automne, and awarded the Légion d'honneur as the possessor of an outstanding art collection. Then, of course, there was the matter of disposable income: the tragedy of the Russo-Japanese war brought millions in profits to firms which received orders to supply the military. Hundreds of thousands of rubles were paid into the personal account of the director of the Tver Textile Mill Company as a result.

If, for Matisse and his Fauvist friends, the turning point came in 1905, for Ivan Morozov, collector of modern French painting, the turning point came in 1906. The modest red ribbon in the buttonhole (which, unlike the French, who greatly coveted this inconspicuous badge of honour, he probably never wore) quite changed his attitude to his as yet small collection. For the first time he found himself not just one of the many visitors to the Salon, but one of its important participants: works from the Morozov Collection were shown at a Russian exhibition under the aegis of the Salon d'Automne.

A vast exhibition of almost 750 works called for serious investments, but Sergei Diaghilev was a great persuader. He had once so enthused Savva Mamontov and Princess Maria Tenisheva that they helped to sponsor his journal *Mir iskusstva* (The World of Art) for almost five years.[10] Diaghilev managed to draw five art collectors into his French project. Industrialist Vladimir Girshman (son of the 'railway king' Vladimir von Meck), Doctor Sergei Botkin (son-in-law of the late Pavel Tretyakov), and Prince Vladimir Argutinsky-Dolgorukov agreed to finance the planned exhibition *Two Centuries of Russian Painting and Sculpture*. Ivan Morozov was the last to join the exhibition committee.

It was not an easy decision for him. Ivan Abramovich did not particularly care to support artistic and cultural projects. When he did make charitable donations it was, for the most part, to schools and hospitals, out of an affinity, as it were, with his mother's efforts. He did not in general care for honours and did not aspire to ranks and membership of committees and societies. It proved impossible to persuade him to join the Board of the Tretyakov Gallery: he refused all proposals, saying that he did not consider he had anything useful to contribute to the gallery. How many other art collectors would have given their eye teeth for that honour! If his brother Mikhail had been alive, we can be sure he would have jumped at the chance.

Sergei Diaghilev, a champion of culture, man of the theatre, art critic, and one of the founders of the World of Art association, closed his magazine and mounted a dazzling exhibition of Russian portraits in the Tauride Palace in St Petersburg. A new chapter was beginning in the life of that indefatigable impresario, and he could not wait to conquer Paris. In twelve halls of the Grand Palais, Diaghilev and Bakst[11]astonished the Parisians with a display of icons on glittering gold brocade and exhibited paintings from the era of Peter the Great and Catherine II, portraits by Levitsky, Borovikovsky, Kiprensky and Bryullov. Perhaps even more importantly, they showed contemporary Russian painting, as represented by Levitan and Serov, Vrubel and Somov, Malyavin, Roerich and Yuon. Truth to tell, it was for this latter purpose that Diaghilev had initiated his European exhibition project in the first place. Morozov not only acted as one of the sponsors, but agreed also to lend his paintings for the exhibition. No one had suspected that the brother of Mikhail Morozov had managed to acquire so many interesting paintings by his compatriots. Diaghilev selected only a few. He took *Portrait of a Lady in Blue* by Borisov-Musatov, views of old Moscow by Apollinary Vasnetsov, *The Castle of Chernomor* by Golovin, *Café in Yalta* by Konstantin Korovin, and *March Snow* by Grabar. Morozov himself bought scenes of Versailles by Alexander Benois, Korovin's *Portrait of Chaliapin* and Grabar's *Tansy* at the exhibition. This time the French were in the minority in the list of his autumn purchases: he bought *Woman Bather* by Manguin and a landscape which had shown up at several Salons by Pierre Lissac, who shortly afterwards abandoned painting to devote himself to caricatures.

Morozov made numerous interesting acquaintances as a result of the Russian exhibition. He was constantly being invited somewhere, or there was someone he himself wanted to know. He was able to meet Baron Denys Cochin thanks to a recommendation from Diaghilev. Ivan Abramovich had heard a lot about the baron's magnificent art collection and mansion, for which Maurice Denis had painted a mural and made a spectacular stained-glass window several years earlier.[12] He was particularly interested in Denis.

Ivan's first painting by Denis was a small canvas, *The Sacred Spring at Guidel*, which he acquired in the spring of 1906 at the Salon des Indépendants. He also liked a scene with bathers, which was listed in the catalogue under the title of *Polyphemus*,[13] but, alas, the picture was not for sale. Artists do, however, often repeat their work, so why not enquire? In any case, paintings could be purchased more cheaply in a studio than in a gallery. After visiting exhibitions, Morozov had previously felt an urge to meet up with the artists. He had never, however, managed to arrange any meetings. With Denis everything was to turn out differently.

Morozov arrived in the Paris suburb of Saint-Germain-en-Laye in a rented car. He chose two works in the studio. Firstly, he asked Denis to repeat the landscape with Polyphemus, which he had marked in his catalogue at the Salon des Indépendants, and to go with it he reserved the unfinished canvas of *Bacchus and Ariadne* which was standing on an easel. His interest was clearly piqued by Denis' ability to combine the mythological and the mundane, not without an added hint of irony about the sublime. The artist transferred classical figures from antiquity to the present, which is how Bacchus and Ariadne came to turn up as ordinary bathers on a beach in Brittany. There seems nothing out of the ordinary in the fact that the giant, Polyphemus, is playing on his pipes in an adjacent cove. Such quirkiness was wholly to the taste of Ivan Morozov.

Having viewed the paintings of Denis in Baron Cochin's mansion, Morozov discovered to his surprise that he was also an excellent decorator. The murals and stained-glass windows made to Denis' design greatly impressed him. Ivan Abramovich decided it would be a good idea to invite Denis to decorate his own mansion, and the following year he did so.

Morozov's visit to rue de Babylone had one other important consequence for him: at Cochin's residence he finally encountered the artist who would become his all-time favourite.

# CHAPTER VII

## 'Cézanne Season'

Time was,

           one season

                      van Gogh was God,

another season,

           — Cézanne.[1]

In terms of the number of paintings in the Morozov collection, the *Hermit of Aix* was well ahead of the rest of the field. Over seven years Ivan Morozov assembled a positive Cézanne Museum which illustrated each of his periods. Sergei Shchukin had an analogous susceptibility to Matisse, whose paintings he bought on an even grander scale. Shchukin declared that he needed to live with a painting for at least a year in order to understand it. 'Very often,' he said, 'at first glance you don't take to an artist, he even repels you; it can sometimes take several years before you recognize his talent, but then gradually the scales fall from your eyes.'[2] Morozov took his time over coming to Cézanne. He first saw the *Plain by Mont Sainte-Victoire* in 1904. 'Here we are touching something completely different from . . . the art of the Greeks, the Renaissance,

Manet and Puvis de Chavannes . . . We are in a realm close to the artless frescoes of the first Christians, Byzantine miniatures. Here we are far from a desire to decorate, delight, regale . . . An artist from a different era, with a way of thinking different from ours. In order fully to appreciate him, we must forget a lot, renounce a lot. You feel that he faces life squarely, oblivious of everything, totally in the grip of a new impression,' Sergei Vinogradov noted in the margin of his catalogue in whose company Morozov was inspecting the Cézanne Room at the Salon d'Automne.[3] Ivan Morozov was to buy the landscape three years later, under the spell of the posthumous exhibition of Cézanne.[4]

Ivan Morozov was not given to making instant decisions. He was one of those people who need dialogue. Listening to qualified advisers chosen from among his artist friends, he seemed to be checking whether he was making the right choice. In the early days his invariable consultant was Sergei Vinogradov, but occasionally the role went to Igor Grabar or Valentin Serov. Of the art dealers, he particularly trusted the judgement of Ambroise Vollard. We are told that, sinking into a soft armchair on rue Laffitte, this impatient Russian customer asked to be shown only those paintings the dealer himself considered the best. Sergei Shchukin, on the contrary, trusted his own eye, and asked to be shown everything there was.

An art dealer must have no qualms about an artist he is betting on. Commercial success hinges largely on that. According to Théodore Duret, Vollard succeeded, through the mediation of Cézanne's son, in buying more than 200 of his father's canvases, investing the greater part of his savings in them. In 1895 Vollard arranged an exhibition of Cézanne (followed in quick succession by two more). For most people it was a revelation. Pissarro tells us there were exquisite items: 'Still lifes irreproachable in their perfection, alongside others which had been much worked on only to be abandoned unfinished, but even more beautiful than the former. Landscapes, nudes, portraits which, although they had not been brought to completion, were truly magnificent, extraordinarily artistic, amazing in their plasticity.' Pissarro recalls that at the exhibition Degas and Monet bought 'some completely stunning paintings'. He himself part-exchanged a fairly indifferent study for 'a . wonderful *Bathers* and a self-portrait of Cézanne'.[5]

Morozov was himself to acquire a *Bathing*, a *Self-portrait* and one of the unfinished portraits which had so enraptured Pissarro. He did not immediately manage, however, to buy *Madame Cézanne in the Conservatory*: the artist's son, Paul, was in no hurry to part with this portrait of his mother. Morozov was a patient man, though, and in the end the coveted painting was his. *Madame Cézanne in the Conservatory*, one of twenty-seven portraits of Hortense Fiquet, had been displayed at exhibitions in Berlin, London and Vienna before it arrived at Prechistenka Street in 1911. It cost Morozov 35,000 francs. Vollard placed the same valuation on *Blue Landscape* and *Interior with Two Women and a Child*. The only artists more expensive in Paris than Cézanne in those years were Renoir and Degas.[6]

It came as no surprise when Morozov suddenly brought back to Moscow an early canvas by the maestro rather than something that was 'absolutely the last word'. Because he was not merely buying paintings for the sake of it, but putting together his own museum (although he never fully admitted that to himself), threading like beads one master-piece after another, he considered it important to present the whole story of a painter's creative quest. In the course of seven years Vollard sold Morozov fifteen paintings by Cézanne, including two early genre canvases of interiors: *Interior with Two Women and a Child* and *Girl at the Piano (Overture to 'Tannhäuser')* painted in a 'Romantic' manner. Morozov also had two still lifes which, according to French art critics, best expressed the soul of Cézanne: *Still Life with a Curtain*, one of Cézanne's best compositions with fruit on a starched white tablecloth, and *Peaches and Pears*. Boris Ternovets, the first curator of the national-ized Morozov Collection, gave the latter painting pride of place, hanging it above the sofa, like an icon in its corner.

For Morozov, autumn 1909 was 'Cézanne season', when no fewer than seven of the artist's paintings arrived in Moscow. Ivan Abramovich chose works he needed to complete his collection, and money was no object. He found the Impressionist *The Road at Pontoise* at Druet's gallery, and at Vollard's, *Bathing*, *Flowers*, and *The Smoker*, the previous owner of which had been Auguste Pellerin, one of the first to appreciate Cézanne's work. Morozov also bought *Mont Sainte-Victoire* from Vollard, after which he had two paintings of the celebrated mountain. (Cézanne painted this amazing view year after year.) The artist did not take particularly good care of his paintings, and often kept them rolled up, quite badly damaging his canvases, but Morozov was undeterred. He also took the scratches on *Flowers* in his stride. This beautiful still life was not mutilated by some mindless viewer indignant at what he saw as pointless daubing, as many believe, but by the artist himself. He had a tendency to rip and mutilate his own paintings. The flowers got off relatively lightly, Cézanne only having scratched through the paint with the top end of a paintbrush before reprieving the picture, recollecting the *Flowers* by Eugène Delacroix hanging over his bed. Everyone who visited Cézanne in Aix recalls Delacroix's watercolour, which the artist was exceptionally fond of. Unlike the free copy of it he had made, and which Ivan Morozov acquired.

Before his visit to Vollard, Morozov had fitted in a visit to Durand-Ruel, whose gallery he frequented less and less. 'I have already gone round almost all the dealers in paintings. Durand-Ruel has positively nothing, unbelievably boring,' he had complained to Ostroukhov a year previously.[7] Durand-Ruel was conscious that he was losing a client who had cooled towards the Impressionists: in the previous year he had managed to sell Morozov only one painting, by Renoir. He knew, of course, about the new enthusiasm for Cézanne and Gauguin, whom Ivan Abramovich was regularly buying from Vollard, and indeed there had been a time when he and Vollard were buying Cézannes for 150–250 francs. Those days, however, were long gone and the artist now commanded higher

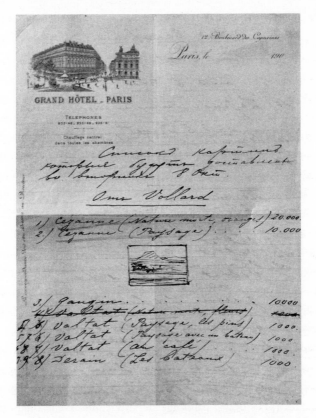

15 A list of paintings acquired by Morozov from Ambroise Vollard with a sketch of Cézanne's *The Plain by Mont Sainte-Victoire*, Morozov's own handwriting, October 1908.

prices. It made sense to buy back paintings already sold in order to resell them to new, wealthy enthusiasts. Immediately before Ivan Morozov's arrival in Paris, Durand-Ruel had succeeded in obtaining two excellent Cézanne paintings from New York.

Louisine Havemeyer, now the widow of a 'sugar king', decided to dispose of the paintings. Her loyal friend and adviser, the American artist Mary Cassatt, recommended that she should purge her collection. The young Louisine Elder, the future Mrs Havemeyer, had met Cassatt long ago in 1874 in Paris, where she had been staying with her mother and sisters. When Louisine returned a second time, Mary Cassatt took her to Père Tanguy's shop in rue Clauzel, where the young American bought a beautiful Degas pastel. When Louisine married Henry Osborne Havemeyer in 1883, she and her husband began actively buying works of art. Thanks to Cassatt, who became their main consultant (just as Vinogradov became Morozov's adviser), by the mid-1890s the Americans had shipped across the Atlantic masterpieces by Courbet, Manet, Monet, Degas and Renoir. After the sudden death of her much-loved husband, Louisine was profoundly depressed, something of which, she claims in her memoirs, Durand-Ruel took advantage, persuading her to sell *The Banks of the Marne* and *Self-portrait in a Cap*.[8] In reality, it was at the prompting of her mentor, Mary Cassatt, whose attitude towards Cézanne had shifted decisively, that Mrs Havemeyer decided to part with the paintings. In her old age, Cassatt, who had been a loyal champion of the Impressionists, decided that Cézanne's art was having a bad influence on younger artists, whose innovations she found unacceptable. Cassatt not only sold several of her own Cézannes, but persuaded her friend to follow her example.

Durand-Ruel had worked with the Havemeyer couple for a quarter of a century.[9] He located paintings they aspired to have in their collection, and later helped sell them when his clients wanted to be rid of them. It was a routine matter. 'I am glad we were able to sell your two Cézannes so rapidly because, despite the furore around this artist's name, there are still very few buyers for his work, especially if they are not of high quality. For some reason not entirely clear to me, it is only in Germany and Russia that high prices are being paid for them.'[10] Having notified Louisine Havemeyer of the successful sale, Durand-Ruel did not go into further details, but she soon became aware of them. Two weeks after the paintings arrived in Paris, her Cézannes had been sold to a Russian collector for 30,000 francs, of which Mrs Havemeyer herself had received precisely half.[11]

Amicable relations between Louisine Havemeyer and Paul Durand-Ruel were soon restored, but Durand-Ruel's collaboration with Morozov, which had been so much to the advantage of both parties, came to an end with the sale of the Havemeyers' Cézannes. The gallery where Ivan Morozov had made his first purchases in spring 1903 lost its best Russian customer. Ivan Abramovich did, however, continue to buy Cézannes. Visiting the mansion on Prechistenka Street on one occasion, the critic Sergei Makovsky noticed that the wall for works of the *Hermit of Aix* had a blank space.[12] The paintings were equally spaced in two rows, so it was immediately noticeable that a place to one side had been left empty. Morozov serenely explained that this was where he intended to hang a 'blue Cézanne'. He had been looking closely at the work of the artist's last period for some time but had yet to find a painting worthy of his collection. For over a year the reserved space remained empty.

The tale of the buying of the 'blue Cézanne' typifies Morozov's approach to collecting. He would go to absurd lengths in his single-minded pursuit of just the right canvas, leaving a place on the wall because he knew exactly the kind of work he wanted to see there, sooner or later. 'I. A. Morozov has a gift (and it is an immensely valuable gift!) for acquiring an artist's most vivid and expressive paintings. If need be, he can exercise patience like nobody else, waiting at great length for the opportunity to acquire a work he wants, searching for years through artists' studios and in the shops of *marchands de tableaux* for the perfect painting, the missing example of a favourite maître,' Makovsky was to write.[13]

In the catalogue of the posthumous Cézanne retrospective, Ivan Morozov put a prominent question mark against No. 54. Three years later, the question was answered and the empty space on his wall was occupied by *Blue Landscape*. 'When the collections of Pellerin[14] and Vollard are finally sold, in order to judge the work of the great citizen of Aix it will be necessary to travel from Paris to Moscow.'[15] If 1914 had not happened, and after it 1917, Sergei Makovsky's prediction would undoubtedly have come true.

# CHAPTER VIII

## 'A Russian Who Doesn't Haggle?'

Two visitors who came into Ambroise Vollard's gallery were speaking a foreign language he did not recognize, but which he later discovered was Russian. Russian customers were not that uncommon in the galleries of Paris, but purchasers of Monet and Pissarro, let alone Cézanne and Gauguin, you could count on your fingers. Having bought a painting by Gauguin, one of the visitors left, but his companion continued looking at the canvases. A conversation ensued, and Vollard mentioned he had had a buyer from Russia who bought a picture without bargaining. 'A Russian who doesn't haggle? He must have been a Pole,' the visitor retorted. From which Vollard concluded that 'buying without bargaining goes against the grain of a truly Russian person'.[1]

The phrase 'A Russian who doesn't haggle' became firmly attached to Ivan Morozov, after which almost no article on Russian collectors failed to quote the hallowed expression. The 'Russian who doesn't haggle' in fact missed no opportunity to do just that, and in no way did he lag behind his brother, Mikhail. In Paris they were, of course, much more restrained and did not pressure exhibition organizers the way they would at home, with demands for a discount of a hundred or two.

In any case, the art prices were much lower in Paris than in Moscow. We have only to restate the price of French paintings in rubles to see that. It might well be why the brothers preferred to buy paintings in Paris, where the cost of living was also cheaper. One French franc was worth thirty-seven and a half kopecks. What could Ivan buy for 100 rubles in Moscow? Actually, nothing worthwhile, unless perhaps watercolours by Somov.[2] In Paris for the same money you could acquire all sorts of interesting things: Valtat, for example, Cross, Derain, or one of the Fauvists, and upcoming new talents like the Spaniard, Picasso. Renoir and Monet, needless to say, could not be picked up for kopecks. For them the bill would run into the tens, and sometimes hundreds, of thousands of rubles.

When trying to acquire a painting at a reasonable price, Morozov did not, of course, miss an opportunity to haggle. In the few letters of Ivan Abramovich which have survived, the word 'haggle' recurs constantly. 'I'm haggling with Vollard over a large landscape by Claude Monet. This painting is the same size as the one I have and, although it is less interesting, it nevertheless has very considerable merits. I am also haggling over a pretty Degas pastel and a wonderful Cézanne landscape,'[3] he advises Ostroukhov, who understood him better than anyone else.

Ilya Ostroukhov was a rare type of painter-collector. He began collecting long before he began painting, and was very single-minded about it. He lived, moreover, in almost ideal conditions for a collector, because for many years he was the director of the Tretyakov Gallery. This put him in a unique position to hold in his hands absolutely any of its items. Practically every day he was in contact with the owners of paintings and drawings. Often enough, canvases, sheets of paper and albums were brought directly to him at home, where he would deliver his august judgement on them. Buying works for himself (all the best things he bought for the Gallery), Ostroukhov never overpaid, and in favourable circumstances might even acquire an item without payment at all. He followed the example of the marchands of Paris: buying two and selling one for the total price he had paid.

It is not difficult to understand Ostroukhov. He was an obsessive collector, and literally bought up everything – drawings, paintings, sculptures, porcelain, bronze, icons. Not having a business of his own, he found himself obliged to finance his hobby from the capital of his wife, the heiress of the Botkin sugar empire. Accordingly, Ilya Ostroukhov would have felt shamed if he missed acquiring any available first-class work, but also if he paid the kind of money rich men like the Morozov brothers could afford.

In fact, however, although an exceedingly wealthy man, Ivan Morozov too was much averse to throwing money away, and, if he could not get a price down to what he considered a reasonable level, would allow a transaction to fall through, purely as a matter of principle. 'I regret to inform you that I have been unable to agree to your offer of 600 marks for the painting by E. Munch *The Port in Lübeck*, No. 181 in the exhibition of the Secession. I have been successful in obtaining 1,000 marks for it,' Paul Cassirer advised his Russian client.[4] Mikhail Morozov, on his last visit to Paris, had acquired *The Girls on the Bridge*, and Ivan could easily have equalled his brother, but for some reason struck a pose and decided the dealer was not being square with him. 'If you won't come down,' he seemed to be saying, 'then you can just keep your old Munch!' Given the sums he was spending by this time, the amount was, frankly, risible.

Morozov never stinted, however, when buying Gauguin,[5] and he reaped the reward. His Gauguins were little inferior to Shchukin's famous 'iconostasis' in the formal dining room of his Moscow mansion, which so amazed everyone with its flaming yellows and oranges, the sweetness of its pinks, and the sumptuousness of its deep blues.[6]

Describing Moscow as 'the city of Gauguin, Cézanne and Matisse', Alexander Benois had, obviously, both collections in mind. Shchukin's collection of Matisse was unrivalled, but it was far less easy to decide on who had the better selection of Gauguin, Cézanne and van Gogh. The cognoscenti were divided over that. The Belgian poet and playwright,

Émile Verhaeren, who came to Moscow on the eve of the First World War, took the view that Shchukin had the better canvases of Gauguin, while in Morozov's collection he was struck by the power of the works of Cézanne.[7] Alfred Barr, arriving in the USSR in early 1928, noted in his 'Russian Diary' that Morozov's collection was no less beautiful than Shchukin's, and his selection of eleven Gauguins, although less numerous, was of higher quality.[8] Barr was fortunate enough to see both collections in their original settings, before they were merged less than six months later.[9] Having visited both of them twice, the founder of New York's Museum of Modern Art definitively pronounced the quality of Shchukin's Gauguins and Cézannes inferior to those of Morozov. Morozov's collection of Cézannes was the more extensive, with twice as many paintings by the *Hermit of Aix*. As for Gauguin overall, he deemed both collections to be of equal merit.

It makes no sense to ask whose collection was 'better': each was good in its own way. Can we see Shchukin and Morozov as competitors? Hardly. There were no instances of one poaching a painting from the other, although in respect of some artists their tastes coincided almost entirely. The main difference was in their approach to collecting. Morozov preferred to 'wait, rather than rush in and make mistakes', as Boris Ternovets put it. He was incredibly discriminating and thorough, carefully considering which work of each artist he would choose as representative, where exactly he would hang the canvas, and how it would fit in with the others. Sergei Shchukin gave not a moment's thought to such matters. His elder daughter Ekaterina recalled that paintings greatly excited her father, and that if he liked one he passionately wanted to possess it.

In October 1906, Sergei Shchukin and Ivan Morozov met at the great, posthumous retrospective of Paul Gauguin at the Salon d'Automne.[10] Morozov, as usual, put a cross in the catalogue against paintings he liked. If we were able to glance into the catalogue with Shchukin's notes, we would doubtless be amazed by the degree of coincidence.

Not one to deliberate at length, Shchukin promptly bought three paintings, which Morozov had marked in his catalogue but not resolved to purchase, including the 'brilliant nude' Gauguin himself rated so highly, *What! Are You Jealous?* Morozov mulled such things over for a whole year. To bring something so provocative to Russia required considerable courage. He was a decorous, prudent man, in no hurry to 'shock the bourgeoisie', unlike Shchukin, who took pleasure in showing off his acquisitions, 'not sparing the feelings of people in commerce'. 'Here is an artist who was derided and mocked all his life, and now, after his death, his paintings are worth their weight in gold,'[11] he would explain to guests when they waxed indignant over the 'garish colours' of Gauguin's unconventional paintings.

At all events, Gauguin was the only painter to hold quite the same powerful fascination for both collectors. Curiously enough, the reason for this may have been their line of business. Shchukin and Morozov were both textile manufacturers: one produced fabrics, and the other sold them. In order to succeed professionally, artistic taste was essential, a feeling for colour, shapes, patterns. It is far from coincidental that most of Moscow's art collectors were textile magnates, beginning with Pavel Tretyakov and ending with our protagonist. The textile business, hard but highly profitable, generated huge profits for Russian merchants in the nineteenth century, and enabled them to invest in the purchase of works of art.

It was perhaps precisely Gauguin's decorativeness that so bewitched the textile magnates Shchukin and Morozov.[12] 'His colours are a large part of Gauguin's enchantment, colours the like of which European painting had not known for a long time, because for centuries it shunned decorativeness,' Petersburg critic Sergei Makovsky exclaimed in delight over Morozov's Gauguins. 'No wonder Gauguin was drawn away from Europe, from the civilization of moderation and timid ideals to exotic, barbarous lands, to the sun of Oceania, to the "Isles of the Blessed", where the bounty of nature dazzles and primal man is magnificent, as if he has stepped down from the fresco of an ancient temple into a fairy-tale kingdom of palm groves, rainbow-winged hummingbirds, emerald coastlines and sapphire skies.'[13]

Sergei Shchukin bought his seven best Gauguins in 1906. In 1908 Ivan Morozov brought five Gauguin canvases to Moscow, each more beautiful than the last: *Flowers of France*, *Woman Holding Fruit*, *The Great Buddha*, *At the Foot of a Mountain* and, painted before Gauguin left for Tahiti, *Night Café in Arles*. Sergei Makovsky emphasizes the meticulousness with which Morozov selected his Gauguins. 'One by one, images of Tahitian life pass before the viewer, and you are hard put to decide which best conveys the grandeur of its simplicity: the women by the idol of the Great Buddha, the women picking fruit, the women in the meadows with exotic, strangely curving flowers and strangely branching trees . . . Perhaps, though, of all the works by Gauguin in this collection, the most captivating in its colours and the subtlety of its painting is *Still Life with Parrots*. This is a pearl among pearls.'[14]

The beautiful, but at the same time poignant, *Still Life with Parrots*, painted by Gauguin in the last months of his life, was the acme of Morozov's Gauguin collection: with this purchase he showed himself no less acute than Shchukin in his artistic instincts, or in his willingness to spend insane amounts of money on paintings. Sergei Shchukin was prepared to pay for *The King's Wife* whatever price Gustave Fayet might ask. And pay he did: this Gauguin painting, which hung over the fireplace in Fayet's Paris mansion, set Shchukin back 30,000 francs – until shortly before that an unimaginable price.[15] Morozov paid Fayet almost as much for the vivid *Still Life with Parrots*. Eugène Druet acted as mediator, earning his ten per cent on the deal. Gauguin's friend would never have parted with either *The King's Wife* or *Still Life with Parrots* if he had not just bought the ancient Fontfroide Abbey in the Eastern Pyrenees and desperately needed ready cash to restore his grand Cistercian monastery.

At 27,000 francs, *Still Life with Parrots* was an exceptional purchase. The going rate for a Gauguin at Vollard's gallery was 8,000 francs.[16]

Morozov was to pay just under that amount in autumn 1908 for Gauguin's *Night Café in Arles*. He obviously acquired it as a pair for van Gogh's *Night Café*, which he had bought that spring at an exhibition organized by the St Petersburg magazine *The Golden Fleece* for 7,500 francs or 3,000 rubles, 'taking the exchange rate as 40 kopecks to the franc, including translation, telegrams and customs expenses'.[17]

The Moscow exhibition of *The Golden Fleece*, referred to in the Parisian style as a Salon, was wholly exquisite, as was anything touched by the hand of Nikolai, one of the nine Riabushinsky brothers.[18] Boris Pasternak long remembered the stupefying aroma of hyacinths in the dark rooms of the Salon. Not only French artists were exhibited: there was also a Russian section, where Morozov found three compatriots, Mikhail Larionov, Petr Utkin and Martiros Sarian, worthy of his collection. (We are adopting as Russian the Armenian, Sarian.)[19] Sarian's *Oriental Motif*, Utkin's *Lovers of the Storm*, and Larionov's *Springtime* were hung on the ground floor of the mansion on Prechistenka Street, which was reserved for contemporary Russian painting, and van Gogh went to the prestigious first floor. Six months later it was joined by Gauguin's *Night Café in Arles*.

The two *Café*s hanging side by side were a reminder of the friendship of their painters, who had lived and worked shoulder to shoulder in the autumn of 1888 in Arles. Gauguin and van Gogh not only depicted the interior of the same station café, but gave the paintings the same name. 'I have also painted a *Night Café*, which Vincent likes tremendously, but I less so. Truth to tell, the picture is not to my taste: I do not care for the vulgar local colour. I like it in other people's works, but for some reason I myself always shy away from it. It is all a matter of one's upbringing, a person cannot change himself,' Gauguin wrote to the artist Émile Bernard,[20] with whom van Gogh also corresponded. 'At the present moment Gauguin is working on the same painting, with the same night café I painted, but peopled with characters we saw in brothels. The picture promises to be interesting.'[21]

Van Gogh's *Night Café* turned out much more sombre. The combination of red and green (with which van Gogh said he wanted to 'express the baneful passion that drives people') was to amaze the Russian poet Osip Mandelstam. 'Van Gogh spits blood, like a suicide in furnished lodgings. The floorboards in the night café are tilted and flow like a gutter in electric fury; the narrow trough of the billiard table resembles a dugout coffin. I have never seen a palette which barked like that.'[22]

It is difficult to determine the principles underlying the way Morozov hung his paintings. Perhaps he chose the canvases by their colouration. The colour of autumn 1909 was red: the *Tahitian Pastorals* of Gauguin were plainly bought to go with the orange and red in his *Sacred Spring, Sweet Dreams* and also, of course, with van Gogh's *Red Vineyards at Arles*. 'But on Sunday if you had been with us, you would have seen a red vineyard, all red like red wine. In the distance it turned to yellow, and then a green sky with the sun, the earth after the rain violet, sparkling yellow here and there where it caught the reflection of the setting sun,' Vincent wrote to his brother Theo after returning from a walk with Gauguin, who came to join him in Arles.[23]

It would be interesting to know whether Morozov was aware of the history of *Red Vineyards*. It was believed to be the only painting by van Gogh that was ever sold during his lifetime, and its first owner had been Père Tanguy, a Montmartre celebrity who sold paints in rue Clauzel, and also paintings with which impecunious artists paid him. In May 1891 Tanguy sold the canvas for 350 francs to the Belgian artist, Anna Boch. Such, at least, is the legend. Passing from one owner to another, *Red Vineyards* finally came into the possession of Alexandre Berthier, the Prince of Wagram.[24]

Eugène Druet, who was readying a van Gogh exhibition in his gallery, was not only well acquainted with all the owners of his paintings, but also well aware of their intentions. In particular, he knew that the Prince of Wagram was prepared to part with several works. Druet had already managed to sell one van Gogh[25] to Morozov and did not want to miss out, the more so since his Russian client was highly enthusiastic. 'I have just had a meeting with the owner of the paintings we saw. He is asking 30,000 francs for *The Red Vineyards* and 25,000 francs apiece for the other four paintings hanging on the wall next to *The Vineyards*. This totals 130,000 francs for five paintings, but if they are bought together, they will be marked down to 100,000 francs.'[26]

Morozov was, as usual, staying at the Grand Hotel. It was to Suite No. 60 that letters arrived on the headed notepaper of *Galérie Druet: Contemporary Paintings*. 'Tomorrow is the eve of the vernissage of the Salon d'Automne. I shall be going to it at 10 o'clock in the morning,' Druet wrote. 'If you would care to visit it with Madame Morozoff, I could accompany you. In that case you might call for me at rue Royale at 9 ¾. I also have a new and very fine painting by Van Gogh, and I would be delighted to show it to you.'[27]

The letters of Eugène Druet, which their addressee carefully kept, are our sole documentary source on the purchase of van Gogh paintings in the autumn of 1909. We know from Boris Ternovets that none other than Valentin Serov, who was brought in as a consultant, advised Morozov to select *The Red Vineyards* and *Prisoners Exercising* from the five paintings. At the exhibition, which opened at the gallery in November, both paintings were already listed as belonging to Monsieur Morosoff.[28]

The 'Russian who doesn't haggle' managed to talk down the price of *The Red Vineyards* by a third and, with the money thus saved, bought from Druet the van Gogh painting he had mentioned in his letter. *Landscape at Auvers after Rain* was an exception from van Gogh's dramatic canvases, with its romantic mood and extraordinary luminousness. Nothing in this idyllic picture, painted in June 1890, portends his tragic end: on 27 July 1890 Vincent van Gogh mortally wounded himself with a shot from a revolver and died two days later.

# CHAPTER IX

# Cupid and Psyche

Ivan Morozov brought to the designing of his mansion in Moscow the same detailed and methodical thoroughness as he did to buying paintings. At first the old house had stayed exactly as it had been when its new owner took possession of it, but when it began to fill with paintings, Morozov was obliged to undertake a succession of alterations.

The first issue was, of course, whom to appoint as the architect. Of the three architects most popular in Moscow at the time – Shekhtel, Zholtovsky and Kekushev – Morozov settled on the latter. Lev Kekushev designed commercial apartment buildings, and built fashionable mansions for wealthy industrialists and successful businessmen – for the most part, in the Arbat, Prechistenka and Ostozhenka districts, which were being abandoned by aristocrats on the verge of bankruptcy. Buildings by Lev Kekushev were distinguishable by their abundance of stucco moulding and exuberant ornateness. They invariably featured statues of lions or lion masks, alluding to their designer's name. In the interior of Morozov's mansion, however, the architect's commission was to eliminate decorative excesses.

It was decided the Baroque mouldings and other decorations of the grand enfilade on the first floor should be done away with altogether, leaving in their original state only the dining room and Gothic study with their wooden panelling. A grey-green hue was chosen for the walls, which immediately gave the rooms an austere, dignified appearance. In the ornate and capacious room called the Music or Concert Salon, Kekushev removed, in addition to the mouldings, the mezzanine. This made it possible to raise the ceiling to a height of six metres. A final touch was the lantern in the roof, providing the salon with the natural light so necessary for viewing paintings.[1] The Morozov mansion on Prechistenka Street was gradually turning into an art gallery, which was, indeed, the logic behind the transformations. The eclectic finishes of the 1870s, and the Art Nouveau style that replaced it, disappeared, leaving behind only wood panelling, which gave the dining room and study a certain solidity.

The Music Salon with its pillars and caryatids, well illuminated during the day by the glass lantern, was crying out for murals. Ivan Morozov had long been wondering whom to commission for the task. His artist friends encouraged him to select a Russian, one of their number. The trouble was that Vrubel, who had created panels for Morozov's relatives (*Faust and Margarita* for his cousin Alexei Vikulovich, *Day, Morning and Evening* for his uncle Savva the Second),[2] was terminally ill. Viktor Borisov-Musatov, who would have been well able to undertake the commission, had recently passed away. Building work on Prechistenka Street was in full swing when Morozov found himself in the Paris mansion of Baron Cochin in rue de Babylone, which had been decorated by Maurice Denis. Morozov did not just like Denis' work: it was at the top of his list, immediately after Cézanne.

Morozov never had an opportunity to meet Cézanne, but he knew Denis personally, and had even been received in his home. It was late spring when he first visited him in Saint-Germain-en-Laye. The garden in full bloom gave the estate an ineffable charm. It was idyllic, but

Morozov was not there to admire the garden: he had come to buy paintings. His visit had the agreeable outcome for Denis that his guest not only purchased two paintings but, shortly afterwards, offered him the major, lucrative commission of painting decorative panels for his mansion in Moscow.

Few people in Moscow were in a position to invite a celebrated foreign artist to work for them. The Kharitonenkos commissioned portraits of their daughters from Albert Besnard, and brought François Flameng to paint the ceiling in the concert salon of their elegant mansion on Sofiya Embankment, which enjoyed the best view of the Kremlin in the entire city. Flameng's manner was ideal for sumptuous Belle Époque-style interiors, such as the paintings in the buffet of Paris's Gare de Lyon,[3] where passengers of the Orient Express could wait in style before embarking on a long train journey. Morozov, having employed Kekushev to rid his interiors of ornate clutter, wanted something more pared down for his concert salon, and Maurice Denis was just the man for the job.

The artist was in great demand in Paris, which may explain why, for such a long time, he was unable to finish the paintings Morozov had commissioned. Indeed, Denis was just at that moment completing a panel titled *The Latin Land, Inspirer of Art and Poetry*, commissioned by Jacques Rouché, the owner of the *Grande Revue* and future director of the Paris Opera, for the entrance hall of his new mansion. Denis was hoping Morozov would change his plans and be among the chosen few invited to admire his murals at rue d'Offemont[4] and, of course, not miss his personal exhibition at the Bernheim-Jeune Gallery.[5] 'Two paintings, destined for you, will be on display at the Société Nationale. I sent them there over a week ago. On 8 April my exhibition of 60 paintings and drawings opens at Bernheim, and in addition on 10 and 12 April I would like to invite you to visit the Rouché mansion, where I painted the vestibule this winter. I am sorry you will not be able to attend the opening of these exhibitions, but hope that in a few days I shall be able to show you my exhibition and murals . . . The Salon is to open on 13 April and my exhibition will close on the twentieth. Could you by any chance come to Paris a few days earlier than you planned?'[6]

Whether Ivan Morozov was in time to see the exhibition we do not know, but he certainly visited the Bernheim Gallery, and even bought a landscape by Henri-Edmond Cross. At the end of the Salon des Indépendants he also bought a Paul Signac.[7] Morozov seems to have been no less aware than Shchukin that, without the neo-Impressionists,[8] the story of the evolution of French painting in his collection would be incomplete. After viewing the Salon des Indépendants, Ivan Abramovich went to the Grand Palais, to the salon of the Société Nationale, where Denis was showing *Bacchus and Ariadne*[9] which, along with *Polyphemus*, would shortly be on its way to Moscow.

In 1907 alone, Ivan Morozov spent 210,000 francs on paintings, and that is before counting the 50,000 he paid Denis to paint panels for his home on Prechistenka Street. After visiting the mansion of Rouché, he was determined that his Music Salon should look just as poetic.

'I've already thought about the subjects I would like to choose for the decorative panels,' Denis wrote after receiving the exact dimensions and photographs of the Morozov salon. 'You wanted me to take subjects from the world of classical mythology, and the story of Psyche, idyllic and full of mystery, seems to me ideally suited. I have put together five scenes which are completely distinct from those of Raphael in the Villa Farnesina, but nevertheless wholly consonant with the tale told by Apuleius. I don't, of course, harbour any ridiculous intention of even remotely imitating Raphael, but I would be happy to make a modern transposition of this ancient legend, so beautiful and full of visually striking images. Before continuing work on my sketches, I would like to be sure that you will afford me complete freedom and have no objection to the subject: the story of Psyche.'[10]

The letter from Denis was delivered to Prechistenka Street on the very eve of the wedding of Ivan Morozov and Evdokiya Kladovshchikova.

The mysterious tale, transposed to a modern idiom, of the union of Soul and Love (that is, of Psyche and Cupid), which would soon adorn their shared home, seemed a wonderful wedding present. Ivan Morozov departed with his young wife to Biarritz, adored by all Russians, for their honeymoon, where his Dosya was finally able to show herself in society, dazzlingly dressed and sparkling with jewellery.

The millionaire merchant, amicable towards his family and friends but fiercely private towards outsiders, proved to be a romantic at heart. How else are we to explain how someone with such wealth and status would take it into his head to marry a former cabaret singer?

It all started at Yar, a restaurant out on the Petersburg Highway which was popular with rich Muscovites. It was famed for its conjurors, circus wrestlers and wonderful Russian and gypsy choruses. Or, more precisely, chorus girls. These enticing lovelies enlivened merchant dinner parties with French songs and Tyrolean ditties and in Yar, quite unlike any other Moscow restaurant, the singers were at liberty to leave, after their performances, with their admirers. Ivan Morozov was something of a regular, even though at that time Petrovsky Park was considered almost on the outskirts of Moscow. At the beginning of the new century the restaurant established a garage, and luxurious cars would be sent for customers on demand:

Why so sad? Take a guitar,
Sing a song about love's pain.
Better still, drive out to Yar
And warm your blood up with champagne![11]

At Yar the thirty-year-old Morozov's eye fell upon a lively, pretty singer with the pet name of Dosya. The object of Morozov's passion was barely eighteen. Two years later, Little Dosya was born. Only a few intimates knew about the child, which Dosya's married sister immediately took to foster. Filling out a questionnaire in 1916, Ivan Abramovich indicated that he did have a daughter, but that she was adopted. In order to preserve the family secret, he decided against going through the complicated adoption procedure. His own step-brother and step-sister, the children of Vasily Sobolevsky, were also for many years deemed illegitimate, just like Little Dosya. Sobolevsky adopted his son Gleb shortly before he was due to enter university, but not Natalya. As a result, Varvara Morozova's daughter could attend higher education classes only as an *auditeur libre*: the laws of the Russian Empire, upholding the sanctity of the bonds of matrimony, were very rigid. A secret liaison, a child given up to a foster mother . . . but this story of romance did have a fairly happy ending: the millionaire married the chorus girl. In July 1907, Ivan Morozov and Evdokiya Kladovshchikova, whose stage name was Losenbeck and who turned out to be a member of the gentry,[12] were married in a quiet ceremony. There were no newspaper announcements, no lavish banquets at the Hermitage such as his brother had had. There was only a modest dinner with the witnesses, the Bakhrushins, and a few close friends.

Alexei Bakhrushin was an obsessive collector. He began collecting works of art almost by chance, for a bet. His cousin was boasting about his theatre memorabilia and Bakhrushin bet he could outdo him.[13] He was scrawny and, because of his short-sightedness, invariably wore a pince-nez, which made him look very much the part of the Chekhovian intellectual. In fact, however, his father was a millionaire, a tanner in the commercial Zamoskvorechiye district of Moscow who happened to own the biggest cloth factory in Russia. Alexei Bakhrushin himself, by temperament and in his manners, remained a true merchant: quick-tempered and stubborn. He devoutly observed ritual and made the sign of the cross after lunch and dinner. He made the sign of the cross over his children at night and strictly observed Lent. This did not prevent his decamping on New Year's Eve to the Côte d'Azur, staying at the most luxurious hotel in Nice, and demanding that *eau de vie russe* be served at dinner. When the waiter brought him the spirit in a liqueur glass, he sent it back and demanded a full carafe of vodka, with sardines to accompany it.

Morozov, perhaps his only close 'capitalist' friend, was welcome just to drop in on him at his house on Luzhniki Street (renamed Bakhrushin Street under the Soviet regime). Unlike Morozov, Alexei Alexandrovich was a very public figure. When he began holding 'Saturdays', artists and theatre people began frequenting his house. These 'jours fixes', when guests were free to stroll through the rooms viewing his theatre-related memorabilia, became the joy of his life. The architect, Ilya Bondarenko, recalled, 'Bakhrushin would take from a glass case, say, the shoes of Asenkova, a ballet dancer famous in the 1850s, give them a peck with his lips and say, "There, I found them. I searched for such a long time." There would then follow the pedigree of the curio, and the display would turn gradually into a talk about a particular actor, theatre, or a whole theatrical epoch. Bakhrushin would sit a new visitor down, open an album bound in brocade, and ask them to leave a memory of themselves ... Then everybody went up to the dining room for dinner at a huge table. The accompanying libation would enliven the general conversation, which usually continued until two or three in the morning.'[14] Their host never begrudged his 'Theatre Saturdays', unlike the banquets for his fellow merchants, at the end of which he would always count up how much he could have bought for the museum if he had not had to splash out on a chef from the Metropole, musicians and cut flowers.

Together with his young companion, Morozov would often visit the red-and-white mansion with its idiosyncratic turrets. Initially he did not venture to bring his lady any further into society than Luzhniki Street. Alexei Bakhrushin's son, Yury, has left a detailed account of how his father and mother, anxious to see a family friend happy, urged him to formalize his clandestine relationship. 'Each time she came, my father warmed more and more to Dosya. She was modest, she did not try to join in conversations on matters she knew nothing about, she was cheerful and jolly, and there was not a speck of vulgarity about her.'[15]

16  Ivan Abramovich (standing in the middle) and other guests at the Odintsovo-Arkhangelskoye estate of his cousin Alexei Vikulovich Morozov (standing first from the right), 1907.

Bakhrushin himself dealt with the issue of marriage as expeditiously as he did with collecting: he spotted his future partner in life at a fancy-dress ball and – just like Levin in *Anna Karenina* – offered her his hand and heart three weeks later at the ice-skating pond. Unlike Kitty Shcherbatskaya, who turned Levin down, the daughter of cloth manufacturer Vasily Nosov accepted his proposal. 'Well, have you seen my fiancée? Isn't she pretty?' the successful suitor crowed to his coachman. 'She's pretty enough,' was the answer, 'but with your kind of money you could have managed a better deal.'[16] The Leather and Cloth Manufacturing Company of A. Bakhrushin and Sons really did rank several notches higher than the Trading and Industrial Manufacturing Company of the Nosov brothers.

The Tver Textile Mill Company ranked even higher in the hierarchy of Moscow's merchants. In today's terms, Ivan Morozov was not a millionaire but a billionaire, and might have been expected to choose a bride, if not from a wealthy family, then at least from a prominent one. If he was going to marry a young woman with no dowry, she ought at least to have had a distinguished ancestry, like the bride of his elder brother. Dosya had none of these attributes (although she was at least of noble origin). Since the Bakhrushins had themselves married for love and not 'by arrangement' as was customary in the merchant class, they continued to urge Morozov to formalize his relationship. They instanced one happy couple after another, and in every case the groom was a merchant and the bride an actress. There had been many such cases. Mikhail Bostanzhoglo (the man who had won a million rubles off Mikhail Morozov in a single night) was married to a dancer, but did find that an embarrassment and claimed on a form to be unmarried. Ivan's cousin, Sergei Morozov, had a 'kept woman', a Hungarian dancer. Ivan Vikulovich Morozov was married to a ballerina, as were the Karzinkin brothers and several other sons of the wealthiest merchant families. That was all very well, Ivan objected, but there was a big difference between a dancer in the Imperial Ballet and a chorus girl from the Yar. The stalemate continued.

Morozov hesitated for quite some time, solely, he said, for fear of putting Dosya in an awkward situation. What if society did not accept her? It was difficult to argue against that. When at last the relationship was sanctified by marriage, Bakhrushin and his wife undertook the mission of presenting Madame Morozova to the world and threw a dinner party. 'The high society of Moscow's merchant community met young Evdokiya Morozova coolly, with obvious misgivings. There was close observation of how she ate, how she conversed and comported herself. The young lady in fact comported herself so straightforwardly and was so manifestly at ease that one might have supposed her entire life until that moment had been lived exclusively in such society. By the end of the evening the more amenable hearts had softened and the young couple received several invitations. The battle had been won.'[17] Moscow's high society had admitted Evdokiya, but with reservations, and behind her back she continued to be called 'Dosya la-la-la' or, at best, plain 'Dosya'.

The memoirs of Yury Bakhrushin, who at that time was just ten years old, are not wholly objective. Bakhrushin junior sincerely loved Ivan Morozov and did not want to upset him. 'He never gave me any gifts,' he recalls, 'never spoiled me, but there was always something companionable in his manner of talking to me, unpatronizing, and that I really appreciated.' It is understandable that Yury should have written supportively of Morozov's lawful wedded wife. More often, however, young Madame Morozova evoked a different reaction. Valentin Serov, for example, called her 'a painted doll' and never did change his attitude towards her. This is clearly visible in the portrait he painted of the newly wed lady. The plunging neckline, the sumptuous dress, the fingers freighted with rings, the bejewelled gold bracelets, the earrings, the pendant. Serov did not fail to include every last extravagant detail of his model's toilette.

Mikhail Morozov's wife, the regal beauty, Margarita, has been captured in a dozen photographs, costumed in all sorts of ways, with a hat and without, full length, in profile and full face – but there is not a single photograph of poor Dosya and hence nothing to compare her portrait with. Either Serov deliberately turned her into a 'painted doll', or Evdokiya Morozova really did look like that: a self-satisfied, slightly haughty look, her hair piled up, her smile seductive. Serov never fawned on his clients, even the most illustrious. By no means all his fellow artists were equally rigorous. Some, indeed, began currying favour with Madame and obsequiously soliciting her opinion about their paintings. It is unlikely that

Dosya welcomed their unexpected attentions, although her husband may have found them flattering.

Ivan Morozov, director of the Tver Textile Mill Company and warden of the Merchants' Club, adored his wife. It is entirely possible that it was with an eye on his imminent marriage that he decided to commission the mural panels from Maurice Denis. The theme of love which Denis suggested may well have been dedicated to the new mistress of the Music Salon.

# CHAPTER X

# Maurice Denis, or the French Occupy Moscow

Having received the go-ahead from Moscow, Denis immediately set to work. Five huge panels, each 4 x 3 metres, was an important and lucrative commission. He was intending to depict Italian landscapes on his canvases. Taking with him sketches he had begun in Saint-Germain-en-Laye, he went with his wife to Lake Maggiore, using it as a base for travels around Italy. Meticulous researchers have identified in his background landscapes the cypress avenues, marble statues and fountains of the gardens of Palazzo Giusti in Verona, and the picturesque terraces, grottoes and arbours of the Boboli Gardens in Florence.

The Italian expedition lasted several months.[1] 'I have worked a lot but, I think, without any major results or discoveries,' Denis wrote from Fiesole in mid-December to André Gide. 'I have prepared my future Psyche (for Moscow), which will be very chaste in comparison with Giulio Romano's.'[2]

Few artists dared to portray love scenes as unashamedly as Giulio Romano did in the Palazzo Te; only selected friends of the Marquis of Mantua were allowed into the private hall of the country villa of Federico II Gonzaga.[3] 'The Chamber of Psyche surpasses everything: the wedding, the bacchanalia, the coffered ceiling, a triumph of painting, sensuality, and more painting ... Splendour, deification of the animal in man, amazing paganism,'[4] Denis noted in his diary. In the Moscow mansion of his Russian patron, however, everything must be irreproachably respectable lest, God forbid, there should be occasion for gossip about the kind of stage on which Madame Morozova had pursued her career.

During the months spent in Italy, Denis managed not only to complete eighty sketches, but to exhibit them in the Druet Gallery and sell them.[5] It was only in April 1908 that the client and his artist finally met up. Morozov was able to view three large panels as work in progress, but the other two were only sketches. Denis finished all five panels in under a year, but it would have been impossible in the time available to complete such huge canvases working on his own, and he resorted to the help of assistants. This he was to rue.

The Morozov panels had to be ready by autumn 1908 in order to be on view at the Salon. 'My life in Paris from 30 July until 21 August is to spend every day at the Grand Palais ... this vast building that has been placed temporarily at my disposal,'[6] Denis notes in his diary. 'At the present time I am chained to *Psyche*. I am currently alone in Saint-Germain, without my wife, and every morning I travel to Paris to work in the Grand Palais, where *Psyche* awaits. This will continue until the end of September, when the Salon d'Automne opens,'[7] Denis tells his confidante, Madame de la Laurencie. 'I am nonetheless concerned about what people will think of *Psyche* and, more importantly, what kind of impression it is going to make on me. A little more than a month has passed since I left it in rather a problematical state,'[8] Denis writes in another letter to the Countess. In actual fact it was he himself who at that moment was in rather a problematical state. He did not dare to put in writing how worried he was: the bulk of the work had been done for him by his assistants, and the 'teamwork' had left its mark on the quality of the painting.

Denis was in fact desperately worried as, two years later, Henri Matisse was to be no less worried about exhibiting panels, also at the Grand

Palais, which had been commissioned by Sergei Shchukin. The displaying of *Dance* and *Music* created a major scandal, which for a time made Shchukin doubt the wisdom of his decision to acquire the highly controversial panels. With *Psyche*, however, everything passed off smoothly. The client was happy and showered the artist with praise. 'When I had the pleasure of talking to you at the Exhibition there was insufficient time for me to express fully the satisfaction and admiration I felt when viewing your beautiful canvases. They display an elevated understanding and magnificent rendering of the subject, and from now on I shall consider them pearls of my art gallery. Moreover, from the bottom of my heart, I am certain that these works will delight not only myself but all those like me who are closely following everything that the talent and hard work of an artist like yourself, dear maître, can bestow.'[9]

The paintings were rolled up and sent to Moscow. In December they were affixed to stretchers, adorned with brocade ribbon, and fixed to the walls of the Music Salon.[10] In early January 1909 the artist and his wife Marthe followed the panels to Moscow, travelling together as was their custom. Madame Denis was 'in an interesting condition', but that did not deter her.

At first Moscow failed to impress the French couple particularly. Denis noted in his diary, 'Arrived in Moscow, small station square, low houses, snow, weather very mild, cab drivers in long, heavy blue coats stamping around their light sleighs. In Berlin and Warsaw, which we passed through quickly, it was muddy, with puddles, but here everything is white, a hushed realm, little traffic in the streets. We set off immediately to the Kremlin, it was already half-past three, and it quickly begins to get dark. Overcast, the first lights, flocks of ravens, pealing of bells, curious silhouettes, but nothing particularly impressive, except, perhaps, for the view of a snow-covered city with countless bell towers which is discovered from the terrace in front of the statue of Alexander.'[11]

Ivan Morozov was not there to meet his guests – he had to rush to Tver for the funeral of his younger brother, Arseny. The death of Arseny

Morozov was enigmatic, his burial site was kept secret, and the attention of journalists was so focused on this story that the arrival of a fashionable French painter did not make it even into the newspapers' news section. While Denis was sightseeing in Moscow, Ivan was spending days and nights in St Petersburg lawyers' offices. His brother's papers had unfortunately all been notarized in the capital.

He was obliged temporarily to entrust the care of his guests to Prince Sergei Shcherbatov and his companion Vladimir von Meck.[12] They duly organized a programme of tourism for the French visitors: a service in the Cathedral of Christ the Saviour, the Faceted Palace and cathedrals of the Kremlin, the Novodevichy Convent, a sleigh ride, Morozov's box at the Bolshoy Theatre, the Tretyakov Gallery, and the Rumyantsev Museum, where Denis admired Alexander Ivanov's biblical études.

And of course there were invitations: to visit Shcherbatov and von Meck, to the editorial offices of *The Golden Fleece* for tea with Nikolai Ryabushinsky, who then took Denis to his studio, full of 'revolting paintings – little Persian études by Sarian. Many sketches, large and small, by Kuznetsov[13] . . . there are fountains, bowed heads reminiscent of my own subjects of ancient times, but visualized quite vaguely. He is a poet and knows nothing. He has a lot of imagination but there is no colour.'[14]

Next, to Petr Shchukin on Gruzinskaya Street to see his museum of Russian antiquities, which Denis described as 'a junk shop'.[15]

To Sergei Shchukin on Znamensky Lane, in his aristocratic palace 'in the style of the eighteenth century where, among all the old furniture and Barbedienne statuettes there is a collection of French paintings . . . a lot of Monet, Cézanne's last period . . . Brangwyn, Thaulow, Pissarro and even Moret . . . In the dining room the table is set with blue plates, there is a large Burne-Jones tapestry and two rows of Tahitian Gauguins, radiant and yellow, like oriental rugs . . .'[16]

Then to Margarita Morozova, the widow of Mikhail Morozov, in her 'Pompeian, Egyptian, Moorish house . . . There is a full-length portrait of

Samary, a Degas nude, two of my little items, a large *Faust and Margarita* by Vrubel, a charming Corot (*Motherhood*).'[17] Next on to the Girshmans and Free Aesthetics,[18] to Ilya Ostroukhov in Trubnikovsky Lane and 'In the evening, an unexpected invitation to M'sieu Ostroukhov, director of the Tretyakov Gallery, for an evening of piano and chamber music performed by Madame Landowska.'[19]

If Matisse was to be greatly impressed by Ilya Ostroukhov's icon collection, what Denis remembered in his house was an abundant cold dinner with caviar, fish and suckling pig in aspic, which he did not omit to note in his diary. Denis did not see Ostroukhov's icons because he had not at that time begun his collection. In most other respects, however, he fared better than Matisse. When two years later, in 1911, Matisse arrived in St Petersburg together with Sergei Shchukin, the Hermitage had closed for the winter and Shchukin was reluctant to inconvenience its director. The frosts also came unusually late that year, the snow not having fallen even by the beginning of November, so Matisse's hopes of seeing the Russian winter were frustrated. Denis made a brief two-day trip to St Petersburg and, thanks to his Moscow patrons, saw a good deal there.

Returning in high spirits to Moscow, Denis once more carefully inspected the collection of 'my' Ivan Morozov ('*le mien Ivan Abramovitch*') and recorded the impressions in his diary. Alas, with the exception of the Music Salon and the main staircase, not a single room in the house was photographed during Morozov's lifetime. As a result, Denis' diary is the only source from which we can glean any idea of the layout of the rooms in the mansion.

The first thing the Frenchman noted was 'the large number of Russian painters' ('*beaucoup de peintres russes*') on the ground floor: Morozov 'held' them there, rarely allowing any of his compatriots to aspire to the first floor. Denis particularly noted Malyavin's large, vivid *The Whore*.[20] He praised the simplicity of the furniture, upholstered in modest greys, and the abundance of fresh flowers – lilac, lily of the valley, cyclamen. He mentions Somov, Vrubel, Golovin and 'the fine landscape painter, Levitan' – whose études occupied an entire wall in Morozov's study.[21] A predilection for Levitan's lyrical landscapes ran in the Morozov family: his brother Mikhail had collected them, and his cousin Sergei even surrendered to Levitan the studio he had fitted out for his own amateur painting.

What the Morozovs' Parisian visitor described in the greatest detail was the location of his own work, starting with the small *Sacred Spring at Guidel*, which was hanging in good company between Cézanne's *Peaches and Pears*, *Overture to 'Tannhäuser'* and *Large Pine at Aix*,[22] and Tahitian canvases by Gauguin. 'Being next to Cézanne is not to my advantage, admittedly, but Gauguin is not so much above me,' Denis recorded proudly. 'My Italian and French forms are at home beside his oriental carpet colours.'[23] Denis was more gracious in respect of Renoir, and acknowledged that his three paintings were very good (*'Trois très beaux Renoir'*), especially *Girl with a Fan*. Monet and Sisley did not merit even a mention. He praised Friesz and *La Toilette* by his friend Bonnard. The paintings of Valtat, Vuillard, and indeed of Matisse, were dismissed as 'weak'. He noted particularly the two Arles cafés: 'One is Gauguin, with an Arlésienne, a bottle, and smoke'; the other is Vincent's (as he calls van Gogh): 'Dazzling and all wrong, but so profoundly experienced, so *felt* that it makes Gauguin's *Café* seem academic.'[24]

When he saw his panels, Denis was rather upset. They were hung properly, but the interior of the Music Salon was not quite right for them. What particularly detracted from the overall impression was empty space above the doors and between the panels. That was what came of working from drawings and photographs without ever having visited the house. 'My large murals look rather isolated in this cold, cavernous room of grey stone with mouse-grey furniture. We need to add something to draw everything together into a single whole,' Denis recorded in his diary.[25] Five picturesque scenes in a narrow hall with a six-metre-high ceiling were clearly not enough. It would really be quite hard to imagine a less felicitous setting. The only solution that suggested itself was to paint two further horizontal panels to fill the space above the doors. Additionally, Denis decided he needed to flank the door to the next room with thin floral borders and insert narrow vertical panels with the figures of Cupid and Psyche on the piers between the large panels. These panels should be grisaille, a monochrome painting technique imitating sculptural relief.

Denis had a vivid image in his mind of how the room would look after its makeover, but felt there was still something missing. How about placing large ceramic urns in the corners? He could paint them with female nudes himself and they would be the work of a single hand. The urns, of course, would give the salon a special charm, but should there perhaps also be full-sized bronze statues? Nobody in Moscow had anything like such an ensemble . . . Morozov readily approved it.

It was all decided. The panels were touched up and their harsh colouration mitigated. Denis blamed his assistants who had not met his own high standard, meaning that he had now to correct their mistakes. He tried to deflect attention from this obvious blunder and steered the discussion to other topics. To his diary he did, nevertheless, confide that 'of all the criticisms of my *Psyche* panels, the only one that matters is that it is not always my hand which is visible. Rysselberghe says that in future he will entrust other hands only to apply the size, and that only in a thin, not a thick, layer.'[26]

The two large horizontal panels, *Her Family Leave Psyche at the Mountaintop* and *Cupid Transports Psyche to Heaven*, are undoubtedly the most perfect constituents of the entire artistic ensemble of the salon, and every last centimetre of them was exclusively the work of Denis himself.[27] The sculptures were to be the work of his friend, Aristide Maillol, of whom Julius Meier-Graefe wrote in his *Modern Art* that he was the only sculptor capable of creating work consonant with the decor of Maurice Denis.

Before departing, the French painter gave one last instruction: to remove all the furniture from the Music Salon. He just had time to sketch the design of the new furniture: on one sheet he sketched narrow benches, and on another, using watercolour, he put brushstrokes of the hues for fabric to tone in with the panels.[28] Denis insisted that the banquettes must be upholstered in exactly such white and gilded silk. Morozov did not argue, trusting the maître implicitly. Madame Morozova also found everything to her taste, and the old furniture which, in the opinion of Sergei Vinogradov, was in perfectly good taste, was promptly removed. The white banquettes and sofas were positioned along the walls and were, by all accounts, extremely uncomfortable, the seat being terribly low and the back and armrests too high. In terms of style, however, they fitted the room to a tee.

The Music Salon ensemble, produced and directed by Denis, was undoubtedly impressive. There were the huge, picturesque panels framed by gilded brocade ribbons, the bronze figures of Maillol's virgins (Pomona, Flora, Spring and Summer),[29] the snowy white painted urns on their tall pedestals,[30] the gleaming silk of the refined, if somewhat theatrical, furniture. Everything together was spectacular, stylish and expressive, but, oh dear, the murals . . . The figures themselves looked false and sugar-sweet, and then there was the cloying colouration, which Prince Sergei Shcherbatov aptly likened to pink caramel. Despite his best endeavours, Denis could not wholly tone down something lurid in the colours. Comparison with a chocolate box from the Abrikosov factory would be entirely just.

Alexander Benois was also disappointed, and considered himself partly responsible for his favourite's downfall. 'It was inevitable that this kind of pretension to "high art" would inexorably reveal that artist's insubstantiality and, even worse, his lack of taste,' Benois wrote brutally in his memoirs half a century later.[31] When he grew old, Benois, like many people, turned on his former idols. He it was who had promoted Maurice Denis in Russia with such abandon that it was simply impossible not to be influenced by his raptures. As a result, Sergei Shchukin bought three paintings by Denis. His brother Petr bought one, but it was a capital work of the maître, namely the idyllic *Sacred Grove*. Mikhail Morozov bought two, while Ivan Morozov, according to Benois, 'threw caution to the winds and gave Denis free rein to show himself up completely'. He is, of course, alluding to the panels.[32]

Benois could see clearly that his protégé had fallen on his nose with *The Tale of Psyche*, and felt immensely awkward viewing the panels in the presence of Denis' happy customer, who was exultant. Benois and Prince Shcherbatov were, however, clearly in a minority. 'Elegant roses, delicate greenery, vivid violets and pale, translucent blue hues. What joy, what tranquillity Maurice Denis has brought into this light, wealthy house. It is as if he has managed to capture, in the midst of the Russian winter, a memory of a Greek, or perhaps rather, a French springtime.' Émile Verhaeren, 'the modern Dante', could not conceal his enthusiasm.[33] The Music Salon was such an unbelievable success with the Morozovs' guests that even Sergei Shchukin was a little envious, perhaps even jealous, which was really quite out of character.

# CHAPTER XI

# The Mediterranean–Moroccan Suite

Very early in 1910 the last painting by Denis arrived at Prechistenka Street: *Green Coast at Perros-Guirec*, a classical idyll in an antique frame, with nymphs lying on a hill. It was painted in Perros-Guirec in Brittany, where Denis had recently bought a villa. 'This is a splendid work. The artists who have seen it showered praise on it!',[1] the picture's jubilant owner wrote, joining his voice to the chorus of acclamation but never buying another Denis painting, despite the fact that proposals from the marchands, some very tempting, were received.[2]

During the previous two years, more than a hundred French paintings had arrived at the mansion. It was time to think about where to hang them, something Ivan Morozov was glad to make a start on. In any wealthy Parisian house, the art met him at the front door: painted ceilings, stained-glass windows, sculpture. The entrance hall of his Moscow mansion was too modest for cultural display, but painted panels could fit very nicely into a shallow recess on the landing to which the long, narrow flight of his main stairs led. And who better to commission them from than Pierre Bonnard?

Judging by the markings in the margins of his catalogues, Morozov did not at first much care for Bonnard's work. Quite soon, however, he changed his mind and bought two landscapes. At the 1908 Salon d'Automne he was very taken by a still life with a mirror reflecting a nude. Valentin Serov, who considered *Mirror above a Washstand* almost the best work in Morozov's collection, agreed wholeheartedly. Morozov went on later to buy another ten paintings by Bonnard, six of which he commissioned from the artist. Sergei Shchukin behaved in exactly the same way, buying picture after picture from his favourite artist, Matisse.

Shchukin had a taste for edgy, exciting paintings and bought not a single Bonnard. Back in 1899 he had acquired one small work of his, but found he could not live with it and sent it back to Paris.[3] 'Bonnard's miracle-working eye reveals in even the most humdrum things amazing treasure troves of colour. When talking about him it is impossible not to compare his painting to music. Bonnard's colours really do sing, and chime, and merge into wholly unique chords . . . France at the end of the nineteenth century has, perhaps, created no artist to rival Bonnard as a colourist . . . And yet, despite that, overall his art seems empty, often even ridiculous.'[4] Such was Alexander Benois' merciless verdict. Perhaps it was something of the sort that Sergei Shchukin too had sensed. Shchukin had his own approach: he would buy a painting, hang it on the wall, and wait to see whether the picture continued to excite him, rather like soberly assessing an initial infatuation. For Shchukin, it was a test which Bonnard failed. For Morozov, he passed it.

Having bought *Mirror above a Washstand*, Ivan Morozov asked Bernheim to introduce him to the artist. It is unclear whether they agreed immediately on the subject for the future panel between the columns but, in respect of his second commission (a diptych, of course), Morozov made it very clear that he would like something relating to life in Paris, which he had always found alluring and intriguing.[5] Bonnard had to postpone the two-part *Paris Suite* for a while to concentrate on the labour-intensive four-metre panels for the the staircase landing. In spring 1911 the triptych *On the Mediterranean* was completed and exhibited at the Salon d'Automne. After the exhibition, the panels arrived in Moscow. In their wake came crates delivered to the Prechistenka mansion containing two bronze virgins by Maillol for the Music Salon.

The upper landing could be viewed admirably from below. You had only to enter the front door and look up for a fairy-tale picture to open before your eyes: a blue strip of sea, the sun, golden sand, children playing. *On the Mediterranean* was a kind of trompe l'oeil: three separate tall canvases with a southern landscape were affixed to the wall between semicircular pillars. The marble volutes of the ionic capitals were in the way, so the upper corners of the canvas had to be cut, but only slightly.

Bonnard's art filled the mansion with the colours of the Côte d'Azur, whose delicate fragrances lingered in its rooms because lilac, cyclamen and lily of the valley were delivered to chilly Moscow directly from the warmth of Nice. 'I seemed to be in a tale from *The Thousand and One Nights*: the sea, yellow shadows, the reflections of light as bright as the light itself,' wrote Pierre Bonnard, expressing his delight at the intoxicating riot of colours of the French Riviera.[6]

As he began painting a park on the Mediterranean coast, Bonnard had only a sketchy idea of the Moscow mansion: photographs of the staircase and the measurements of the space between the semicircular pillars were all he had to go on. Maurice Denis had found a dissonance between his paintings and the architecture of the Music Salon only after he arrived in Moscow, and Bonnard was to have no opportunity to visit Russia at all. He was never to realize that his panels were sandwiched between the broad spaces of the side walls. His client could see for himself that these great empty surfaces violated the illusion of immersion in a Mediterranean paradise.

Morozov naturally thanked Bonnard, assuring him that his panels had decorated the space between the columns pleasingly, but ascending the marble stairs yet again he could see that *On the Mediterranean* on its own was not enough. He ordered two more panels, this time on the theme of the seasons.[7] Bonnard had evidently no shortage of commissions because, instead of expressing gratitude for the confidence being placed in him, he argued over the proposed fee. 'I regret your decision not to raise the sum of 20,000 francs for the new panels, whose dimensions you have sent. The area has increased and accordingly the volume of work may also increase. I would prefer to decline to paint them, notwithstanding my great desire to be pleasant to you.'[8] Morozov was usually the one to do the bargaining. This time the roles of client and artist were reversed.

'As regards the proposed price, it is insufficient, because this work is at least as substantial as the previous one, and possibly more so. I would request the same amount, namely 25,000 francs.'[9] Bonnard explains his reasoning to Fénéon, who is negotiating with Morozov on behalf of the Bernheim-Jeune Gallery. Morozov yields and adds a further 5,000. It is a hefty sum: for that kind of money you could buy two Marquets, two Derains, or paintings by Russian artists. The objective, however, made it worthwhile: Morozov really did want to create a unique decorative ensemble in his palace.

Renowned for his slowness, Bonnard completed the commission in record time. After the exhibition at Bernheim, *Autumn. Fruit-Picking* and *Early Spring in the Countryside* arrived in Moscow. The huge, nearly four-metre canvases seemed to have been woven by individual brush-strokes and resembled ancient tapestries. Morozov hung them immediately next to the triptych. The effect was amazing: the upper landing was instantly transformed into a kind of stage tableau on the theme of the seasons. The present-day Mediterranean world captured on Bonnard's canvases served as a prelude to the ancient myth which came to life on the walls of Maurice Denis' Music Salon. But for Morozov this was not yet perfection. He had *Early Spring* and *Autumn*, but the 'Mediterranean suite' lack a conclusive, final chord. That was to be provided by the further five-square-metre canvas, *Summer*.

It is as if the owner of the palace on Prechistenka Street was intent on covering every bare surface with the carpet-like canvases of Bonnard, just as the owners of medieval castles adorned their walls with costly Gobelin tapestries. 'Monsieur Morozov . . . was going to commission you to decorate a certain room, but now . . . he has purchased a large canvas by Bonnard for it,' Shchukin writes to Matisse, dismayed at Morozov's 'treachery'.[10] Sergei Shchukin is sure the reason for this must be Morozov's advisers, painters who do not understand how his own favourite is evolving. Certainly, Morozov was influenced by his consultants, but the owner of the Tver Textile Mill Company chose Bonnard by himself, and Bonnard was weaving him one beautiful 'carpet' after another. Perhaps his wife, the lovely Dosya, was also entranced by the sparkling kaleidoscope of colours? It seems that Evdokiya simply agreed with whatever her husband desired, and naturally shared his tastes. Her husband even made a commission on her behalf, asking none other than Henri Matisse to paint a still life for her.

Shchukin, then, was mistaken about Morozov's attitude towards Matisse. Ivan Abramovich was by no means spurning Sergei Ivanovich's favourite, whom he had met even before the beginning of his 'romance' with Bonnard. In spring 1908 Shchukin had himself taken Morozov to the studio on the corner of Boulevard des Invalides and rue de Babylone, although, unlike Morozov, he did not particularly care for tramping round the ateliers of Paris. At that time Matisse had yet to sign his three-year contract with Bernheim and was free to sell his paintings himself, without paying a commission to the gallery.[11] A year later, he was obliged to forward all his new work to the gallery and, if a painting was sold before it had been completed, he was obliged to pay the gallery a full fifty per cent of the sum received.

Matisse was never to forget the April day when two Russians visited his studio in the deserted Convent of the Sacred Heart. From then on, Sergei Shchukin was his loyal customer and an ideal patron. Who, other than the grey-haired Russian, would regularly write to him requesting an update on every detail of each new picture? And buy one canvas after another, telling everyone – with complete sincerity – how much he admired Matisse's art. Matisse's relationship with Morozov was completely different. Morozov ordered and paid and Matisse carried out the commission (if not always on time). Both were satisfied. 'Morosoff, a Russian colossus, twenty years younger than Stchoukine, owned a factory employing three thousand workers and was married to a dancer.'[12] That is all Matisse could find to say about him a quarter of a century later, misremembering a singer as a dancer and 13,000 workers as 3,000, evidently because he found such wealth unimaginable.

Shchukin fell head over heels in love with Matisse's painting, and did not waver. He had never previously commissioned paintings, but with Matisse everything was different. Sergei Ivanovich first asked him to paint two still lifes. Matisse quickly fulfilled the order, and in October 1908 exhibited the two-metre *The Dessert: Harmony in Red* at the Salon d'Automne. In the spring, even before visiting the studio of Matisse, Shchukin bought *Nude (Black and Gold)* from Bernheim. Morozov tried to keep up and bought the nude *Seated Woman*. Two such dissimilar paintings depicting the same model are an ideal example of different readings of the theme 'nude'. Morozov's canvas has a real model, posing for students of the Matisse Academy and the master himself. Shchukin is much bolder in his choice, trying to understand what the artist is striving for. As Matisse himself explained, 'Suppose I want to paint a woman's body . . . I must give something more. I will condense the meaning of this body by seeking its essential lines.'[13]

The fact that the painting of nudes was a sensitive issue did not trouble Ivan Morozov in the slightest. He had plenty of such paintings in his mansion, especially in the Music Salon. People might like or dislike his voluptuous Cupid and Psyche, but there was nothing provocative in Denis' decoration. Matisse's nudes are much more stylized than Denis' nymphs in Morozov's mansion, which were painted in full compliance with all anatomical proportions. Shchukin, however, was worried. 'Russia has something of the Orient in it,' he tried to explain to the French artist after receiving sketches of the panels he had ordered from Paris. Sergei Shchukin urged Matisse to replace his nudes with clothed ladies, assuring him that he was doing so only out of concern for his adopted daughters. The young girls he had recently undertaken to bring up lived, he explained, together with him in his mansion on Znamensky Lane. Quite where Ivan Morozov's 'adopted' daughter was living we do not know. Morozov and his lady wife were clearly in no hurry to take in Little Dosya.[14] This could be the reason he was less embarrassed by the nudity on Denis' canvases. Even without them, there was no shortage of paintings of nudes in his mansion.

After some hesitation Shchukin decided, nevertheless, to flout bourgeois respectability and hang a painting with nude figures on his stairs, as he informed Matisse. By this time Morozov too was 'ripening' and ready to commission two still lifes from him, but Matisse was completely engaged in painting the huge panels of *Dance* and *Music* for Shchukin. By the beginning of 1910 he had managed only to finish the first still life for Morozov and had not even started on the second. Morozov, meanwhile, was sending him letters asking for information on the exact size of the paintings he had commissioned: he was busy hanging pictures in his mansion and wanted to reserve a place for the still lifes. Matisse was anxious, only too aware that he should not test the patience of this other wealthy Russian client any longer. He found a way of satisfying everyone.

He painted *Fruit and Bronze* specially for Morozov. *Fruit, Flowers and 'The Dance'* was painted while also working on the Shchukin commission, as we are reminded by a fragment of *The Dance* in the background. This, however, is not *The Dance* with the famous red figures on a background of blue and green, soon to adorn the staircase of Shchukin's mansion. In Morozov's painting the figures in the round dance are pink: this is the first version of *The Dance*, which was eventually to find its way to the Museum of Modern Art in New York. In terms of size and price

(5,000 francs each), the canvases were much the same and made an excellent pair, something Ivan Abramovich loved. The client could not but express his appreciation. 'I have just received the two paintings and find them amazing. The frames are very beautiful too.'[15]

Matisse was not one of Morozov's favourite painters, but Valentin Serov nevertheless placed *Fruit and Bronze* in the background of his portrait, a vivid red, yellow and blue still life with a carpet, apples, pomegranates, lemons and one of Matisse's bronze statuettes. 'Matisse: although I feel the talent and the nobility in him, he just gives me no joy and yet, strangely, that makes everything else seem boring. That is something to think about,' Serov debated with himself. He admitted on more than one occasion to not being able to make much sense of Matisse. 'Hard to deny it is brusque, askew and awry, but you shy away from looking at the canvases of the masters hanging nearby, painted in a long familiar manner. Technically Matisse's paintings are good, but still something is lacking – it is vapid.'[16] 'You are fated to simplify painting,' Matisse's teacher, Gustave Moreau, once predicted. Serov was himself unwillingly moving in that direction, since otherwise he would hardly have chosen *Fruit and Bronze* for the background of Morozov's portrait, painted in such bright colours that it conceded nothing to Morozov's Gauguins and van Goghs.

Abram Efros called Serov 'the most self-willed of Russia's portrait painters', and believed he had flattered Morozov by moulding him 'from different clay than nature had used'. Morozov, according to Efros, was 'big and flabby', 'with a typical goatee beard', but in Serov's portrait he looked 'like a very dapper, very emasculated European, with the overall appearance of either a fashionable member of parliament or a fresh-complexioned, art-loving banker who buys whatever those who whisper in his ear say is the latest thing, only immediately to hide it away in order not to offend against the code of decorum'.[17] Serov did indeed have a unique ability to convey the inner nature of his models, a core of their personality invisible to profane eyes. He was closely acquainted with Morozov, and had more than once watched him choosing paintings and haggling. He had seen his eyes light up when he managed to get his hands on a treasure he desired. In Serov's portrait we see not only the European gloss but also the Russian features of this individual. We see a Moscow merchant of a new kind, 'a Russian rough diamond, polished by civilization'.

Serov completed the portrait of Ivan Morozov in late 1910, when *The Dance* and *Music*, which had so scandalized Paris, arrived in Moscow. A young sculptor, Boris Ternovets, amazed by what he had seen, wrote, 'This is the best of anything Matisse has created, and perhaps the best the twentieth century has given us so far. This is not painting, because there is no form here; it is not a picture – it is a different kind of monumental decorative art – it is a thousand times more powerful and astounding.'[18] In 1918, after nationalization of the Morozov Collection, it was Ternovets who was sent to Prechistenka Street as an expert assessor, and who then went on to become director of the Museum of New Western Art.

Almost everyone liked Maurice Denis' panels, but for the most part the Matisse panels met with outright hostility. Ostroukhov thought them so awful that he asked Shchukin to grant him a waiver, enabling the Tretyakov Gallery not to accept them after his death, and even to provide a formal declaration to that effect. (Shchukin had bequeathed his collection to the gallery, which had recently had the collection of the late Mikhail Morozov donated to it.) How Ivan Morozov reacted to Matisse's panels we do not know, but by the beginning of the following year, 1911, he had sent Matisse a further commission, emphasizing that this time the order was on behalf of his family. His adored wife requested that Matisse should paint a still life for her, and he himself hoped he might acquire two landscapes (where would he be without a pair!), because he already had no fewer than seven still lifes himself, which was quite enough.[19] They included a recent purchase from Bernheim, a very early Matisse painting created under a strong influence of Jean-Baptiste

Chardin's still lifes, which he had made in the Louvre during his studies with Gustave Moreau.[20]

'I have been thinking about your landscapes ever since I arrived in Collioure, but I am afraid that this summer I won't be able to paint them. Most probably I will work on them in Sicily, where I am planning to spend the winter,' Matisse wrote,[21] but changed his mind and in late January 1912 was not in Sicily but in Morocco. The only merit of the modest hotel with the grand name of Hôtel de France in which he and his wife were staying was a pretty view of the roofs of the old city and the bay. Amélie Matisse stayed with her husband in Morocco for two months, before returning to France on a mail boat which sailed once a week between Tangier and Marseille. Matisse continued to work, reporting regularly to Amélie on how it was going. 'This morning I wrote a letter to Shchukin . . . I added a sketch of a still life and of the two landscapes for Morozov. One is deep blue and one is periwinkle. It was a delightful sketch and came out as a triptych.'[22] The blue landscape may have been *Window at Tangier*, and the other was evidently *Periwinkles (Moroccan Garden)*, now in the Museum of Modern Art in New York.

In the summer, Matisse raised Morozov's hopes by writing that his paintings would be finished any day now: he had begun them in Morocco and was continuing to work on them at home, so Monsieur would certainly see them at the Salon d'Automne. However, Matisse evidently overestimated his stamina. 'I am extremely embarrassed to write to you about this, but I have not been able to finish your two landscapes, and they will not, therefore, be in the Salon. Tomorrow, however, I am going to Morocco, where I hope to paint them.'[23] Of the still life for Madame, we note, there is not a word.

On his second trip to Morocco, Matisse travelled to Tangier alone, and for an extended stay. There would be nobody to disturb him, he was going to get through a lot of work, and would surely manage to finish the commissions from Shchukin and Morozov. Just before their first trip to Morocco, he and his wife had purchased a house in Issy, which they had previously been renting. The down payment of 25,000 francs used up all the family's savings, so the Russian commissions were very welcome.

Matisse was full of artistic plans. The weather was good in Tangier, he was not suffering from insomnia, and his work was going well. When his wife came to join him in November he had finished *Window at Tangier*. The couple were even photographed with the painting in the background. It is not a simple matter to determine its genre: *Window at Tangier* with its vases of flowers on the windowsill is as much a still life as a landscape. The entrance to the Kasbah (the old part of Tangier where the Sultan's palace was located) is more like a landscape. But where is the still life for Madame Morozov? Shchukin was to acquire no fewer than four Moroccan still lifes, but Madame Morozov, instead of irises and mimosa, would have to make do with Zorah, an Arab girl, sitting on the terrace. We have no reason to suppose Matisse would wish to offend Madame. Art historians surmise that he had not abandoned the idea of painting a triptych, and accordingly replaced the vase of flowers with the figure of an Arab girl and linked the three canvases with the colour blue.

Locating a female model in the Orient was not easy. The French owners of the hotel had great difficulty finding a girl who would agree to pose, and the sessions in any case soon came to an end. 'Her brother appeared. I think he would have killed her if he had found out she had been posing,' Matisse complained, having been deprived of a good model. Returning to Tangier in the autumn, he searched for a long time for Zorah before coming across her in a brothel. The Muslim laws forbidding women to show their face did not extend to prostitutes, so the sessions resumed. The flat roof of the brothel, on which the girl posed in the intervals between her main jobs, was transformed by Matisse into a terrace. Wistful, pretty Zorah in her gold-embroidered caftan, an exotic flower of the Orient, became the centre of the future triptych.

In mid-February 1913 Matisse sailed back to France, taking with him four paintings destined for Sergei Shchukin's Pink Salon, two landscapes for Ivan Morozov, and a still life for Madame Morozova. That is how he describes the paintings in his letters, and Morozov in return wrote to emphasize again and again that the two paintings were for him, while the third was for his wife: 'The three paintings . . . at the present time are on display with Bernheim. They have been a great success, and I hope you will be pleased, despite having had to wait so long. I also believe that Madame Morozova will be satisfied. The three paintings are composed in such a way as to belong together and in a particular order.'[24]

Matisse even provides a sketch in the letter, showing *Window at Tangier* on the left, *Entrance to the Kasbah* on the right, and *Zorah on the Terrace* in the middle. The artist proposed to put them in simple frames, which he painted grey. These three large paintings are in no way inferior to the panels. He is sure Morozov will appreciate that, but he is going to have to wait another two months. Ivan Abramovich does, looking forward patiently to further adorning his mansion with this latest ensemble.

In April, Matisse exhibited the Moroccan triptych in Paris. In effect, almost the entire Moroccan series of eleven paintings, with the exception of two small canvases, became the property of the Russian collectors.[25] On their way to Russia the paintings were held up for a week in Berlin, for exhibition at the Fritz Gurlitt Art Salon, finally arriving at Prechistenka Street only in June. Once again, Ivan Morozov lavished praise on them, making haste to report to Issy-les-Moulineaux that he and Madame Morozov found the works delightful. This expression of gratitude for work very well done was accompanied by a cheque for 24,000 francs, 8,000 for each painting, as agreed.[26]

'Mr Morozov is enchanted with your Moroccan paintings. I have seen them and share his admiration. All three are splendid. He is now thinking of commissioning three large panels for one of his living rooms. He is returning to Paris on 20 October and will discuss it with you,' Shchukin wrote, hastening to pass the good news on to Matisse. It was important to him to know that his enthusiasm for Matisse was shared by many of those he considered 'sincerely devoted to art'.

Sergei Shchukin had himself just received *Arab Coffeehouse*.[27] Matisse had more or less promised *Coffeehouse* to Morozov, to go with the Moroccan triptych. He had mentioned that in April, in the letter with a sketch of the triptych, diffidently surmising that, after receiving the three paintings, Monsieur might wish to visit his studio and view two large canvases depicting a Moroccan,[28] and an Arabian café. In late May, Morozov received another letter from Issy: 'May I hope to see you during your forthcoming trip to Paris? I have two important paintings from Morocco: I would prefer not to send you photographs.'[29]

Matisse did not send photographs, anticipating that Morozov would visit him in the summer. Instead, he sent a copy of *Les Cahiers d'aujourd'hui* with an article by Marcel Sembat, who had written the first book about his work. The laudatory article, he evidently supposed, would have a more favourable effect on Morozov than black-and-white photographs which could give no appreciation of *Arab Coffeehouse*, the most abstract of all his Moroccan paintings. It consisted of scattered shapes painted on a pale bluish-green background.

The *Arab Coffeehouse* and the Moroccan triptych seemed to have been made for each other. If they had been united, the Moroccan Symphony of Matisse would have rivalled Bonnard's Mediterranean Suite. In the summer of 1913, however, the first Russian to appear in Matisse's studio in Issy was not Morozov but Shchukin. Sergei Shchukin not only bought *Arab Coffeehouse*, but commissioned four more large paintings for his Pink Salon, aspiring to transform it into the ultimate Garden of Eden. Circumstances conspired to ensure that Ivan Morozov never sent Matisse another commission.

# CHAPTER XII

# A Place in History

Morozov kept his collection hidden from outsiders 'with the jealous love of a miser'.[1] Once more we can only lament the paucity of gossip and rumours surrounding our protagonist. We have a few sentences in the memoirs of his brother's widow and an essay by Abram Efros, 'The Man Who Tweaked', an obituary of sorts on the death of an outstanding collector. There is even less information about the youngest Morozov, Arseny. Of the three brothers, he was the most unpredictable, and was no less well known than Mikhail and Ivan. It was enough to build a castle in the proximity of the Kremlin to reserve yourself a place in history. Arseny proved quite right when he retorted to his brothers that there was no telling what might become of their collections, but that his house would stand forever.

It really was impossible not to notice such a bizarre building. Even Leo Tolstoy in his novel *Resurrection* decided to give Castle Morozov a mention: Nekhlyudov, driving along Vozdvizhenka Street, wonders why they are building 'a foolish, unnecessary palace for some foolish, unnecessary person'. The 'Spanish Hacienda' was constructed adjacent to the

17  Arseny Abramovich Morozov and his wife Vera Sergeevna Morozova, early 1900s.

18 & 19  The interior and exterior of Arseny Morozov's mansion at
16 Vozdvizhenka Street, early 1900s.

palazzo of his mother, the plot having been presented by Varvara Morozova to her son upon his coming of age. The land had previously been occupied by the Carl-Magnus Hinne Equestrian Circus, but in 1892 that burned down and Madame Morozova made haste to acquire Plot No. 16. Having cleared away what remained of the earlier buildings, construction of the mansion began. For his architect, Arseny Morozov chose Viktor Mazyrin, a close friend of Konstantin Korovin, Sergei Vinogradov and Valentin Serov, who was famous for having designed the Russian pavilions at the World Exhibitions in Paris and Antwerp, as well as the pavilion for the Central Asian Exhibition in Moscow. Arseny travelled with Mazyrin to Europe in search of ideas. They went first to Spain, and thence to Portugal. In the old town of Sintra near Lisbon both were ecstatic about the Pena Palace, whose fantastic intermingling of Moorish and Gothic styles left them dumbstruck.

Arseny Morozov was fired with enthusiasm to build a mansion in the Manueline (or 'Cable') style which had been popular in Portugal during the Age of Exploration. If the romantic legend is to be believed, in order to obtain the plans of the Pena Palace, the young Morozov was obliged to seduce the daughter of the estate manager. The upshot, at all events, was that the mansion on Vozdvizhenka Street was copied from the palace in Sintra, after adjusting certain details to take account of the much colder climate. The palace in Portugal was densely covered in grapevines, but that problem was overcome by decorating the Moscow mansion with ornamental carved vines. Scholars in Moscow are inclined to see less a Portuguese than a Spanish influence in the architecture, and this is partly justified: the stylized shells on the façade were inspired by the whimsical Casa de las Conchas in Salamanca.

The castle on Vozdvizhenka Street took a full four years to build and became something of a primer on architectural styles: the formal reception room, known as the Knights' Hall, was Romanesque; the Great White Hall was Baroque; the Golden Hall was *Empire* with walls covered with gold damask. In the mistress's boudoir, Art Nouveau jostled with neo-Rococo, and the master's study was designed in the Moorish ambience which Arseny so loved. The heads of wolves and wild boar were everywhere, albeit carved in wood. Viktor Mazyrin was a devotee of mysticism and went to great lengths for his eccentric customer, placing knotted hawsers wherever he could, as symbols of prosperity and longevity. As it transpired, the talismans and charms failed to protect the master of the castle.

Arseny spent most of his time on his estate in Tver. He had taken to hunting in England, where he had been sent to learn the ropes of the textile business. His mother had been hoping that her youngest son would be part of the factory management team, but that was not to be. The wealthy young heir chose instead a life of pleasure, abandoning his wife and little daughter for a femme fatale, but not initiating divorce proceedings in order to minimize fuss. He did, nevertheless, soon feature at the centre of a grand scandal.

If his brother Mikhail's passions were wine, women and paintings, Arseny's was hunting. During a dinner in his hunting lodge a dispute arose over willpower, and the owner, having drunk not wisely but too well, boasted he had no fear of pain. Before the guests had time to think what was happening, he seized a rifle from the wall and, completely out of control, shot himself in the foot. A few days later, Arseny Abramovich Morozov, in his thirty-fifth year, died of blood poisoning.[2] A hereditary citizen, a shareholder of the Tver Textile Mill Company, a member of the Moscow Philharmonic and other societies, he was buried on his estate of Vlasievo, near Tver.

The ubiquitous journalists immediately picked up on rumours that Arseny Abramovich had bequeathed his entire fortune to his common-law wife, the Caucasian beauty, Nina Okromchedlova-Konshina,[3] who was said to have bewitched half of Moscow. It was a huge sum of money: three million rubles with, in addition, the mansion on Vozdvizhenka Street, valued at no less than another one million, which Arseny had already transferred to Madame Konshina.

Arseny's lawful wife, Vera, decided to challenge her husband's last will and testament, and Arseny's family did everything they could to help her.[4] 'Long before his death,' Vera declared, 'both the physical and mental health of the deceased had been profoundly compromised: his physical health had been reduced to a state where it was unable to resist even the inflammation of the minor attack of erysipelas which led to his death; the mental disorder was manifest principally in a loss of will-power and total submission to persons in his environment.'[5] Perseverance over many years was rewarded only in 1913, when the will was declared invalid. The mansion, however, remained the property of Madame Konshina, and for a time she luxuriated in the unimaginable sumptuousness of her Moorish castle, until it was taken off her by the new masters of Russia after the October coup.

The details of Arseny Morozov's personal life provided rich pickings for the newspaper reporters, and this compensated to some extent for the lack of juicy details about the family life of his elder brother. The private life of Ivan Morozov, businessman and art collector, remained sealed and inaccessible to the gossipmongers. Nobody even knew of the existence of Little Dosya, so meticulously did Ivan and Evdokiya preserve their family secret. Otherwise, Serov would assuredly have painted not only the portraits of the Morozovs, but also of their daughter, and he would have made Little Dosya every bit as charming as her cousin Mika, the son of Mikhail, was in his portrait.[6]

Mikhail and Margarita had had four children. Their daughter, Marusya, was born three months after her father's death. The widowed Margarita the Younger left shortly afterwards with her children for Switzerland, returning to Moscow only in 1905 at the height of the events of the first Russian revolution, into which she plunged headlong. There remained in Margarita Morozova not a trace of the former 'lady with a yearning for life'. She was fully occupied organizing lectures on historical topics and discussions of current events. In the past, people had come to the Morozovs' mansion for balls (the buffet from the Hermitage restaurant, Labadie as master of ceremonies, the orchestra Romanian, the singers from Naples). These invariably ended with a cotillion, and the ladies were given flowers sent from Nice and cockades of colourful ribbons. Now, however, instead of balls Margarita arranged literary and musical evenings and lectures, attended by at least 200 people. 'The lectures were on the two main topics preoccupying liberal circles of society: the difference between constitutions (English, French, German and American) and socialism . . . The second topic . . . was, of course, much more complicated,' recalled Margarita, trying to think through everything for herself.[7]

'Fortunatov[8] gave lectures on constitutional law to M.K. Morozova and E.K. Vostryakova (her sister) . . . It was in Morozova's house that, for the first time, a group of public figures came together with Milyukov:

the Constitutional Democrat Party was formed there,' Andrei Bely recalled. 'It is a pity Breshko-Breshkovskaya exists![9] Otherwise, it would be Margosha who was called "the grandmother of the Russian revolution!" they joked, having in mind her willingness to host the Kadets, the Bundists, and other irreconcilable individuals who never met each other outside her house.'[10]

There was a lot of disagreement at that time in Moscow about how serious the political interests and intellectual questing was; about whether Margarita was intelligent; about how well she really understood the 'complex debating at her green table'. 'I do not think she understood everything. Without specialized philosophical training not even the cleverest person could have understood Yakovenko's paper on "Immanent Transcendentalism". What I am sure of is that she understood all the people. She invariably sat in an armchair near the green table, and sometimes in the front row with the public,' recalled the philosopher Fedor Stepun. 'Her dazzling eyes, with their gleam sometimes of sapphire, at other times of emerald, were impossible to forget. The blackness of her long eyelashes, emphasized by dark eyebrows, gave them, in combination with the bluish tint of the whites, the particular iridescence of steel.'[11]

'Yes, she intuitively understood the subtlest rhythms of the most intimate human relationships, but with her innate gentility, beneath which there lay a concealed bashfulness, she did not always open out. Very many people were disdainful, seeing in her just a Lady Bountiful, and failed to notice what an amazing person she was,' Bely said, seconding Stepun, and writing in his memoirs that at the time Margarita was 'pursuing ideologies, often ridiculous but often colourful. In her, Nietzsche, Kant, Skryabin and Vladimir Solovev met in the most ridiculous combinations.'[12] 'An amazing woman in terms of intelligence and good taste. It has become evident that she is not just throwing her money about, but is mentally alert and taking an active part in everything. This is more important than hospitals, refuges, and schools,' the philosopher Vasily Rozanov exclaimed admiringly.

Meanwhile, Margarita Morozova continued to spend her three million ruble inheritance on all manner of good causes, her generosity no less than that of her mother-in-law, but not publicizing her charitable deeds in any way. She bought the estate of Mikhailovskoye in Kaluga province and gave it away to a saintly teacher, who first organized a school and a club for peasants in a neighbouring village, and then a home for street children, which Margarita financed. She greatly admired the talent of Alexander Skryabin and lavished care on him: she took lessons from him, paid a decent allowance for several years (2,000 rubles a year) and, in addition, paid for the publication of his music and the organization of concerts. It was the support of Margarita Morozova that enabled the composer of *The Poem of Ecstasy* to live abroad and create in peace. For this good deed alone Russian culture should be immeasurably grateful to her. If her correspondence with Andrei Bely had not been preserved, we would never have known what contradictory feelings overwhelmed the young widow. 'I am obsessed here with Skryabin and regret your absence! I need you in order to make better sense of him. I will say one thing: it is not he who captivates my heart, not he, I think, but his destiny! But he himself is subjectively sweet and the beauty of his artistic nature is very attractive. Talking to him, however, is terribly *unpleasant*, even embarrassing. But when he begins to play, it is so good!' Margarita wrote to Bely in Switzerland just before the outbreak of war.[13]

In early 1910 she decided to sell her huge house on Smolensk Boulevard, whose contents had become too burdensome, and to donate her husband's collection to the Tretyakov Gallery. She stated that during his lifetime Mikhail Morozov had expressed the wish that his collection of paintings by Russian and foreign artists should eventually become the property of the gallery of the Tretyakov brothers, and that she was only carrying out his wishes. On those grounds, Margarita Morozova donated sixty paintings to the gallery immediately after her husband's death, and decided to keep the remaining twenty-three. Among the works she did not want to part with were Degas' *Toilet of a Woman*, landscapes by Boudin, Díaz, Gallen-Kallela, Jongkind, Corot, the beautiful white marble *Eve*, commissioned by her husband from Rodin, studies by Levitan, and Vrubel's *Swan Princess*. At the same time, Margarita stipulated that after her death these canvases too should be donated to the Tretyakov Gallery.[14]

The happiest days of the donor's childhood were associated with the gallery:

> The Tretyakovs' house in Lavrushinsky Lane was on the site where the gallery stands today, directly opposite the gates. It was a spacious white two-storey mansion . . . there was a white room with plants by the windows and two grand pianos . . . The furnishings of all the rooms were very simple and modest. . . . Pavel Mikhailovich was tall, thin and haggard, with a big, dark, silky beard and luxuriant dark hair. He was extraordinarily quiet, modest, and taciturn. He said almost nothing. His face was pale and lean, ascetic somehow, like an icon . . . Sometimes in the hall of the house, sometimes in the gallery there would be a new painting Pavel Mikhailovich had just acquired, covered with a white sheet . . . At that time there were no members of the public in the gallery on holidays, and we ran through it alone.[15]

Margarita particularly remembered the dance lessons: 'Because these lessons were taking place in the evening, the hall was plunged in darkness. There were candles only on two small side tables, and the light falling from them faintly illuminated the lower paintings. Their golden frames flickered slightly, and in the half-light we could see familiar paintings as we practised our steps to the scraping of a violin.'[16]

Margarita did not, however, choose the Tretyakov Gallery only out of nostalgia, but because there was simply no other location in Moscow worthy of the collection. After the death of his brother Sergei in 1892, Pavel Tretyakov had donated his own collection of Russian artists, together with his brother's collection of foreign paintings, to the city of

20 *New Treasures of the Tretyakov Gallery: Russian and Foreign Artworks Donated by Mikhail and Margarita Morozov, Iskry* (Sparks) magazine, 1910. Left, Russian paintings; right, Western paintings.

100 „ИСКРЫ". Художественно-литературный и юмористическій журналъ. „ИСКРЫ". № 13

# Новая сокровищница Третьяковской галлереи.

(Картины, пожертвованныя М. А. и М. К. Морозовыми).

## ИНОСТРАННОЕ ИСКУССТВО.

Фот. А. И. Савельева.

1) Море. Карт. Гогенъ. 2) Ночь. Туловъ. 3) Мать. Морисъ Дениса. 4) Поцѣлуй матери. Каррiеръ. 5) Samary. Ренуара. 6) Труженики моря. Каттетъ. 7) У пристани. Валлотонъ. 8) Пейзажъ. К. Монетъ. 9) Танецъ. Англада.

Moscow.[17] He allocated two rooms to his brother Sergei's foreign paintings, little suspecting how much more room would be needed in the future. During Pavel's lifetime (he died in 1898) the prospect of supplementing the gallery's Western section was only an aspiration.

For his part, shocked by the sudden death of his greatly loved wife, Sergei Shchukin in January 1907 also made his will in favour of the Tretyakov Gallery, bequeathing it his collection of French paintings. Shchukin did not make his intention public, and at first only a few people, including Ilya Ostroukhov, a trustee of the gallery, knew of his decision. Needless to say, the news soon leaked to the press and when, in 1910, the newspapers reported Margarita Morozova's donation, art critics and historians were greatly enthused. 'In the very near future, the massive collection of Shchukin and of some others whose names I am not presently at liberty to reveal, will merge with the wonderful foreign collection (mainly of the French masters of Sergei Tretyakov and Mikhail Morozov). At that point it would appear that nowhere else in the world will French art of the nineteenth and early twentieth centuries be so fully represented as in our gallery,' Ostroukhov wrote in anticipation.[18]

Margarita Morozova, meanwhile, moved out of a house on Novinsky Boulevard (which, at her own expense, she would turn into a hospital during the war) to a mansion redesigned for her by Ivan Zholtovsky between the Arbat and Prechistenka Street. It was the complete opposite of the grandiose palace on Smolensk Boulevard. She was not only moving house but moving on to a fundamentally new chapter of her life, almost mirroring the life of her mother-in-law, Varvara. Both women had endured the same twelve, far from idyllic, years of marriage, which served as a kind of prelude to real life, a new age. Margarita seemed like Varvara to be seeking 'self-determination', unsure, as Andrei Bely comments, which direction to move in. 'Towards art? Towards philosophy? Towards a role in public life?' There was another parallel: a new love in her life too. The man of her dreams was very different from the late Mikhail Morozov: he was a philosopher, a thinker, a writer – and a prince.[19] Unlike Professor Sobolevsky, however, Evgeny Nikolaevich Trubetskoy was married, had three children, and would never leave his family. They were able to meet in secret only abroad, and while in Moscow had to restrict themselves to polite social relations. Their ten-year romance is encapsulated in letters which Margarita preserved. 'Russia needs our love,' she wrote to her prince.[20] 'Of course the life of a withered old maid or a matron full of high-minded rules is not for me. My life will either be a blaze or it will be extinguished. Only then will I be alive, able to work and bear my cross, when my soul is fired up in contact with that radiant world where I have my wonderful sunlit horseman, where we become one to create the bright, beautiful thing which alone makes life worth living . . . If we cannot have a personal life, then let there at least be a life of jubilation and creativity in living and working for Russia!'[21]

It seems a repetition of the Khludova–Sobolevsky drama, complete with all the subplots. He is a thinker and she helps to arrange his lectures. His ambition is to publish Russian philosophers, and for that and for him she sets up first a newspaper and then, in 1910, the *Put'* [Path] publishing house, at whose board meetings they can see each other in public.[22] At these, 'among lilies of the valley blooming in January . . . against a background of Vrubel's *Faust and Margarita in the Garden*', the members of the Religious-Philosophical Society would gather of an evening and, seated at a long oak table, try 'to resolve the burning issues of the age'.[23]

It is unlikely that Ivan Morozov was ever seen at these meetings in the house of his sister-in-law, but we can be sure that Margarita would have been among the guests invited to his mansion on Prechistenka Street. From Dead Lane, now Prechistensky [Blessed Virgin] Lane, to the Morozov estate was a matter of only a few minutes.

Morozov was not like Shchukin, who threw open his gallery on Sundays to the general public and did not consider it beneath his dignity to act as a guide, because who could show off the collection better and provide a more informed commentary on the paintings than he himself? In order to be admitted to Shchukin's mansion on Znamensky Lane and view Gauguin and Matisse you had only to register by phone, but to penetrate Prechistenka Street letters of recommendation and other guarantees were required. Matisse, for example, had to write twice to Morozov, asking him to allow Karl Osthaus to view his gallery, advising him that this was the German art collector's main reason for visiting Moscow. It was unthinkable at that time to imagine Ivan Morozov ever acting as a guide like Shchukin, yet after the 1917 revolution he had little option but to act in that uncongenial role. Fortunately, not for long.

It is much easier to write about Sergei Shchukin: he falls in love with an artist, buys his paintings, stops buying them, transfers his interest to a new talent. He experiences tragedy in his life, a Gauguin appears in his gallery; another misfortune befalls him, and the house is filled with paintings by Matisse bringing affirmation of life. Plotting the course of Ivan Morozov's collecting is far more difficult. The death of two brothers has no effect on his collecting preferences. He leaves no private letters or diary entries, but an abundance of communications from Parisian art dealers and their invoices for paintings. From these invoices and prices and the names of painters we have to reconstruct the course of a life.

On the evidence of currency transfers, Ivan Morozov broke with his usual routine in 1912 and did not go to Paris in the spring or summer. Apparently other obligations prevented it. There were the celebrations of the Battle of Borodino, anniversary exhibitions to commemorate the French invasion in 1812, and an exhibition *One Hundred Years of French Painting*, to whose committee Morozov was appointed for his services in collecting French art in Russia. Many people knew that the director of the Tver Textile Mill Company owned a first-rate art collection, but only a select few had had an opportunity of seeing it. In 1912 all that changed. An essay was printed in the spring issue of *Apollon*, the

St Petersburg magazine of art and literature, by its publisher and editor, Sergei Makovsky.[24] It was about the Morozov collection, and illustrated with fifty-two reproductions of paintings by French artists. Only, alas, in black and white. There were also photographs of the interiors of the Music Salon with the panels by Maurice Denis.

'Moscow can be justly proud of Ivan Abramovich Morozov's "French gallery" on Prechistenka Street. There are few comparable collections, not only in Russia but indeed in the West. Here is a museum of painting which is infinitely precious and essential for anyone seeking an under-standing of contemporary art . . . It is a museum reflecting one person's taste, of course, not by any means the impartiality of an institution.'[25]

When, in early 1914, an issue of *Apollon* reviewing Sergei Shchukin's collection appeared, it would never have occurred to its author to describe it as a museum, let alone to reproach its creator for being guided solely by personal taste. Indeed, what private collector could ever aspire to encyclopaedic thoroughness in his collection, or indeed, to remain impartial?

It was unjust to accuse Morozov of having assembled 'a museum reflecting one person's taste'. He was fully aware himself that his collec-tion was less than comprehensive. No doubt if his life had been different from how it turned out he would have managed to fill the gaps. It was something he was to talk about a lot with Boris Ternovets in the winter of 1918–19. The first director of the Morozov Museum, when working in the 1920s on a scholarly description of the collection, was neverthe-less to blame its former owner for 'insufficiently bringing out' first one and then another artist. He personally, for example, found Morozov's selection of the paintings of Claude Monet unsatisfactory. To say nothing of Édouard Manet, whose work was completely absent from the collection.

# CHAPTER XIII

# Elusive Manet

Figuratively speaking, Édouard Manet was at the top of Ivan Morozov's wish list. His brother Mikhail had bought the wild *In the Bar 'Le Bouchon'*, and Ilya Ostroukhov had acquired *A Portrait of Antonin Proust*.[1] These were the only works by Manet in Russian collections. Morozov was not looking for portraits or genre paintings by Manet: what he needed was a landscape – not a sketch, a finished landscape – in order to demonstrate and emphasize the continuity between Manet and the Impressionists. He advanced doggedly towards that goal, his actions sober and calculated. It is simply impossible to imagine Shchukin being that rational. Sergei Shchukin fell in love, became a 'fan' of an artist, then evicted him from that place in his heart and bestowed his favour on the next talented painter. It is not without reason that Shchukin's collection is described as a history of his obsessions. Ivan Morozov was never so obsessed with his artists or his mission: he waited for the appearance of the work he needed, paid what was asked, and departed with his picture, gleefully rubbing his hands.

Everybody whose opinion Morozov valued and whose advice he listened to was recruited to search for the 'right' Manet for his collection.

The first to respond was Igor Grabar. 'I have just, in passing through Paris, seen one masterpiece at Durand-Ruel's place which unambiguously and dazzlingly passed the difficult test of standing comparison with the old masters themselves, of which I had seen so many in Italy. It was Édouard Manet's *Chasseur de lions*.[2] It is available. (Durand-Ruel has priced it at 60,000 francs but I think he will come down.) I so much wanted to see this piece, undoubtedly one of the five or ten best Manet created, find its way to Moscow that I have been unable to resist the temptation to inform you immediately. You will never regret it. I think, moreover, that that is very inexpensive and I simply cannot understand how no one has yet snapped it up,' Grabar wrote, beside himself with joy.[3]

Morozov respected Grabar as an authoritative art critic and regarded him highly as an artist (he had four landscapes by Grabar in his collection, including *March Snow*, perhaps the best of Grabar's Impressionist paintings). Nevertheless, he ignored the suggestion that he should buy *The Lion Hunter*. An imagined portrait of a famous explorer, posing in front of the enormous carcass of a dead lion and pointing his gun at the viewer, was not allowed into the collection. Morozov, as Makovsky rightly noted, regarded as worthy only what he liked, and what conformed to his intuition and views on the purpose of painting. He was not going to be satisfied with a painting merely because it bore the signature of Édouard Manet.

Ivan Morozov was much more enthusiastic about a proposal from Vollard, who told him he was agreeing a major deal with Auguste Pellerin[4] and could obtain from him one of the most beautiful and rare paintings by Manet in his Paris collection. The work was being offered as part of an exchange. 'I do not know whether you saw this picture when visiting Monsieur Pellerin. It was in a room we could not enter when you came with your Russian painter friend. A photograph will make the subject matter clear to you, but can convey no idea of its wonderful colouration . . . I am asking 50,000 francs for it . . . The photograph will be put in the post tonight.'[5]

21  A letter from Valentin Serov to Ivan Morozov featuring Serov's sketch of Édouard Manet's *Rue Mosnier with Flags*, 10 December 1909.

When he received the photograph, Morozov was wildly enthusiastic. He had just returned from Paris and was staying in the mansion of the French 'margarine king' in Neuilly, where he and Serov were examining his collection. Had Vinogradov or Grabar been in Paris at that time, the Manet might well have ended up in Moscow, but just at that moment the person to hand was Valentin Serov. 'Valentin Severe' (as his friends called him behind his back) categorically rejected the work.

'The item, in my opinion, is uninteresting, as I telegraphed. All it amounts to is a hastily painted sketch of the Paris streets on some political celebration of the July Revolution: the sun is shining, masses of French flags.' In his letter Serov even sketched the composition of the picture, which in fact depicted a holiday in honour of the 1878 World Exhibition. In passing, he heaped abuse on Vollard, whom he called a 'fraud' and 'compulsive liar', having made up his mind that the owner could not much value the painting if he was offering to exchange it. 'The overall tone is disagreeable. The study is in fact not too characteristic of Manet and is not a success (I repeat, in my opinion).'[6] The blurred black-and-white photograph, together with Serov's negative characterization, proved decisive and *Rue Mosnier with Flags* did not make it into the Morozov Collection. It found a home shortly afterwards with the Hungarian collector, Marczell Nemes.[7]

From time to time, French artists would venture to make recommendations to Morozov. These included Maurice Denis, who was personally acquainted with many owners of paintings. For several months Denis stalked the owner of Manet's *Le Déjeuner sur l'herbe*. No, not, of course, the actual legendary painting which had recently come to adorn the galleries of the Louvre, but the original version of it, about which Denis was not just well informed: many years earlier he had been given the task of removing an old layer of varnish from the picture. He decided to chance his luck. Who knows, the son of Hippolyte Lejosne,[8] who had been a friend of Manet, might decide to part with *Le Déjeuner* for a goodly sum of money, and then the painting could be added to the collection of his patron in Moscow. 'I know how much you admire the painting by Manet which I own, and so I am not at all surprised that you spoke about this painting with an enthusiasm capable of sparking off a desire to possess a work so interesting and characteristic of the artist.'[9] Although there was no question of his selling the painting at that moment, its owner indicated that he would certainly bear the offer in mind, and might consider selling if future circumstances so required. Those circumstances materialized after the First World War, but by then Morozov was no longer among the living, and the earlier *Le Déjeuner sur l'herbe* was bought by British industrialist, Samuel Courtauld. He also acquired the beautiful *A Bar at the Folies-Bergère*, which would equally well have filled out the Morozov Collection.

To acquire *A Bar* Morozov would not even have had to travel to Paris. Baron Nikolai Wrangel and Sergei Makovsky brought the painting to the exhibition *One Hundred Years of French Painting*, hosted by *Apollon* and the Institut Français in St Petersburg. The organizers managed to collect some 600 works, and had hoped that Morozov, who had just granted *Apollon* the exclusive right to publish photographs of his collection, would agree to lend his paintings. It was not to be: allowing someone to take photographs for a magazine was one thing, but sending his paintings to an exhibition? He flatly refused. Sergei Shchukin lent not a single item, but Ivan Morozov did at least accept an invitation to join the exhibition's Russian organizing committee, which consisted mainly of the top echelons of St Petersburg's aristocracy. No doubt everyone had reasons of their own.

Ivan Morozov dragged his feet over whether to travel to St Petersburg, while many Muscovites were raring to go to the exhibition. A contemporary recalled, 'I prepared furiously for the visit, making notes from Tugendhold's articles on French art and the relevant chapters of Richard Muther's *History of Painting from the Fourth to the Early Nineteenth Century.* I never again had an opportunity to see Édouard Manet in all his glory. Imagine it: *A Bar, Nana, Woman in Black: Berthe Morisot, Argenteuil.*'[10] Then there were ten days left before the exhibition ended and still Morozov had not appeared.

'I grieve that you have not yet visited the French Exhibition! May I nevertheless hope that you will come to St Petersburg before it closes? That is, before 18 March, Palm Sunday? I.S. Ostroukhov has several times written and told me you will definitely visit us, but now I am beginning to fear that the closing date will be upon us before you visit. I have, moreover, a feeling that when you see one of Courbet's paintings, you will want to buy it, because it is being sold really very cheaply and is a quite exceptional example of Courbet's art,'[11] Sergei Makovsky fretted.

We do not know whether Morozov did manage to visit the exhibition, or whether business affairs and family problems prevented that. It is, however, a fairly simple matter to reconstruct his plan for expanding the collection and filling the empty surfaces on the walls of the first floor. In addition to Gustave Courbet and Édouard Manet, the intention was for paintings by Honoré Daumier and his contemporary Constantin Guys to be acquired.[12] His 'Paris theme' was to be continued with Toulouse-Lautrec, but Morozov was not destined to buy any of them.

If we count Ivan Morozov's collection as having begun with *Frost in Louveciennes* by Sisley, then its foreign section was collected over a period of ten years. Let us not in the process forget that there was a Russian section, with almost twice as many paintings as the foreign section, and to which we shall return a little later. A collection assembled in such a short time was, of course, uneven and could not be otherwise. Many masters who are important in the history of art of the late nineteenth and early twentieth centuries did not find their way into the Morozov Museum, but the Impressionists, those 'beloved and celebrated teachers from an already departed generation', as well as their successors, 'Matisse and the "wild" young artists inclined to Cubism', were, as Makovsky rightly remarks, exquisitely represented. The works chosen were without exception exemplary. That dimension of illustrativeness and the underlying methodical approach were the hallmarks of Ivan Morozov.

The Impressionists – Monet, Renoir, Pissarro, Degas and Sisley – were allocated the largest room on the second floor. Next to them hung Cézanne and Matisse. Neither were the neo-Impressionists – two Signacs and one Cross – forgotten. Adjacent to them were the landscapes of Albert Marquet, despite the fact that his manner differed fundamentally from the bright colours of the Nabis, who were Morozov's great love. The large formal hall known as the Music Salon was entirely the realm of Denis, and the stairs were given over to Bonnard. In the dining room, Morozov hung van Gogh and Gauguin, and the intention was to add still lifes by Matisse. Next to Marquet, Valtat and Friesz hung Derain's *Fishing Boats, Collioure* – the first Fauve landscapes. All that was missing were the views of Collioure by Matisse. 'The general impression is extraordinarily vivid,' Makovsky concluded admiringly.

Abram Efros derived his own formulation to describe Morozov's approach to collecting: 'Shchukin's maîtres, tweaked by Morozov'. What

Efros had in mind was that the list of artists represented in the collections of both Moscow collectors was almost identical: the difference was only in the principles underlying the approach to the choice of a particular work. As a result the collections were in fact completely different: 'Coming into the Morozov Collection, people were first amazed, then disappointed, then their curiosity revived, and finally they felt a wonderful satisfaction at the completely different kind of human organization . . . manifested in such an approach to collection.' In the French half there was no 'latest sensation'. The same Frenchmen hung on his walls as on those of Shchukin only, for some reason, in Sergei Shchukin's collection they were utterly sensational, while in the Morozov Collection:

> . . . they seemed meek; the artists seemed meek; Ivan Morozov himself seemed meek. Everything had been tweaked and everything, in turn, effected a tweak. Nothing changed radically. Shchukin's favourites retained their same qualities, remained in their same places, only Morozov introduced in their very concentrated, very tribal, very defiant appearance a small, subtle change. Perhaps what we should say is that in Shchukin's collection the celebrities of Paris were always on stage, in full make-up and highly charged. In Morozov's collection they were quieter, more intimate, more transparent. Morozov . . . searched at great length in his discriminating way for something he alone could see in a new artist. Finally he made his selection but, in the act of choosing, he always introduced his 'golden tweak'.[13]

In the ten years since his brother Mikhail's death, Ivan Morozov had had his revenge. He possessed a magnificent palace, a beautiful wife but, most significantly, he had a collection which was not only several times more extensive, but also more important than that of his brother. The sibling rivalry and jealousies were long forgotten, but now it was not he but Mikhail who trailed behind as the extra. Ivan Abramovich's main competitor, however, was still in a different league: compared with Sergei Shchukin, Ivan Morozov would always be in second place. Abram Efros, renowned for his paradoxical epithets, was only articulating this situation when he spoke of 'Shchukin's maîtres, tweaked by Morozov'. It seemed an authoritative pronouncement.

Except that, on closer examination, this summation is in fact open to challenge. It implies that Ivan Morozov has to be measured against Shchukin, and that the greater part of his collection – Bonnard, Denis, Maillol, whom Shchukin had ignored – remains, as it were, outside the equation. On top of which, is it really possible to characterize the Fauves, Vlaminck and Valtat, as 'meek'? Wild beasts, more like, not at all meek and mild. Unexpectedly, it is Morozov who manages to present the broader panorama of the era with all its currents and subtle nuances, and that makes his collection the more objective in respect of the artistic movements of its time. We have no choice, however, but to agree that Shchukin's collection was revolutionary, while that of Morozov was evolutionary.[14]

Shchukin and Morozov often bought the same artists. Sometimes their tastes coincided so exactly that even the 'Morozov tweak' proved powerless. Looking now at paintings from the Shchukin and Morozov collections, hung on the same wall, it can be difficult to guess which work was acquired by whom. It is easiest to be mistaken with the Gauguins and Marquets, or to be tripped up by Derain's late works: Morozov's *Tree Trunks*, painted in Martigues, and Shchukin's *The Grove* are all but indistinguishable. They both bought Derains from Daniel-Henri Kahnweiler, the son of a German businessman who, in 1907, took the apparently foolhardy step of opening an art gallery in Paris and enthusiastically buying Cubist paintings, an investment generally considered highly speculative.

Morozov found his way to 28 rue Vignon in 1912, when Derain and Picasso were already under contract to Kahnweiler, which obliged them to sell all their new works through him. Such an arrangement, guaranteeing the artist a regular income, regulated the relationship between the Bernheims and Matisse, between Druet and Marquet.

Sergei Shchukin had been a regular customer of the gallery since 1910. He at first systematically bought paintings by Picasso, but then became infatuated with André Derain. 'All of Pee-pee-pee-casso pales before this poo-poo-poo-poortrait,' he is supposed to have shouted. This passion had been aroused in him by Derain's *Portrait of a Man with a Newspaper*, the sixteenth and last of Derain's paintings he bought, which arrived at Shchukin's mansion on Znamensky Lane in the spring of 1914. Morozov did not show off his purchases, and was even less likely to vent his feelings about them in public.

Derain had come to Morozov's attention back in 1907, when he bought *Drying the Sails* from Vollard, which Louis Vauxcelles dismissed as suitable only for decorating a nursery, considering the artist's impudent, ironic palette and disorderly colour contrasts childishly pig-headed.[15] Moving closer to the Cubists, Derain repudiated his earlier vivid Fauve colours but did not go on to become a pure Cubist. Instead he created his own, so-called neo-Gothic style, which so appealed to Shchukin. In 1913, Morozov acquired two Derain landscapes and one still life from Kahnweiler, painted in a brown-green palette adopted from the Cubists. Ivan Morozov advanced no further than Derain's moderate Cubism, with the exception of the most avant-garde work in his collection, Picasso's *Portrait of Ambroise Vollard*, which consisted of painted blocks. It was not something he regretted, although he later kicked himself for never having bought a single Manet, and having overlooked Seurat.

# CHAPTER XIV

## Last Acquisitions

In January 1913, Renoir's *Boy with a Whip* and *Head of a Woman* were delivered to Morozov's Moscow mansion. Together with them came a last, eighteenth, painting by Cézanne, *Interior with Two Women*. This was to be the earliest painting by the *Hermit of Aix* in the Morozov Collection. Next came Ker-Xavier Roussel's paired *Triumph of Bacchus* and *Triumph of Ceres (Rural Festival)*, which the artist had significantly altered since Morozov had seen the paintings. Understanding from Vollard that the buyer was intending to hang his pastorals alongside Matisse, Roussel hastily repainted both canvases before they were sent to Moscow, unwisely, as Ternovets put it, exaggerating the colours. This did nothing for the paintings' artistic merit, although Degas liked them. Vollard recalls that he stopped before *The Triumph of Bacchus*, stroked the canvas and, when told the name of the painter, remarked, 'This has nobility.'[1]

The panels set Morozov back 10,000 francs, a substantial sum. He could have returned paintings which had been subjected to such unexpected alteration; he could have summoned the artist to Moscow where, like Denis, he might have toned back down the excessive enhancement of his 'rural festivals'. Visiting Vollard in rue Laffitte in autumn 1913, he could have complained to him and even refused to accept the Roussels. None of this happened, but something in the relationship between buyer and seller had clearly gone wrong. If early in the year Ivan Abramovich had spent almost 100,000 francs on paintings from Vollard, just like in the good old days, in the autumn he limited himself to inexpensive sculptures. A delivery of bronzes arrived in Moscow on the eve of the new year: three bronzes by Rodin, *Abandon* and *The Implorer* by his student Camille Claudel, and two torsos by Maillol's assistant, Richard Guinot, whom Vollard had hired as a pair of hands for the aged Renoir, whose severe arthritis made him unable to model sculptures.

In fact, however, Morozov had his eye on large, expensive marble statues. Vollard, at his request, had already begun negotiating with Rodin for the purchase of *Triton* or *Romeo and Juliet*, but the sculptures were just too heavy: the one-and-a-half-metre-high marble *Triton* weighed around one and a half tons. As a result Morozov had to limit himself to three small bronze compositions: *Amor fugit*, *Eternal Spring* and *The Kiss*.

Morozov had been foiled, not by the price of 110,000 francs which the sculptor was asking, but by the sheer weight of the marble. Ilya Ostroukhov had, with considerable difficulty, persuaded the mayor to ask the Moscow Duma for an emergency loan of 16,000 francs to enable him to buy something by Rodin, and Morozov was quite at home dealing in hundreds of thousands. Ostroukhov was concerned that the marble *Eva*, promised in her will by Margarita Morozova, would end up being the only work in the Tretyakov Gallery by that 'giant among giants, Rodin'. His problem was that the gallery's regulations at the time allowed it to accept works by foreign artists only if they were donated, but not to purchase them.[2]

Although devoted to the ethos of the gallery, Ostroukhov remained a passionate collector and secretly longed for Rodin to let him have 'some piece of his work for which he would not charge too much . . . just a bit, part of a torso, a thigh, a muscular shoulder, just any characteristic chunk of the genius of Rodin'.[3] For that, however, he, the son-in-law of the tea and sugar magnate, Petr Botkin, was not prepared to pay more than 3,000 francs. He could only envy Morozov, who had paid Maillol almost 60,000 for four bronze virgins. Neither Ilya Ostroukhov nor the Tretyakov brothers' gallery, which now belonged to the city, could have thought for a moment of paying that sort of money.

Ivan Morozov did not always buy expensive pieces. Sometimes he paid 200 or 300 francs for a canvas, and instead of Rodin's marble he settled for seven small bronze figures by Maillol, which Evdokiya Sergeevna put on her dressing table. The figurines were most likely bought for her. The *Bouquet of Flowers* by Ascanio Tealdi was also for her. As Matisse hadn't got round to painting flowers for his wife, let her have a beautiful bouquet from somebody else – perhaps that was his reasoning. Why else would the owner of an outstanding collection on his last visit to Paris be tempted by the canvas of a little-known Italian painter which only cost 1,000 francs? His Dosya loved still lifes with flowers. So, indeed, did Lydia Shchukina. Her son, Ivan, recalled that Cézanne's *Bouquet of Flowers in a Blue Vase* hung in his mother's boudoir. Of all the paintings her husband had bought, that was the one she chose for herself.

Sergei Shchukin's wife passed away in 1907. He had not bought any Cézannes for a long time, and in recent years had been desperately struggling to find his way to Picasso. He had already run out of space for the Spaniard's canvases on the walls of his 25-square-metre study, but Shchukin still wanted more, and continued buying one Picasso after another. He never said to visitors that he was besotted with Picasso's work or that the artist was better than others, but Picasso entranced Shchukin, bewitched him, and he did not conceal the fact. Perhaps this can explain why he went ahead and bought the two-metre canvas, *Three Women*, although he had refused it a year previously. There was really no longer any free wall space in the mansion on Znamensky Lane.

The painting belonged to Leo and Gertrude Stein.[4] The brother and sister decided to separate, and split their collection. Both needed money.

Leo needed a new place to live, and Gertrude had finally decided to live with her friend, Alice B. Toklas, and was planning to refurbish the apartment on rue de Fleurus. The Steins continued to live on a grand scale, but their financial situation had deteriorated. In terms of wealth they were as far removed from Shchukin and Morozov as they were from J. P. Morgan and John D. Rockefeller. Apart from paintings they had once bought at knockdown prices, they had nothing to sell. When they divided the collection, Gertrude got nearly all the Picassos. Leo had long since cooled towards Picasso and kept only a few drawings for himself. Everything else he surrendered to his sister. She decided to sacrifice three works by her favourite artist. Kahnweiler bought *Three Women* and *Young Acrobat with Ball* from her, and immediately resold them to his Russian customers.[5] The Cubist masterpiece went to Shchukin and the masterpiece of Picasso's pink period went to Morozov.[6]

The Muscovites were well familiar with Stein's paintings. Both had several times visited the spacious American studio at 27 rue de Fleurus, where canvases by Cézanne, Gauguin, Renoir, Matisse and Picasso hung in several rows. The brother and sister bought their first Picasso in 1905 in the little shop of Clovis Sagot, a former circus clown, in rue Laffitte.[7] The vulnerable pink *Young Girl with a Flower Basket*, whose thin 'monkey' legs irritated Gertrude, cost them 150 francs. Even before that, Leo had brought home from Sagot a large gouache *Family of Acrobats with Monkey*. Leo and Gertrude bought the girl acrobat on the ball directly from Picasso. He became a regular visitor at the house on rue de Fleurus around the time that Morozov was acquiring *Two Acrobats (Harlequin and his Companion)* from Vollard. Ivan Morozov took a shine to this work by an unknown artist: the vivid colours and strong, fluent outline, melancholy Harlequin with his whitened face, and his girlfriend whose face resembled a Japanese mask. *Harlequin and his Companion* fitted admirably into his Paris theme – his paintings by Maurer, Lempereur and Morrice – especially since there was nothing on the theme of the circus in his collection. The picture, he decided, was worth its 300-franc price tag. It was only when he was preparing for the *Apollon* publication that Morozov realized he had not even bothered to find out the full name of the artist.

'First name of Picasso: Pablo.' Vollard volunteered no further information. By that time he had ceased to buy Picasso, although he had organized Picasso's first exhibition and been the first to sell his paintings. There might also have been a more personal reason. Many of the artists Vollard sold painted his portrait. So did Picasso, but in his Cubist style, which Vollard found unacceptable. The dealer lost interest in his protégé, although he did describe the portrait as very much out of the ordinary.[8] He sold it to Morozov for 3,000 francs.

Vollard's behaviour is not too puzzling, but whatever made Ivan Morozov buy a Cubist painting, which was so clearly not to his taste, remains a mystery. There are two possible explanations: either his instinct told him that Cubism deserved a place in his museum, or he simply trusted a Parisian marchand from whom he had bought almost all his Cézannes and Gauguins, as well as most of his works by Valtat, Vlaminck, Degas and Renoir. It seems unlikely that Morozov was taken by the uncanny resemblance of the portrait to its sitter, which was acknowledged by everybody at the time.

Unlike Shchukin, Morozov was not bewitched by Picasso's painting. The tension and concentration of the Spaniard's art was clearly not to his taste. In painting, Ivan Morozov was looking for tranquillity and joy, which is why he so loved the Nabis. Trying to decipher the meaning of paintings with complicated geometrical shapes did not suit his temperament. Perhaps, however, there was something in this Cubist visual conundrum which piqued his interest. There is now no telling the direction in which he might have gone on to develop his collection. The war turned everything upside down. Its tragic consequences would derail the future. In any case, in the summer of 1914 it became impossible to make trips to Europe.

# CHAPTER XV

# Citizen Morozov

The war proved a golden age for the owners of the Tver Textile Mill Company, with a vast order for 5 million arshins (3.56 million metres) of fabric and 10,000 covers for grenades. In just one year they earned as much as they had in the previous twenty. Almost 15,000 people were working in the Morozov enterprises. The spinning factory processed over 10 million kilograms of cotton in a single year and produced over 8 million kilograms of finished yarn.

The Morozovs quickly reorganized their business to meet the demands of wartime. A Chemicals Committee was formed under the National Artillery Board for the procurement and production of explosives, asphyxiating and incendiary agents, directed by Lieutenant General Vladimir Ipatiev,[1] a research chemist.[2] A joint stock company, Koksobenzol, was set up by Nikolai Vtorov and Ivan Morozov to produce explosives and chemical products with military applications: the army needed not only cloth for greatcoats, but also gas masks.

The war did not at first have any great impact on Ivan Morozov's art collecting. He continued never to miss an exhibition, of which, in 1915 and 1916, there were a great many in Moscow. 'It is as if Russian artists have been conscripted to paint pictures rather than into military service. The Union Exhibition, the Itinerants' Exhibition, Ostroumova's engravings, the World of Art, the Students' Exhibition at the Academy of Painting, Free Creativity, Ukrainian Artists, Contemporary Painting, Art of the Past and Present, Konenkov's sculptures and, to top all that, an exhibition of industrial design. A total of eleven. For such an eventful year, that might be thought rather a lot of exhibitions,'[3] one critic suggested. Now, however, only Russian art was on sale. All contact with Paris had been lost.

By the end of 1916 interruptions in the supply of cotton, dyes and wool to the Tver factories were increasingly common. Production was periodically halted and, in addition, there were problems with food supplies. Some of the workers were mobilized, and those who remained were involved in disturbances and went on strike, demanding increased pay to cover food and lodging, for their holidays not to be disrupted, and for none of those who went on strike to be dismissed. The owners refused. Then came the revolutionary events of February 1917, the Tsar's attempt to prorogue the State Duma, and his subsequent abdication.

On 4 September 1917, Varvara Khludova-Morozova died suddenly. Until her dying day she had not let the reins slip from her hands. The matriarch had long ago made her will: her shares in the company, estimated at 3–5 million rubles, were to be sold and government bonds purchased with the proceeds. These were to be lodged with the National Bank and earn interest. The Tver Textile Mill Company was to use these funds to build houses and dormitories for the factory workers. Just as she had hoped in her youth, Varvara Khludova was going to have done something useful with her life.

In October 1917 the Bolsheviks seized power, and in August 1918 the Tver Textile Mill Company, which produced twenty-seven types of textile products in forty-nine varieties, was nationalized. Its old management was replaced by a workers' committee. Ivan Morozov personally handed over the keys to the safes and the ledgers of the company to the workers' representative, a carpenter called Ivan Rakov. The Morozovs' enterprise became the Tver Proletarian Manufacturing Company or, more simply, the *Proletarka*.

The house at 9 Varvarka Street,[4] where the board sat, was, unsurprisingly, requisitioned. Ivan Morozov, the widows of Mikhail and Arseny, and with them their children and relatives were stripped of a huge fortune. The value of the company's real estate alone was estimated at 26 million rubles.

Morozov's art collection of some 500 items was nationalized four months later, but, unlike that of Shchukin, it was not judged deserving of a special decree. The title of the decree of the Soviet of People's Commissars of 19 December 1918 was 'On the Nationalization of the Art Collections of I.A. Morozov, I.S. Ostroukhov and A.V. Morozov'. That is, the Ivan Morozov Collection was one item on a list, albeit enjoying the questionable distinction of being first. Alexei Morozov, the son of Vikul Morozov, who was the cousin of Abram Morozov and had founded the manufacturing company of Vikul Morozov and Sons, was third. The second name in the 19 December decree was Ostroukhov. As formerly the director of the Tretyakov Gallery, Ilya Semenovich might seem to have been a candidate for greater indulgence than the factory-owning Morozovs. He had always positioned himself as primarily a painter (his landscape, *Siverko*, to this day hangs in the Tretyakov Gallery's Levitan room) and a museum administrator, rather than as an official of the Botkin tea and sugar empire of his father-in-law.

His kinship with the Botkins debarred Ostroukhov from classification as an artist which, under the categories of the new social hierarchy, would have seen him deemed a 'proletarian element'. The studios of 'artists' were not subject to nationalization and their art collections, which as a rule were modest, remained under their ownership and that of their heirs.

Alexei Vikulovich Morozov, like Ostroukhov, did not consider himself a businessman. He had passed the running of his father's textile factory in Orekhovo-Zuyevo to his brother back in 1895 and, having received the share due to him, devoted himself exclusively to collecting. The remit of his collection extended to porcelain, miniatures, engravings, *lubok* woodcuts, glass, crystal, silver, snuffboxes, carved wooden toys, fabrics, embroideries and icons. Ivan Morozov's second cousin also did not care to show his treasures to outsiders, a penchant for privacy evidently being a family trait. At the same time, Alexei was very much a man of the world who adored female company, but remained a bachelor until he was sixty. He was always dressed to the nines, with never a wrinkle on his trousers or jacket. His hands were manicured and his moustache perfectly dyed and twirled. He invited guests for the sole purpose of delighting them, decorating the table with flowers and serving sterlet, lobster, sturgeon and caviar in silver bowls. He drank and ate very little himself, watching his waistline.

In the spring of 1918, anarchists seized twenty-five wealthy mansions in the very centre of the city. Among them was the house of Alexei Vikulovich Morozov. The Moorish castle of Arseny Morozov on Vozdvizhenka Street suffered the same fate. Konstantin Paustovsky, in his autobiographical *Story of a Life*, thus recalls the misbehaviour of the anarchists:

There they lived their merry, uninhibited lives amid the fine antique furniture, chandeliers and rugs, which they used in their own, unorthodox way. Pictures became targets for revolver practice. Instead of tarpaulin, valuable rugs covered the stacked cases of cartridges left in the yard. Windows were boarded up for safety with collectors' items from the library. Ballrooms with patterned parquet floors were used as night shelters . . . Prim old ladies spoke with horror of abominable orgies. In fact, there were no orgies, only drinking bouts of the most pedestrian sort, at which hooch was drunk instead of champagne to wash down salted fish as hard as rock. The mansions housed a collection of riff-raff and neurotic boys and girls – an early version of a Makhno gang in the heart of Moscow . . .[5]

On 12 April 1918 Felix Dzerzhinsky, the head of the Cheka political police, gave the order to end the anarchist occupations. Paustovsky was an eyewitness as they were neutralized. They had occupied 'a curious building which looks like a castle and has sea shells encrusted in its grey walls'. This was the mansion on Vozdvizhenka Street, presented by Arseny Morozov to his femme fatale. In Aleksei Vikulovich Morozov's house the uninvited guests left behind them a pile of engravings tossed out of their filing cabinets and the shattered fragments of porcelain figurines. But then the mansion and all its contents were requisitioned, and Citizen A.V. Morozov was issued a preservation order certifying that his museum apartment was registered and protected by the commission of the People's Commissariat for Enlightenment, and that 'as nationalized property, and without the consent of the commission, it is not to be requisitioned or subjected to consolidation'.[6] By that time, however, Alexei had already been 'consolidated' to the greatest degree possible. 'After his father's death his house (in Vvedensky Lane on Pokrovka Street) was inherited by Alexei as the eldest. It was enormous and had innumerable rooms,' Margarita Morozova recalled. She was very fond of her late husband's second cousin. 'All the rooms on the first floor were full of glass display cabinets containing his porcelain collection and icons. He himself lived on the floor below, where he had two dining rooms, a living room and a study. His study was double-height, with two rows of windows, panelled with dark wood, and with five panels painted by Vrubel depicting Faust, Mephistopheles and Margarita.'[7]

Now, however, the times were such that even one dining room was considered an inexcusable luxury, let alone two. At first, Alexei Vikulovich was allowed to retain four rooms, but then they had second thoughts and took away two of them.

This process of consolidation is memorably described in a dialogue in Mikhail Bulgakov's play, *The Heart of a Dog*, between Professor Preobrazhensky and representatives of the new regime:

'Excuse us, professor, but a general meeting of the residents of our house requests you voluntarily, as a matter of labour discipline, to give up the dining room.'

'Nobody in Moscow has dining rooms nowadays. Not even Isadora Duncan. Isn't that right, comrades?'

'Where, then, am I to dine?'

'In the bedroom.'

The Anarchists did not make it to Prechistenka Street and the third Morozov. However, when disturbances began, Ivan Morozov made haste to take down his paintings from the walls and move them to a 'fireproof storeroom' as a precaution.[8] Inside this secure storeroom, with its thick stone walls and vaulted concrete ceiling, stood an enormous chest, 3 x 1.5 metres, where the most valuable paintings could be kept safe. The last inventory of the collection was taken in January 1917. Its insured value was declared to be 560,000 rubles. Including the mansion, the estimated value was over one million.

A double door leading to a huge safe installed at the beginning of the war could be opened by a combination known only to Morozov. By 1918 only someone as naive as Ivan Morozov could have imagined he could rely solely on this kind of secure storage facility. He supposed that, if facing force majeure, he would have time to export the paintings.[9]

Alas, no one was to have time to export anything. Only Prince Felix Yusupov had a measure of success in managing both to save his life, and also two portraits painted by Rembrandt, which he and his wife took with them when they sailed from Crimea in spring 1919 together with the Tsar's surviving relatives and what remained of the White Army.[10] Princess Sofiya Meshcherskaya, who tried in spring 1918 to take *Madonna and Child*, School of Botticelli, out of Moscow, had considerably less success. The picture was requisitioned and, to put anybody else off the idea, a special decree prohibited all further export abroad of items of special artistic or historical value. The curtain came down abruptly.

Preservation orders[11] which, it was promised, would protect 'art property' from requisitioning, and protect those awarded them from consolidation, did not last even six months. Such high hopes had been reposed in those pieces of paper. Good-natured Ivan Morozov put his trust in them like a young boy. He was handed the document with its official seal with some ceremony, the order being brought to him not by just any official from the People's Commissariat for Enlightenment, but by the sculptor, Sergei Konenkov. Before the war, Morozov had bought three one-metre-high female figures from him. A marble *Torso* sculpted by Konenkov made a pair with *Torso* sculpted by Richard Guinot and brought from Paris. Konenkov's *Young Woman*, carved from wood, was part of an ensemble together with Maillol's naked virgins. Then, when the war was at its height, Morozov also acquired two nudes from the 'Russian Rodin', who had just returned from Greece. There were not a few interesting sculptors in Moscow, many of whom had studied in Paris under Bourdelle, and who had visited Rodin's studio, but out of all of them Morozov chose only Konenkov.

A few years earlier, when he had first visited the mansion on Prechistenka Street, Konenkov had been quite aggressive. Instead of looking round the collection, he began, perhaps after having had too much to drink, to berate the owner for his addiction to foreign maîtres. An eyewitness thus describes the incident:

It's muck, all this stuff you've got by Maurice Denis and Manet and Degas and Maillol. Muck – all of it. Maillol is shit. Call those forms? Where are the feet, where is the muscle? It's all rushed, crude, trite. Do you think that by stuffing your wallet full and going to France you are doing something useful by buying all this muck? France is taking money from us, and we are borrowing money from France, and there's absolutely no call to support them!'

Then Ivan Abramovich told him, 'I just love you, Sergei Timofeevich!' And Konenkov retorted, 'Who cares if you love me?

I don't need you and you don't need me. Does it matter a fig if you love me or not?' Morozov replied, 'I don't know what it is I love about you, but you are the first person to speak out so bluntly. Korovin was here. He first gave me a dressing down, but then sent a letter of apology.'

'Well I'm not going to be apologizing,' Konenkov replied. 'Maybe Korovin was dazzled, all this set-up, all the outward tinsel, but I won't take back a word.'

'I'll show you something else,' said Ivan Abramovich, and took him through other rooms, and there, hidden in his bedroom, were Vrubel and Borisov-Musatov. 'This,' said Konenkov, 'is good, but you are hiding it from everybody. In your place I would take Vrubel out for everyone to see. "Look, everybody," I would say. "Study that!" But you don't understand your own Russian stuff. You're forever doing new artists. In ten years, I know, you have had ten idols: first Claude Monet, then Degas, Gauguin, and the rest. You go wild about them one after the other, but you don't have real love for them. You pick up all sorts of muck. Look, Gauguin there is good. But do they understand?'[12]

We need have no doubts about the veracity of this account, which comes to us from the diary of an eyewitness. Sergei Konenkov, the son of a peasant, did not pull his punches, and was not in the habit of grovelling in front of millionaires.

In April 1918, puffed up with his own importance, Konenkov appeared again at Morozov's mansion, but this time as a Bolshevik official. 'Upon my arrival, Morozov cheered up noticeably. He was genuinely pleased that the state would not let his collection, which had been assembled with great artistic taste, be dispersed and destroyed,' the ninety-year-old sculptor wrote in the 1960s, by now rather mechanically, in his memoirs *My Times*. He had brought Morozov the preservation order.[13]

The paper brought by Konenkov afforded at least a glimmer of hope. Who knows, perhaps there might even be a resolution to move the local military unit, billeted on the ground floor, out of the mansion? In those days it was not regarded as a mistake to requisition luxurious mansions for Bolshevik institutions. The deplorable consequences of the use over many years of palaces as offices by the new government are well known. Fortunately, dozens of Moscow mansions were allocated to diplomatic missions, who preserved the interiors designed by Kekushev, Shekhtel and Zholtovsky in pristine condition.

The worst thing was not, however, the destruction of exceptional mansions and priceless art collections. There was also eradication of a whole way of life. Even the most intelligent and far-sighted people did not immediately recognize the root-and-branch nature of the changes. The ground was giving way beneath their feet. Paustovsky accurately defines the situation of someone deprived of their familiar landmarks:

> Day after day, with a ruthless logic, these harsh, pitiless decrees demolished our familiar background and shovelled it aside, making way for the new foundations of our life. It was still difficult to imagine what this life would be like. The change of concepts was so startling that at times the very ground of our existence seemed to give way, quaking and deceptive as quicksand. Everyone felt a warning chill. The weak staggered like drunkards.[14]

People really were not given time to take in the new reality. It seems strange to us now that they did not realize how dire the situation was, did not just pack their bags and flee the revolutionary nightmare. But how could they decide just to up and abandon everything? And where were they going to flee to? Many people, including Morozov, decided to stay in their homes and sit out the revolutionary nightmare in familiar surroundings. Ivan Morozov even carried on buying paintings. The invoice for Konstantin Korovin's *Night with a Campfire by the River* is dated 5 June 1918, literally on the eve of the decree nationalizing major industries. The painting disappeared; his factories were confiscated.

Sergei Shchukin was more far-sighted. Sensitive to market conditions and new trends in art, he also instantly sensed the impending threat. In 1914 the widowed Shchukin had remarried. He now had a three-year-old daughter. Life had taught him many lessons: he knew when to exercise caution. First his wife and daughter, and then Shchukin himself and his elder son, quietly disappeared from Moscow. At the end of August 1918, three months before the Shchukin Gallery was to be declared the property of the people, none of them were in the city. His elder daughter, Countess Ekaterina Keller, stayed behind to look after the collection. For almost three years she continued to be its guardian, never losing hope, like her father, that the Bolshevik government was a passing phase.

Morozov had no one he could rely on and, moreover, his hopes were raised by the preservation order Konenkov had brought him. Overcoming his anxiety for his treasures, he opened his secure storeroom and began to hang the pictures again. The People's Commissariat for Enlightenment viewed this action on the part of Citizen Morozov favourably. A decree, formulated by the Museums Department, with the lengthy title of 'On Registration, Inventorization and Preservation of Works of Art and Antiquities Owned by Private Individuals, Societies and Institutions' had come into force on 5 October 1918. Its aim was abundantly clear: to exercise control over all owners of collections in the Republic, without exception. Igor Grabar was especially enthusiastic: 'I put all my energy into the task of creating an institution that would coordinate the work of all the museums of Russia and systematize protection of works of art and antiquities. Lunacharsky gave complete freedom of action to me and the team of art specialists I had assembled. I wrote an extensive declaration in which I laid out a staged plan for reorganizing all the capital's museums and creating new ones.'[15]

The post of People's Commissar for Enlightenment in the first Soviet government had gone to Lunacharsky. Many of the artists and art historians who remained in Moscow went to work for his Department for Museums and the Preservation of Works of Art and Antiquities, known to its employees as the Museum Collegium, because employment there guaranteed a ration of essential food and firewood.[16] The department's director was Natalya Trotskaya-Sedova, wife of the People's Commissar for the Army and Navy, Leon Trotsky. Her deputy was Grabar, an old friend of Ivan Morozov. Even with such a triumvirate, the authority of the Museum Collegium was not always deferred to.

It was no simple matter to protect collectors from all who cast a covetous eye on their palaces and paintings. Morozov's mansion was constantly under attack. At one moment comrade artists from the provinces would turn up at Prechistenka and demand paintings by Cézanne and Derain because their museums in Vyatka and Saratov did not have any. Next, the soldiers occupying the ground floor would attempt to storm the main staircase to take over the first floor as well. This 'dual power' situation continued at Prechistenka Street for just under four months: the collection had been nationalized, but not yet turned into a Soviet museum open to the public. Accordingly, the former owner was able to continue living there surrounded by his beloved paintings and sculptures, which were being busily registered and inventorized by the staff of the Museums Department. It was at that time that thirteen-year-old Tatiana Lebedeva visited the mansion.

A girl from a good family, she came to see the paintings with her engineer father and, when she got back home, wrote a detailed description of the visit in her diary. A future artist, her memoir is interesting for the freshness and authenticity of her impressions. She compiled a detailed map of the first floor, which she called 'I. Morozov's apartment with paintings hung in it'. She included every detail, not even omitting to mention that she and her father took their outdoor clothing off upstairs. In earlier days fur coats would have been left downstairs with the porter and Tanya was not yet used to the changes brought by 'consolidation'. The ways of the new times were completely different from those of the established customs and manners, and immediately jarred. The painter Oleksa Hryshchenko visited the mansion at about the same time as Tatiana Lebedeva. Morozov had invited him round for tea. 'In a small room he, a big, portly, rich man, poured the tea himself, not from the traditional samovar but from a large kettle.'[17] A symbol of the new way of life, a large brass kettle of boiling water had already found its way into the genteel mansion. Anyone familiar with Soviet films about the war and revolution will recall *Man with a Gun*,[18] in which a soldier wanders through the corridors of the Bolsheviks' Smolny Institute with a rifle and a kettle.

Years later, in an autobiographical sketch, *Paintings and Painters*, Tatiana Lebedeva recalled that January day in 1919:

> One Sunday my father, without saying where we were going, sent for a cab. We drove up in style to a two-storey mansion on Prechistenka Street, to be met by the owner himself. It was clearly deliberate that Serov portrayed this Moscow patron of the arts against the exotic background of a dazzling still life by Matisse, whose pulsing rhythm and 'wild' colour combinations emphasize the flabby features of a merchant's face and the awkwardness of his stereotypical goatee beard à la russe. The precious canvases which lined the walls of the large, bright rooms, no longer belonged to this last representative of a famous dynasty which, for three generations, had clothed millions of Russian peasants in colourful chintz. Hunched up, because it was not warm in the rooms, screwing up his myopic eyes, and smiling languidly at my awkward curtsey, he spoke to me in French.

Here is what Tanya wrote in her diary that very same evening:

> We went down a corridor into the dining room. It is really quite stylish, an oak ceiling, the whole dining room in Gothic style, a huge fireplace. Paintings hanging there by Gauguin, Van Gogh, Picasso.

We passed along a little corridor into a rather large room, where Cézanne, Renoir hung . . . Then we turned left into a large room, where I was struck by a huge painting by Monet, *The Garden at Montgeron*. Wonderful, unforgettable colours combining in gentle harmony. Also his *Boulevard*, and dreamy paintings by Sisley. The next room featured paintings by younger artists. My favourite was Bonnard, *Mirror above a Washstand*. The play of the grey and blue is unlike anything I've seen. Next there was a top-lit room with panels by Maurice Denis. This hall was unlike anything I've seen. The subject was the myth of Psyche. Blue and pink hues. I especially liked the funny, narrow strips with pink flowers. The furniture is all under covers. After that we viewed the study, and here we found pictures by Russian artists: Korovin, Golovin, Serov. Korovin had the most paintings. Golovin had a few. . . The whole study is panelled to halfway up the wall with mahogany, another fireplace finished with reddish marble. Near the study was a small room with a large dressing table on which there were several statues by Konenkov and Maillol, and drawings hanging on the walls by Degas and Legrand in pencil and watercolour.

Altogether I really liked everything. It would be nice to go there again.[19]


Of course, such a viewing was not commonplace: A.A. Lebedev was the chief engineer of the Tver factories and must have been personally acquainted with Morozov. Nevertheless, Tanya's testimony confirms that in that last year Morozov opened his collection to the public on Sunday mornings, with his family and servants providing security. It seems barely believable that Morozov, who was always so off-putting towards strangers, should be acting as a guide for people completely unknown to him, and even providing a commentary. This, however, is confirmed by Boris Ternovets, who was to play an important role in the subsequent history of the Morozov Collection.

Ternovets first appeared in the Prechistenka mansion immediately after it was nationalized, in December 1918. The Museums Department sent two specialists in contemporary Western art to Morozov, choosing from its staff two members who had studied it in situ, in Paris and Munich. The art critic, Yakov Tugendhold, set to work describing the Russian part of the collection, but was soon transferred to the Shchukin Gallery. Boris Ternovets stayed on at Prechistenka and worked shoulder to shoulder with the former owner who, in his words, showed positively paternal concern. They worked jointly on cataloguing the collection. Ivan Morozov, like a true businessman, had kept all the financial records, including bills and receipts. Ternovets methodically wrote down the details from him: when and from whom the painting was bought, how much had been paid for it, etc. By this time Morozov had been deprived of all his land, forests, factories and mansions and now, for the first time, had nothing to distract him from his main interest in life. Indeed, apart from his paintings there was nothing else in it.

Boris Ternovets clearly got on well with Ivan Abramovich. He was thirty-five. Having entered the economics section of the law faculty of Moscow University, he was planning to devote himself to work in the Zemstvo local government institutions, but fate decided otherwise. In autumn 1905 lectures were discontinued because of the revolutionary events, and Ternovets travelled to Berlin, where he became seriously interested in art. In Germany he recognized that economics was not his métier. He enrolled at Szymon Hołoszy's private school, and also became an unregistered student at the Department of Art History of the University of Munich, where Heinrich Wölfflin, who devised objective principles for stylistic analysis, was lecturing.[20] He next attended the Académie de la Grande Chaumière in Paris, and sculpture classes under the direction of Émile Bourdelle. His interest in sculpture was piqued by Hołoszy, who encouraged his students to mould in clay. His classmates proved to be mostly girls from Moscow. The majority did not advance beyond the level of amateurs, but Vera Mukhina, the daughter of a merchant, had a brilliant career as a monumental sculptor under the Soviet regime (for which she had little love).[21]

At the outbreak of war Ternovets, like all Russian citizens, was obliged to return to his homeland. He found working in the Museums Department uninteresting, but the People's Commissariat for Enlightenment provided a steady income and rations. Being an official was burdensome, and he continued to sculpt at night, completing a commission for a monument to Skryabin for Moscow City Council. Cataloguing the Morozov collection, however, took up almost all his time, and Ternovets soon had to put aside his clay and paints.

# CHAPTER XVI

# Emigration

Grabar elaborated a grandiose plan to cover the country with a whole network of museums. He called the largest collections, like those of the Rumyantsev Museum and the Historical Museum, 'department stores like Muir and Merrilees'.[1] He proposed that they should be divided into separate sections to form completely new museums: of Asian arts, of ethnography and archaeology, of everyday life, and a Museum of Old Painting – 'Moscow's very own Hermitage'. Grabar's plan also proposed the creation of small, intimate museums, which is why at the end of 1918 there was a rush to nationalize all private collections.

Shchukin's gallery opened as a museum immediately after nationalization, because for the past ten years, although privately owned, it had been open to the public. The opening to the public of Morozov's gallery was delayed for several months, perhaps in order to complete the inventory on which Ternovets was working all hours.

On the morning of 10 April 1919, Ternovets was summoned to the Museums Department, which was situated nearby, in Dead Lane, in the former mansion of Margarita Morozova the Younger, where he was informed that he was being appointed curator of the Morozov Gallery, which was to be retitled 'The Second Museum of Western Art'. Ivan Morozov became an employee in his own museum. 'I report this to I.A. Morozov, who was appointed my deputy. He is extremely pleased,' Ternovets noted in his diary.[2]

Just two days later, Citizen I. Morozov, new employee of the Museums Department, was asked to immediately vacate the museum, namely his apartment on the second floor where he, his wife and daughter were allocated three rooms: one each. These were luxurious conditions, no worse than those enjoyed by Ostroukhov or cousin Alexei Vikulovich Morozov.

This was too much for Morozov. He was crushed, broken, humiliated. What then happened is less than clear. From the entries in Ternovets' diary we can manage only an approximate reconstruction of events:

14 April. An unpleasant complication. Denisov (the commandant, or political commissar, of the building) is moving Ivan Abramovich downstairs.

3 May. Still no sign of Ivan Abramovich.

13 June. I have not written for over a month. During this time the Morozov Gallery has opened . . . I have hung the Levitan room . . . I have been disturbed by visits from the Department of Fine Arts: Kandinsky, Falk, Kuznetsov, Altman, and others. Their aim is to carry off a number of paintings for the Museum of Pictorial Culture and hang their questionable efforts alongside French masterpieces.[3] Of course, they are aiming to take all that is most characteristic. Agreeing to their plan would completely violate the integrity of the gallery . . . The museum is being visited by tours and artists . . . on Sunday there are usually 100–120 people . . . Twice a week the museum, like all other museums in Moscow, is open in the evenings.

But then, the main worry:

> I.M. has disappeared without trace, his job is unfilled.[4]

Evidently shocked, Ternovets forgot to date this entry.

It made no sense to wait for Morozov once more to ascend the marble staircase, to look up at Bonnard's *Mediterranean Suite* and walk slowly through the rooms of the mansion, peering at his favourite paintings. Ternovets was the first to realize that. He notified the leaders of the People's Commissariat for Enlightenment and they reported the matter to higher authority. A detachment of Cheka policemen was sent to the museum. A report survives in which everything is formulated in clipped, clear, military phraseology:

> A search was conducted of the house on Prechistenka Street. Upon examination of the premises the seals on the steel storeroom and filing cabinets were found to be intact, the paintings and sculptures in the custody of B.N. Ternovets were all present. The former owner of the house and property, Ivan Abramovich Morozov and family, are recorded as having departed in June 1919 to Petrograd.

The Morozovs managed to escape from Soviet Russia. It is unlikely that Ivan Abramovich was able to obtain passports for foreign travel legally and leave, for example, 'for medical treatment abroad', like others prominent in the fields of science and culture. There was no reason to execute him – not, at least, in 1919. As, indeed, there was no reason for the authorities to want to shoot other passengers on the Steamship for Philosophers,[5] on which there would hardly have been a seat for him in any case. The lists of those to be expelled were immensely long, and consisted mainly of people who found the regime unacceptable but had no intention of emigrating. The intelligentsia were forcibly deported on the authority of Lenin personally, who was still suffering the repercussions of his first stroke. In September and November 1922 a first batch of philosophers, economists and writers was shipped out from Petrograd to Stettin on board two German ships. In December a further intelligentsia group was transported from Odessa by the Italians. The exiles were allowed to take with them only two coats, one suit, two shirts and two nightshirts, two pairs of underpants or stockings, but no jewels and no gold other than wedding rings. Everything else was confiscated. They even had personal crosses taken off them.

The Morozovs, unlike the passengers on the Steamship for Philosophers, no doubt managed to bring out some valuables, but leaving their home-land would not have been easy for them, even with their resources and contacts in business and other circles. 'Everything had to be done in deepest secrecy, because escape from Soviet Russia was considered a state crime, and one which the Bolshevik gentlemen punished very severely, even to the point of executing "free" citizens of the communist paradise who were convicted of having had such an intention,' recalled someone who managed to escape from Petrograd in summer 1919.[6] Undertaking the escape was preceded by long research and a thorough analysis of the various methods of fleeing. The first necessity was to find a 'specialist'. 'In Petrograd there was a certain E-d, who had a shop on Nevsky Prospekt, to throw dust in the eyes of the Bolshevik Cheka, where he sold saccharin, vanillin, yeast and all sorts of stuff that had not yet been subjected to price controls.'[7] It was said that for this service E-d demanded 5,000 rubles per person. In spring 1919 people did not much discriminate between Kerensky, Soviet or Duma currency: people paid with whatever they had. Fugitives crossed the frontier, perhaps at Beloostrov or Lembolovo near the Finnish border, and might sometimes have to cover tens of kilometres on foot, dressed as Chukhna, because they crossed the border together with peasants who delivered milk to Petrograd. They could take only a minimum of baggage: as much as would fit into a knapsack.

By the time the Morozovs decided to cross the border, the price had gone up to 7,000 rubles. It remained only for them to agree a day and

22  Passport of Evdokiya (Little Dosya) Ivanovna Morozova issued by the Russian consulate in Geneva, Switzerland, June 1920.

pay the full amount. Payment was upfront, and there was no refund if the clandestine expedition failed.

'Last June [1919], together with his wife, daughter and a niece, Ivan Morozov left Russia (where he had resided without respite for five and a half years) to settle in Switzerland – Interlaken, Ouchy, Lausanne . . .' This was the preamble to the interview Ivan Morozov gave in spring 1920 to Félix Fénéon. It was to be the last interview of his life.

Switzerland was intended only to be a transit point. Morozov, like Shchukin, intended to settle in France. It had taken the family over six months to get to Geneva. During that time the Versailles Peace Treaty had been signed and the First World War had come to an end, having claimed millions of lives. Ivan Morozov's great-grandson has the miraculously preserved passport of the 'juvenile daughter of Industry Councillor Morozov', issued to his grandmother in May 1920 by the Russian consulate in neutral Switzerland.

From the stamps in the passport of Little Dosya, we can trace the family's movements and draw some conclusions. Their departure from neutral Switzerland to France, which had not yet recovered from a terrible war, is confirmed by a stamp from the Russian consulate in rue Grenelle in Paris. At the end of the year the Morozovs spent several days in London: there were funds belonging to the Tver Textile Mill Company deposited in accounts at a bank in London, and very substantial funds at that – over £30,000.

Everything was working out more or less satisfactorily. They had reached Paris, they did have funds, if no longer millions, only Ivan Abramovich was feeling very unwell. It is easy to see that just by looking at his last photograph. The haggard face in the yellowed photograph looks tragic . . . Someone has awkwardly clipped the portrait to an oval shape, and Little Dosya has written sideways on it, 'M-e Ivan Morosoff mon père'.

You would never recognize Russia's richest manufacturer from this photograph. There is almost nothing left of the fat, jovial man in Serov's

23  Last known photo of Ivan Abramovich, 1920.

portrait, apart from the eyes. Nikolai Varentsov had seen those dead eyes of Ivan Morozov before. 'I happened to visit him during the first days of the 1905 revolution, and was shocked by how his face had changed, the eyes filled with despair, the sweat breaking out on his fore-head, and, having given up all hope, he kept repeating, "Everything is lost, everything is lost, and we are all doomed!" There was not the slightest desire to apply his energy and his money to at least partly safe-guarding his situation.'[8] Varentsov is responsible for the assertion that Ivan Morozov committed suicide, supposedly cutting his veins in the bathroom of a Berlin hotel.[9] Varentsov was, however, well known as a rumour-monger and, although distantly related to Morozov through the Khludovs, there is no way he could have known about the last days, let alone the last hours, of Ivan Abramovich: he was unable to travel abroad and lived out his days in Bolshevik Moscow.[10] Because, however, his description of the personality of Morozov is so vivid and credible, even many respected scholars have swallowed this story.

Ivan Abramovich did not take his own life, but had clearly lost his lust for living. Whether or not he was aware that his days were numbered, he did in April 1921 hastily rewrite his will. 'Being in possession of my faculties and with full consciousness, cancelling the will and testament which I made in 1917 in the presence of notary A. P. Kazakov in Moscow, I hereby bequeath all my property movable and immovable, wherever it be and whatsoever it be, to my wife Evdokiya Sergeevna Morozova.'[11] In Europe, Morozov in fact had no 'immovable' property (he rented his apartment on Place Thiers). His estate on Prechistenka Street with all its buildings and land, valued at a quarter of a million rubles, he had already made over in December 1914 to his lawful wife. His daughter was not mentioned in the will: it was as if she did not exist.

Only a year had passed since the Morozovs fled 'Sovdepia'. Recent émigrés had not yet lost hope of an imminent collapse of the Bolsheviks. Many of them, indeed, were to live faithful to the dream of returning to their homeland, until the day they died.

At the end of May 1921, the Morozov family went to their favourite resort of Carlsbad. Life at the spa was as routine and unhurried as before the war, with daily walks to the spring, baths, the traditional promenade along the banks of the River Teplá, and therapeutic procedures in the fashionable Kaiserbad, built specially for the German Kaiser, Wilhelm. During one of these procedures, Ivan Abramovich felt he was having trouble with his heart:

> Kaiserbad, Lutherstrasse. 22 July 1921 at 11 o'clock Ivan (Jean) Morozov died at the age of forty-nine . . . Russian . . . Orthodox . . . married . . . Industry Councillor . . . acute heart failure. Disinfection and other sanitary precautions taken: temporary sealing in a coffin, as prescribed by the regulations for onward transportation. Signed by Dr M. Drum, Municipal Physician.[12]

How dreadful to die away from even his temporary home and then, in a tightly sealed coffin, be shunted around the cities of Europe. Ivan's widow and daughter had to collect so many documents, required before the body could be brought into France, they had no time to mourn him. At the last moment there were further complications over the transportation, and they decided instead to bury the body in the old cemetery in Carlsbad. On a headstone they had his name incised with his titles: *Hereditary honorary citizen. Industry Councillor. Ivan Abramovich Morozov.* A white marble cross was erected.

Three memorial services were held in Paris at the Russian Orthodox Cathedral on rue Daru: the first on 24 July at the request of the family; a second three days later, ordered by the Association of Russian Industrialists; and, on the ninth day, a third commissioned by the Bank of I.V. Yunker, of whose board Morozov had been a member. There were no obituaries, only black-bordered notices that his 'wife and daughter announce with deep sorrow . . .' in the Parisian *Obshchee delo* (Our Common Cause) and *Poslednie izvestiya* (Latest News), and in the Berlin

24  Ivan Morozov's grave in Karlovy Vary (formerly Carlsbad), Czech Republic.

Constitutional Democrat newspaper *Rul* (The Helm). In Soviet Russia, only the journal *Sredi kollektsionerov* (Among Collectors) reacted to Morozov's passing by printing an obituary by Boris Ternovets in their section headed 'Collectors and Antiquarians of the Past', and there was the already mentioned article by Abram Efros, 'The Man Who Tweaked'.[13]

# CHAPTER XVII

# The Palace on Kropotkin Street

The interview which Ivan Morozov gave a year before his death ended on a surprisingly upbeat note. Fénéon advised the ex-collector to think back to his youth and take up painting again, because he now had so much free time. 'I know too much about painting to attempt it . . . Perhaps I'll think about it,' Ivan Abramovich answered, smiled wryly and said, 'You'll need to give me the address of someone who sells oil paints.' He seemed to have no qualms about the future of his collection. 'The collection is unharmed. None of the . . . paintings have suffered. The collection is still in the palace where I assembled it and whose walls are decorated with Bonnard's *Spring* and *Autumn* and the *Story of Psyche* by Maurice Denis,' he had assured Fénéon. Ivan Abramovich did not live to see 1923, when the Second Morozov Section was 'administratively merged' with the First Shchukin Section and, moreover, renamed when someone recalled that the Morozov Collection, in addition to painting, contained sculptures. The word 'painting' in the museum's name was replaced by 'art', with the result that the acronym GMNZZh (*Gosudarstvenny muzei novoy zapadnoy zhivopisi*), already unpronounceable in Russian, was transformed into the only slightly more pronounceable GMNZI (*Gosudarstvenny muzei novogo zapadnogo iskusstva*).

The Morozov and Shchukin mansions were 'consolidated' to the limit. Officialdom not only managed to fit a museum into each, but also carved up the ground floors into cells accommodating several dozen residents. Even so, the Moscow Offloading Commission[1] regularly attacked one or other branch of GMNZI. In 1925 the Morozov mansion on the former Prechistenka Street, now renamed in honour of the anarchist theorist Petr Kropotkin, was very nearly turned into a maternity hospital. It was saved by the intervention of the People's Commissar for Foreign Affairs, Georgy Chicherin. A representative of the *ci-devants* – the son of a diplomat and a baroness, and nephew of a prominent lawyer – Chicherin stood out from other Kremlin officials by the sheer excellence of his education. He spoke all the languages of Europe, and could make himself understood in Arabic; he was au fait with music, and even wrote a book about Mozart. The diplomat who signed the 1918 Peace Treaty of Brest-Litovsk and the 1922 Treaty of Rapallo, normalizing relations between Germany and the Soviet Union, found a convincing argument against the wrecking of Morozov's former home: enemies of the republic would undoubtedly exploit the closing of the new Soviet museum for their own interests. The ploy worked, but in the same year Russian paintings began to be removed.

Morozov's Russian collection was enormous.[2] It took more than two years to transfer it to the State Museum Foundation. Some items were later dispersed to provincial museums, but the Tretyakov Gallery acquired the greater and better part. His brother Mikhail's paintings, we recall, had been bequeathed to the gallery back in 1910. Now the authorities demanded that his widow surrender everything which, under the terms of the donation, was to remain in her possession during her life time. Margarita the Younger was politely asked whether she saw any obstacles to the immediate relocation of works of art which were the property of the gallery. Citizen Morozova did not dare to object. In exchange for ten paintings and Rodin's marble *Eve*, the donor was promised two rooms in the mansion requisitioned from her in August 1918, to enable her to accommodate the few valuable objects which were graciously being left in her safekeeping.[3]

The comfortable Moscow mansion in Dead Lane, restructured for Margarita the Younger by Zholtovsky, became the property of the Department of Museums and Preservation of Works of Art and Antiquities. In the basement there was a well-equipped storeroom, and also a large safe (the equal of the one her brother-in-law possessed). That is what had attracted the Museums Department. According to Marusya Morozova, Natalya Trotskaya-Sedova came to work in a shiny Rolls-Royce borrowed from the Tsar's garage. The daughter and widow of Mikhail Morozov found themselves living next to their old kitchen, from whence came a revolting smell of boiled cabbage and salted fish whenever meals were being prepared for the department's employees.

Margarita settled in to the servants' rooms in the basement. It was a life of candles, carrot tea with saccharin, of cold during the day, and particularly at night when they had to sleep in their coats. But then came Lenin's New Economic Policy, with glittering shop windows, warmth, literary evenings and gatherings for music on Fridays, as in the good old days before the troubles. Marusya was enrolled at the conservatory and studied piano. Margarita's son, Mika, got a government job and married. Margarita could visit the Tretyakov Gallery, where the paintings she had donated hung in a room of their own, the Russian and foreign canvases now all in together. In 1925 the paintings by foreign artists which her husband had bought were moved from the Tretyakov Gallery to his brother's house, while the paintings by Russian artists which Ivan had bought were moved elsewhere.

For almost two decades, Ivan Morozov's old home had housed not one but two museums: in the enfilade of brightly lit rooms on the first floor were the French artists, and in the dark rooms of the ground floor were the Russians. According to Abram Efros, visitors when they

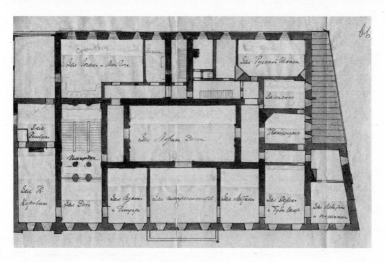

25 & 26  Above, the second section of the State Museum of New Western Art (formerly the mansion of Ivan Abramovich Morozov) on Kropotkin Street, October 1936. Below, a plan of its second floor, 1918–19.

arrived discovered, 'like the discovery of America, that half the Morozov Collection was typically Russian, modern artists, living artists, exhibiting artists who, according to all Russian canons, should never be seated at the same table as aristocratic Parisian painters'.[4] Morozov, however, had brought them all together.

Ivan Morozov was not, in fact, in awe of the Russian part of his collection to the same extent that he revered his Western paintings, although he had acquired half as many Russian canvases and drawings again as he had foreign ones. Vinogradov recalled, 'The Russians were hung on the ground floor. There you could find Vrubel, Levitan, Kustodiev, Ostroukhov, Serov, Somov, Golovin, Sapunov, myself, Grabar, Yuon, and a whole hall dedicated to the wonderful art of Konstantin Korovin. And Krymov, that magician! And Konenkov's wood carvings and sculptures in marble.'[5]

Judging by the number of their works in the collection, Ivan Morozov's favourite Russian painters had been Alexander Golovin and Konstantin Korovin. He had more than forty works by Golovin, not only theatre sketches but also large finished paintings, perhaps the best works the master created before the revolution. *Self-Portrait*, *Spanish Woman with Black Shawl*, *Girl with Porcelain* and *Overgrown Pond* are now in the Tretyakov Gallery. The *Spanish Woman in Red* and *Spanish Woman on a Balcony* went to the Russian Museum. Much was dispersed to provincial museums.

In the Morozov Collection there were even more of Konstantin Korovin's works: fifty paintings and twenty theatre sketches. Morozov had assembled a veritable museum of the works of Russia's first Impressionist. A dozen or two disappeared in the process of nationalization and the carve-up between museums, but the classic Korovin landscapes, depicting cafés in Yalta and boulevards in Paris, found their way to the Tretyakov Gallery. The same was true of the *Portrait of Fedor Chaliapin* and the *Portrait of Ivan Morozov with a Buttonhole*, painted by Korovin in 1902. Morozov told the story of how Korovin had turned up at Prechistenka

Street at four in the morning after a bout with the gypsies and, painting non-stop, completed the portrait in two hours.[6]

Neither Golovin nor Korovin had a single good word to say about Morozov in their memoirs. Golovin has the excuse that he was writing his memoirs in the Soviet Union, but the émigré Korovin might have left some reminiscences about his erstwhile pupil who had gone on to buy his paintings by the dozen! Only loyal Vinogradov did not forget his friend, to whom he donated paintings with touching inscriptions.

Morozov remained a loyal supporter of the Union of Russian Artists to the end. He had a great love of Russian nature, and was constantly acquiring landscapes by such of the Union's painters as Vinogradov, Zhukovsky, Petrovichev and Turzhansky. The World of Art painters also enjoyed his patronage. He began acquiring Konstantin Somov in 1903, even before the French painters. Nine works now in the Tretyakov Gallery, including *Echo of Time Past*, are from the collection of Ivan Morozov. The Tretyakov was buying almost nothing back then: in a year and a half it acquired just three new paintings. Ostroukhov wrote to Alexandra Botkina that there were a lot of interesting paintings at the exhibition of the Union of Russian Artists, and that Serov was 'scuttling round the halls', asking the organizers to reserve this item or that because he was sure the Tretyakov's new board would buy them.[7] Morozov boldly spent his own money and made his purchases. His first acquisitions were decadents of the World of Art and the Blue Rose, and then the currently fashionable artists Mashkov, Konchalovsky, Kuprin and Rozhdestvensky, from the Jack of Diamonds Exhibition.

By the time the Tretyakov Gallery finally plucked up the courage to admit Vrubel within its walls, Morozov already had twenty of his works, although, for the most part, they were drawings. He bought the views of Versailles of Alexander Benois and the decorative fantasies of Boris Anisfeld, who had been discovered by Diaghilev. Neither did he neglect the Russian Symbolists. Of the Blue Rose artists Morozov chose the very best: Petr Utkin, Nikolai Miliotti, Pavel Kuznetsov and Nikolai Sapunov. He commissioned a repeat of *Shrovetide* from Boris Kustodiev, and bought *The Village Fair* by Sergei Malyutin and the enormous *The Whore* by Filipp Malyavin, *The Round Dance* by Andrei Ryabushkin and *The Monastery* by Konstantin Yuon. Mikhail Larionov and Natalya Goncharova also found their way into his mansion. Quite a daring choice! Of the fifty-seven artists represented in the Russian part of the collection, Ivan Morozov was perhaps mistaken in his choice of only five or six. All the others were to become classics of Russian art.

It was often a puzzle what guidelines Morozov followed when choosing paintings for his collection. He seemed sometimes to be buying a picture, not so much because he liked it as because he wanted to encourage a budding talent, intuitively sensing who would go on to greater things and who would not. It was a gift with which nature had endowed Morozov no less than Pavel Tretyakov. This is how Abram Efros recalls Morozov visiting exhibitions:

Serov's 'fashionable member of parliament', so well built and polished in his portrait, surrounded by invisible advisers whispering in his ear, had a somehow highly original way of appearing, large and flabby, at exhibitions, unexpectedly, never at the vernissage days of hustle and bustle when everyone who was anyone in Moscow was there to be seen. He would turn up some time during the week and, unhurriedly, begin making his way, on his own, through the deserted rooms. People said hello, but then left him in peace. He looked around, zigzagging, I would say. There was no evident order or obvious system: he did not walk the length of the walls, or proceed through the enfilade; instead he would approach, and then go off to some other part of the exhibition, come back, and go off again some-where else. I observed him at the 1916 Jack of Diamonds Exhibition, the last at which his figure remains clearly in my memory. When he reserved a picture for himself, artists and critics would cluster round it. There were no disputes: it was self-evident that Morozov had found gold again.[8]

Of course, Shchukin's patronage of art was also admirable, and the Russian avant-garde to an extraordinary extent owes its birth to him and his gallery. But his total eclipsing of 'meek' Morozov is very unjust. The truth of the matter is that it is impossible to overstate how much Ivan Morozov did for early twentieth-century Russian art. Shchukin gave, as it were, moral support, but Morozov gave material support. Of the two of them, only Morozov bought the paintings of the Russian artists of his time, with great enthusiasm, and in wholesale quantities.

It was pointless to offer native Russian painting to Shchukin. The gallery on Znamensky Lane was not interested. The *Head of a Woman* by his cousin Fedor Botkin and Borisov-Musatov's dreamlike lady are exceptions which prove the rule. Vasily Kandinsky believed his non-figurative canvases would have been no less at home in Znamensky Lane than the panels by Matisse, but it was impossible to persuade Shchukin to shift his attention to Russian artists. Morozov, on the contrary, listened attentively to other people's advice, although at times he needed to be guided and prodded. If an artist advising him was one of 'his', he yielded readily. Yakov Tugendhold had no trouble persuading Morozov to buy the work of the young Chagall. Ivan Abramovich was only too happy to give support to a talented painter.

It was 1915. There was a war on. For more than a year and a half Ivan Morozov had not bought any French paintings. Paris was far away, and Tugendhold was relentless, insisting that Chagall, whom he knew from Paris, was one of the 'great hopes of Russian art' and that it was from just such god-forsaken places as Vitebsk, out of these 'untapped, naive provincial backwaters', that fresh forces appear, and so on.[9] Morozov had always been a regular visitor to Russian exhibitions but now, when he was no longer spending his wealth on French painters, Russian painters looked forward to his appearance with even keener anticipation:

'Look, there's Morozov,' and Larionov was off over to a portly, exquisitely dressed gentleman with big red cheeks and cheerful, sparkling eyes.

'Ivan Abramovich, I've been waiting for you for ages. I'm exhibiting my *Cherry Orchard* specially for you – I told you, Diaghilev took it to Paris . . .' and Larionov seized Morozov by the elbow and respectfully steered the occasionally mildly protesting patron of the arts to a distant room, where he succeeded in selling him his *Cherry Orchard*.[10]

Morozov bought four early impressionistic landscapes from Larionov, one of which disappeared in the chaos after the revolution.[11] Chagall also had four paintings in the collection, gouaches from the Vitebsk series purchased between 1915 and 1917.

Chagall came home from Paris in June 1914, intending to return to France three months later, but the war put paid to his plans. He found himself stuck in Vitebsk, where he painted everything he saw around him. Chagall did not walk the streets of Vitebsk with a paintbox to hand but, as he explained, painted solely what he was able to observe happening in the town from his window. In 1915 he was able to exhibit twenty-five Vitebsk paintings in Moscow, which he categorized as studies or documents. On the eve of the war, Tugendhold had helped Klavdiya Mikhailova, who owned the Art Salon, to mount an exhibition of French and Russian painters on Bolshaya Dmitrovka Street. Now he asked her to exhibit the work of his young protégé.

Morozov paid Chagall 100 rubles for a small work: it was a provincial barber's shop painted in gouache on paper. It was 'suffused by a weak sun, dust in the air, and the pitiful smile of cheap wallpaper'. Tugendhold declared it one of the best interiors exhibited in recent years.[12]

With the passage of time Marc Chagall's paintings came to command high prices, but he never forgot that first fee. Thanks to Morozov's purchase he was able to return to Vitebsk and marry Bella Rosenfeld, his beloved, who was to be his muse throughout his life.

In March an exhibition, laconically titled *1915*, opened in the Art Salon on Bolshaya Dmitrovka Street. It was the last great hurrah of the avant-garde artists of Moscow and Petrograd and it brought fame and critical acclaim to Chagall. It was here that Vladimir Tatlin first demonstrated his counter-reliefs, and Vasily Kandinsky his non-figurative compositions. Tatlin, who was no less eager than Kandinsky to be in Shchukin's collection, spread a rumour that Shchukin had gone against his own principles and was about to acquire one of his painted reliefs. Shchukin did not oblige, but Morozov did make several purchases at the exhibition. Out of everything on offer from the gifted young painters of the Jack of Diamonds he chose Alexander Kuprin's lush, vivid *Still Life with Blue Tray*, which could hold its own against the French. Marc Chagall, with his studies of everyday life in a Jewish shtetl, might seem quite clearly not to fit into his collection, but Ivan Morozov acquired three more gouaches from the Vitebsk series: *House in Liozno*, *Portrait of Brother David with Mandolin* and *View from a Window. Vitebsk*. The invoice of 17 April 1917 for the landscape *View from a Window* was signed by the secretary of the Jewish Society for the Advancement of the Arts, the artist Lazar Lissitsky.

Ivan Morozov was Chagall's first Russian customer, together with Yakov Kagan-Shabshai, a wealthy Moscow physicist and engineer who collected only Jewish artists and bought some thirty paintings and sketches by Chagall. Kagan-Shabshai's choices are explicable by the fact that he was aspiring to create a gallery of Jewish art analogous to the Tretyakov Gallery, and to make it a national treasure.[13] But why would Morozov in his palace of nymphs and cupids want Uncle Zusya, the Jewish barber, or the light and dark blue Brother David with his mandolin? What was it in these provincial streets beneath a baleful grey sky, with their jumble of log houses and soft, downy trees, naive signboards and poor horses that appealed to Morozov?[14] It remains a mystery to this day.

Natalya Goncharova was altogether another matter. Her extensive solo exhibition, with over 750 works, had been held at Mikhailova's Salon two years previously. At Bolshaya Dmitrovka Street there was, as usual, great speculation as to whether Morozov would or would not buy anything. 'It seems that Rayonist and Futurist art is becoming fashionable. Any time now Goncharova and Larionov will be recognized as the equals of Korovin and Kustodiev,' reported *Moskovskaya gazeta*. Even Alexander Benois was acknowledging the talent of an artist he had previously reproached for her buffoonery and braggadocio. 'Now I no longer dare to dismiss even her notorious "displacement" as heresy, that nightmarish jiggery-pokery unleashed by Picasso which has infected all the "progressive" young people in the West and here. I still have doubts about these paintings, but do accept that they clearly fall within the definition of art.'[15] Ivan Morozov selected two early paintings by Goncharova: *Boys Skating* and *Orchard in Autumn*. The former, in a folk-art style, would go well with *Snow in Munich* by Friesz, and the latter with his lush Mediterranean landscapes.

Abram Efros notes that Morozov in fact began systematically collecting Russian painters in 1901 when, at the exhibition of the Itinerants, he bought an unremarkable autumn landscape by Manuil Aladzhalov. Friends of Aladzhalov admired his etudes for their sincerity and poetic qualities, forgiving their colleague his careless technique and other failings. But how could Morozov be so taken by him that he bought four more of his sketches? How, having in his collection Bonnard, Cézanne, Gauguin and Matisse, could he be smitten by the landscape of a modest nature lover? That was something of which only Ivan Morozov was capable. In January 1918, Morozov purchased Aladzhalov's *Night*. It seemed a symbolic gesture, the culmination of his collecting. Efros believed that in 1918 Morozov found in Aladzhalov's painting 'something that deserved to be hung alongside Serov, Vrubel, Levitan, Somov and Korovin: he again introduced into our general consensus of negation – his tweak.'[16] Perhaps this surmise has a right to be heard.

At the end of 1924, 300 Russian paintings from the Morozov Collection were moved to storage in record time.[17] A unique museum demonstrating the links between new Russian art and the art of the West was destroyed. A similar fate befell the cosy, intimate museum of Ilya Ostroukhov in Trubnikov Lane (which, very unusually, actually bore his name). The Ostroukhov Collection had never claimed to be first-rate or comprehensive, and after it was rehung, with Russian art in one part and European art separately elsewhere, it was stripped of its earlier charm and unique originality. Ostroukhov fought for his museum until his last breath. In 1929, with its owner barely cold in his grave, the Ostroukhov Museum of Russian Paintings and Icons was closed down. Paintings by Russian artists were moved to the Tretyakov Gallery, which had recently been the recipient of Ivan Morozov's huge Russian collection.

Of course, if there had been more resources and accommodation it would have been possible to fight for particular paintings, the comparison of which with French works gave the Morozov Collection special significance. It was impossible, however, to fight on two fronts, also opposing the proposed merger with the Shchukin Section of the Museum of New Modern Art. With every passing year the threatened merging of the First and Second Sections of GMNZI became more likely. The accursed bourgeois past was to be done away with once and for all, and the former mansion-museums were the obvious first targets. In Shchukin's mansion in Znamensky Lane the leather wallpaper was ripped from the walls in the dining room; the Gauguin 'iconostasis', with its striking primeval power, was dismantled and the walls were lined with a dull grey canvas. The remaining paintings were regrouped and arranged 'in accordance with the principle of historical development' for the purpose of educating the workers and peasants.

The Morozov Section was not allowed to retain a single Russian painting. The representative of GMNZI begged to be left at least a few works, including Chagall's gouaches, on the grounds that an artist born in the Russian Empire had long lived in Paris, and not only had been

213

brought up on the example of Western masterpieces but had been one of those who inspired Expressionism in Germany.[18] Alas, Ternovets was not allowed to retain the paintings of Chagall, three of which went to the Tretyakov Gallery, while David and his mandolin were packed off to Vladivostok. Neither was Ternovets allowed to keep Serov's portrait of Ivan Morozov against the background of the Matisse still life, no matter how he pleaded for it.

In summer 1928 the portraits of Ivan Morozov – who had not only invested immense amounts of money in the museum's collection but also a good part of his soul – were removed to the far side of the Moscow River, to Lavrushinsky Lane and the red brick building of the Tretyakov Gallery. Then too the Shchukin Section of the Museum of New Western Art ceased to exist. From the mansion on Znamensky Lane, already stripped of the remnants of its former glory, the paintings were transferred to Ivan Morozov's mansion on Kropotkin Street, thus bringing the history of Shchukin's gallery to an end. The Gauguin iconostasis, the Matisse Pink Reception Room, the Monet Music Salon and the Picasso Study survive only in photographs.

From the First and Second autonomous sections of GMNZI a single new museum was formed, not de jure, but de facto. It contained nineteen canvases by Claude Monet, eleven by Renoir, twenty-nine by Gauguin, twenty-six by Cézanne, ten by van Gogh, nine by Degas, fourteen by Bonnard, twenty-two by Derain, fifty-three by Matisse and the same number by Picasso. Some fought against the merging of the collections, while others argued for it. It went ahead anyway. Boris Ternovets had long dreamed of merging the world's two best collections into one. 'The impact of such a museum would be astounding,' the future director of GMNZI had imagined at the time of the revolution. Dreams, however, are one thing, while the actuality can prove very different. There were far more paintings than could be fitted into the first floor of the Morozov mansion allocated for displaying them. It was promised that the accommodation problem would be solved during the

First Five-Year Plan, when a new home for the museum would be built, but in the meantime several dozen works would have to be consigned to the storeroom.

The merged GMNZI managed to survive for twenty years, despite the fact that attempts to destroy it were undertaken virtually from the day it opened its doors in December 1929. A brigade from the People's Commissariat for the Workers' and Peasants' Inspectorate of the RSFSR arrived in 1930 to examine the new display at 21 Kropotkin Street and found it unsatisfactory. As well they might. There was nothing proletarian about it. It truly was a spectacle 'for gourmets and aesthetes'. The museum must be reorganized in a new, Soviet way. They tried to rehang the paintings in accordance with a 'thematic, subject-matter principle'. It was the only way to save the collection. Percentages were calculated of how many of the paintings were non-figurative; how many did show something but would be incomprehensible to the mass audience; how many 'were comprehensible but failed to reflect social problems' – all those still lifes and landscapes with no people in them; and, conversely, how many paintings did have people in them but 'without it being clear what class they belong to'. The officials separately added up 'actively revolutionary paintings, campaigning in the right direction', and excluded any which were 'actively reactionary, dimming class consciousness'. There was a further category of 'portraits passively recording the past', which were adjudged neutral.

The conclusion was catastrophic. Only nine paintings could be found with worker and peasant subject matter, a mere 2.18 per cent of the museum's holdings.[19] Such a dire bias obviously needed to be corrected. Practitioners of culture were called upon to set forth on the path of creating equivalents in the arts to rival the Magnitostroy Metallurgical Project.[20] One proposed response to this call was to establish a Russian National Arts Industrial Complex to 'regulate the distribution and use of kinds of art' within Moscow and Moscow province. It was suggested such an industrial centre should be established on the basis of the collections of the Museum of New Western Art and the Tretyakov Gallery, and that it should be under the supervision of an industrial enterprise. The plan was a clear threat to GMNZI but, fortunately, was never implemented.

There was another threat: the extensive Morozov mansion was still exciting interest. This time it was the Military Academy of the Workers' and Peasants' Red Army taking a fancy to it, but again the museum found an intercessor. The new People's Commissar for Enlightenment of the RSFSR, an old Party member, Andrei Bubnov, who had replaced the more intellectual Lunacharsky, came to its defence. The bureaucratic rhetoric of an Old Bolshevik worked its magic: he threatened to inform the relevant Communist Party institutions that an attempt was being made to encroach on 'the minimum quota of the network of museums established for the current period'. Moreover, Bubnov pointed out, the Museum of New Western Art was included in the programme of sights developed by Intourist for visitors to the USSR. The upshot was that the new People's Commissar for Enlightenment saved the museum. The top leaders found it inexpedient to meddle with something that was bringing convertible currency into the Soviet state.

The museum had been saved, but its collection was shrinking inexorably. Some paintings were transferred to new galleries in the provinces or constituent republics of the Soviet Union. This caused minimal harm to GMNZI, because its most valuable items were not involved. The Hermitage, however, was quite another matter. It managed to extract genuine masterpieces from the Shchukin and Morozov Collections by employing an indirect exchange ruse. The Museum of Fine Arts (later the Pushkin Museum of Fine Arts), founded before the revolution by Professor Ivan Tsvetaev, was seen as a teaching museum with casts of sculptures, but now had its own art gallery. It was desperate to obtain high-quality old master paintings, of which the Hermitage had an abundance. Unfortunately, the Museum of Fine Arts had nothing to offer the Hermitage in exchange, so paintings were seized from GMNZI and 'in exchange' the Hermitage donated some of its old masters to the Museum of Fine Arts. This practice continued for only two years, from 1930 to 1931, but seriously depleted the GMNZI collection. The climate in which the exchange took place was tense and sometimes excitable. The Hermitage in Leningrad produced a list of works it wished to receive; the Muscovites resisted desperately, and both museums felt hard done by.[21]

# CHAPTER XVIII

# The End of the Museum

The article 'Muddle Instead of Music', with its murderous criticism of Dmitry Shostakovich's work, was published in *Pravda* on 28 January 1936. This was the signal to commence the battle against 'Formalism'. Given that the fine arts, from Impressionism onwards, were declared 'formalistic', the State Museum of New Western Art found itself the main target of the ideological campaign. In August 1937, People's Commissar for Enlightenment Bubnov was shot, and in 1938 Ternovets was removed as director of the museum. He learned of his dismissal from colleagues who had read about it in the newspaper and then begun bombarding him with phone calls. The museum's days were numbered.

Following the dismissal of its director, GMNZI removed most of the 'Formalist' works from its new exhibition, and provided the remainder with captions explaining in detail the harmful class essence of decadent bourgeois art. Already in the summer of 1936 the Tretyakov Gallery had moved the works of Russian avant-garde artists to its store, to be followed by paintings of the Blue Rose and World of Art painters which Ivan Morozov had bought.

Meanwhile, the ground floor of Ivan Morozov's mansion had finally been vacated by its numerous residents and adapted for exhibitions. Canvases were hung even in the long corridor. The paintings of Matisse, Derain and Picasso fitted into a single room, because the number of exhibited works had been reduced by two-thirds. Against that, the canvas screening which had for many years concealed the panels of Maurice Denis was unexpectedly removed, and the nymphs and cupids, restored by Pavel Korin immediately before the outbreak for Russia of the Second World War, again reigned supreme in the Music Salon. The saccharine, quasi-classical panels Ivan Morozov liked so much would have been ideally suited to any new palace in the Stalinist Empire style, except that a Soviet artist would have coyly draped the nude figures.

In early June 1941 museum staff were busy preparing an anti-Fascist exhibition, composed of photographs, satirical drawings and cartoons from foreign, mostly American, newspapers. 'The exhibition was already prepared, but it never opened. The Fascists had at that time already attacked the Soviet Union and were on the approaches to Moscow. I went to the district committee of the Communist Party to consult them about the possibility of opening the exhibition. Their answer was, "Why excite even greater hatred in them (that is, the Fascists)?" They advised me to dismantle the exhibition,' recalled Nina Yavorskaya.[1,2] By now, however, the staff were no longer thinking about propaganda exhibitions: on 27 June, five days after the outbreak of war, the museum moved on to a war footing. The paintings were removed from their frames and hastily packed into crates, obtained against all the odds, and on 15 July a special museum train took most of the collection east to Novosibirsk.

On the morning of 16 October, instead of the usual bulletin from Sovinformburo, it was announced over the wireless that the Germans were attempting to break through Moscow's defences, and that the situation on the western front was causing concern. People panicked. Many locked their rooms or apartments and fled the city on foot. By the end of October, the capital was virtually empty: anyone who could get out had done so. Here is how one contemporary described the events: 'The vast station square [Kazan station] was jammed with people and baggage. Cars, constantly hooting, could hardly make their way through to the entrances. Familiar faces were spotted: actors, writers, filmmakers were leaving . . . Everyone was rushing past in a great hurry. Someone was crying, someone was looking for somebody, someone was calling out. An actor was dragging a huge trunk, but suddenly looked at his watch, abandoned the trunk and ran towards the platform with only a briefcase . . . Gleaming limousines with foreign flags drove up as the diplomatic corps prepared to leave Moscow. A person I knew whispered to me as they rushed by that the government too was being evacuated: someone had seen Chairman Kalinin in a railway carriage!'[3] Those who remained in the city were up on the roofs on fire-fighting duty at night, extinguishing German incendiary bombs. Morozov's estate was unlucky: the glass lantern proved a tempting target for bombing, and in the night of 28 October a high-explosive bomb hit the Music Salon. Fortunately, the ceiling did not collapse.

And then, in the autumn of 1943, the first trainloads of evacuees moved back, from east to west. People returned to Moscow legally, on instructions (this was called 're-evacuation') and on their own initiative (although without a special pass they could not get a residence permit for the capital).[4] It would be another year and a half before the war was over, but its course was changing dramatically. 'During the whole of the war I do not remember another time like the end of 1943, so full of bright hopes and a feverish anticipation of victory. The Red Army repelled an offensive near Kursk and was advancing on Oryol,' recalled the playwright Alexander Gladkov.[5]

In November 1944, when Soviet troops liberated Belorussia and Western Ukraine and the fighting was already on foreign soil, the collections of GMNZI returned to Moscow. The Morozov mansion was in a terrible state, there was a shortage of building materials, and it was allocated no funds for repairs. In the museum it was not only impossible to think of opening an exhibition, but also to store the crates with the paintings. For over three years the collections had been kept in the Opera House in Novosibirsk, and now they could only find temporary refuge in the Museum of Oriental Cultures.[6] There was no question of unpacking the crates. The most that could be done was to open them for the restorers to reassure themselves.

The future of the museum seemed unclear. During the war the idea had been mooted of expanding the collection's chronological remit by transferring in paintings by artists of the first half of the nineteenth century, French Romantics and Barbizonians, from the collection of the Pushkin Museum. The Arts Committee of the Soviet of People's Commissars rejected that proposal. A counter-proposal, to bring the GMNZI premises under the aegis of the Pushkin Museum, was rejected categorically. 'Interest in the museum has not disappeared during the war, as can be judged from the numerous requests received through the Informburo news agency and VOKS [the USSR Society for Cultural Relations Abroad] from various countries concerning the fate of the museum and when it may reopen. The museum is renowned not only as the largest collection of West European art of the latter half of the nineteenth century, but also as an outstanding architectural ensemble, decorated by leading French artists . . . This effective closure of the State Museum of New Western Art is highly undesirable also in view of the important role it plays in the artistic life of the Soviet Union. Not only artists from Moscow, but those from other cities consider it obligatory to visit the Museum and to study the outstanding skill represented by such painters as Monet, Renoir, Degas, van Gogh and Cézanne, who are extensively represented in the museum.' Such was the conclusion of the Arts Committee.[7]

After resolutions such as these it seemed there could be no doubt that the Museum of New Western Art would shortly reopen and that the Morozov mansion would be brought back to life. In autumn 1946, however, *Pravda* published a report by Andrei Zhdanov, secretary of the Central Committee of the Communist Party, attacking the journals *Zvezda* and *Leningrad*. The vituperation was directed nominally at the poetess Anna Akhmatova and prose writer Mikhail Zoshchenko, but was in reality an attack on everything in any way connected with Western culture. There was a further turning of the screws in the fight against 'formalism'[8] and 'kowtowing to the West', to which was added the struggle against 'rootless cosmopolitans'.[9] GMNZI, as a hotbed of 'formalist' views, and of that kowtowing to the decadent bourgeois culture of the epoch of imperialism, was clearly first in the line of fire:

> The Council of Ministers ... considers that the collections of the State Museum of New Western Art consist mainly of unprincipled, anti-popular, Formalistic works ... devoid of any progressive educational value for Soviet visitors. Formalistic collections ... purchased in West European countries by Moscow capitalists in the late nineteenth and early twentieth centuries ... have caused great harm to the development of Russian and Soviet art. Displaying these collections to the broad masses of the people is politically harmful and contributes to the spread of alien bourgeois, Formalistic views in Soviet art.[10]

The Decree of the Council of Ministers of 6 March 1948 was signed personally by Stalin.

Just two weeks before the issuance of Decree No. 672, the museum staff, ready to begin at any day to hang the paintings again, received an order to 'mount an exhibition' as swiftly as possible. Within a few days it was necessary to unpack dozens of boxes and remove enormous panels from their rolls. By the time of the arrival of the government commission, the conservators had laid out both panels by Matisse on the floor, and nearby placed a large canvas, *Mexican Emperor Maximilian Before His Execution* by Jean-Paul Laurent, to demonstrate that the collection had solidly realist paintings. The deputy chairman of the Council of

Ministers, the collector and amateur painter Kliment Voroshilov, together with the president of the USSR Academy of Arts, the artist Alexander Gerasimov,[11] arrived at the museum early in the morning, accompanied by a retinue. In vain did the team of art specialists try to direct the attention of the top brass to the works of 'progressive Western artists'. The visitors knew exactly what it was they wanted to see, and see it they duly did. To the end of her days, Nina Yavorskaya could not forget the sniggering and meaningful throat-clearing of the 'pack' of senior officials at the sight of Matisse's canvases laid out on the floor. The delegation departed without saying a word.

The idea of exploiting the GMNZI building as accommodation for the Moscow headquarters of the USSR Academy of Arts belonged to Alexander Gerasimov who, in late summer 1947, took over as president of the reborn Academy of Arts. Gerasimov had a visceral hatred of the museum. He went on hating it even after GMNZI had been destroyed and he had taken possession of Ivan Morozov's study. There are tales that the president of the Academy of Arts furiously threatened to hang anyone who dared to exhibit Picasso. '[Gerasimov] bears no resemblance at all to an artist. It is as if he is moulded from completely different clay. He is narcissistic, cold, calculating, thinking only about himself. He is a fat man, a trickster, sly, wicked and greedy, a vulture who quickly finds his bearings and can don the mask of a benevolent, likeable man who cares deeply about affairs of state,'[12] the artist Alexander Labas recalled. Labas was present at the open Party meeting in spring 1948 when Gerasimov announced to the artists of Moscow that the 'poisonous, anti-popular' Museum of New Western Art, which had been 'perverting them for so many years', would be shut down.

The directive to destroy the museum was extremely harsh. Those appointed to ensure its implementation were Polikarp Lebedev, Chairman of the Arts Committee of the Council of Ministers and, as his assistant, Petr Sysoev.[13] They were, within fifteen days, to select and transfer the most valuable works to the Pushkin Museum of Fine Arts.[14] Ten days were allowed for handing over the building and its furnishings to the new owner, the USSR Academy of Arts. Everything which, in the opinion of the responsible officials of the Arts Committee, did not merit categorization as particularly valuable they were to 'atomize', as people said at the time, by dispersing it without unnecessary commotion in the provinces. Manifestly prejudicial matter, like the Cubist Picasso's work, should, in short order, be destroyed.

Of course, there was nothing in the directive explicitly about the physical destruction of artworks, but that option, eyewitnesses insist, was certainly considered.[15] The redundant museum staff[16] did not believe that paintings could possibly be destroyed, and secretly hoped the collection might be saved by some miracle. 'Our greatest hope, given the circumstances, was that all the works would be transferred to the Pushkin Museum of Fine Arts and the Hermitage (rather than to peripheral museums). I almost prayed to God that I.A. Orbeli, the director of the Hermitage, might arrive, knowing that he would never allow the collection to be atomized,' Nina Yavorskaya recalled. 'When I arrived at the Pushkin Museum for a meeting of the commission in the office of S.D. Merkurov, the first person I saw was Orbeli. I called him to one side and implored him to take everything the Pushkin Museum declined. He replied that he had received the same request from A.N. Izergina (who at that time was working in the Western Department of the Hermitage), who, when she heard of the threat to our museum, insisted Orbeli should leave immediately for Moscow.'[17]

Eyewitnesses agree that Andrei Chegodaev, the main curator of the so-called 'special fund' at the Pushkin Museum, was the person most actively involved in the break-up of the GMNZI collection.[18] According to Yavorskaya, it was purely because of his subjective likes and dislikes that the most controversial paintings by Matisse and the work of Picasso ended up in Leningrad. Chegodaev, who was given complete discretion by the sculptor Sergei Merkurov, director of the Pushkin Museum, undoubtedly played the major role in dividing the collection, but he was only obeying the orders of the Arts Committee; these were, to select for Moscow only wholly uncontroversial items which could immediately be included in the exhibition.

'We had to cede a lot that we were reluctant to part with: Renoir's *Madame Samary* [the formal portrait of the actress], two Sisleys, two Marquets, two Pissarros, two van Goghs; I don't remember how many Gauguins and Monets. All of them very valuable for clarifying the broader picture. [Joseph Orbeli] was evidently not that interested in the rest of the paintings, because he agreed to our selection without even looking through the lists. He took absolutely everything we offered, some 400 items. The committee members kept urging us not to give away anything that contributed to the larger picture. They seemed to be burying their heads in the sand . . . For perhaps the first time in my life, I felt very clearly my own little share of responsibility towards the future,' wrote the artist Alexander Lopukhin in his diary.[19] He was involved in assessing the paintings brought to the Pushkin Museum from the mansion on Kropotkin Street.

The break-up of the collection took just five days. 'Orbeli, after some night-time discussions with Leningrad, asks for even more. Our side squander Matisse and Gauguin for no reason at all. I just want to spit and give up,'[20] Lopukhin writes in his diary in desperation. To help out the orientalist Orbeli, his wife, Antonina Izergina, a specialist in French art, comes down to Moscow. Now the Leningraders are emboldened and prepared to take all the 'risky' stuff to the Hermitage: Picasso's Cubist canvases, Derain's brown-black paintings, Matisse's huge panels for Shchukin. Because of a simple lack of space in the Pushkin Museum on Volkhonka Street, the Muscovites also ceded to the Leningraders Morozov's panels of *The Story of Psyche* by Maurice Denis, which were rolled up, and Bonnard's *Mediterranean*. No one was troubled that the pairs so lovingly selected by Ivan Morozov were ruthlessly separated during the carve-up: *The Triumph of Bacchus* went to the Hermitage, while *The Triumph of Ceres* remained in Moscow. Matisse never knew that the Moroccan triptych he composed was split up: its right-hand third, *The Entrance to the Kasbah*, being sent to Leningrad, from whence it returned to Moscow only twenty years later, in 1968.

By the time a session of the USSR Academy of Sciences was calling in January 1949 for a battle against 'cosmopolitanism and kowtowing to the West', the beating heart of 'formalism', the Museum of New Western Art, was a thing of the past. The Pushkin Museum of Fine Arts had allocated a small hall for its new arrivals, and the conservators had begun returning the canvases intended for the exhibition into their frames, when an abrupt order was received to reorganize the museum's halls for an exhibition of gifts for Stalin's seventieth birthday. Within forty-eight hours the permanent displays were dismantled, some of the staff dismissed, and the temple of art on Volkhonka Street was inundated with rugs, vases, panels and an infinite number of statues and busts of The Leader of All Times and Peoples.

Stalin died in March 1953, and within six months several French Impressionist canvases had appeared on the walls of the Pushkin Museum. There then began a slow but steady return of modern French art to the collections on display in the Pushkin Museum and the Hermitage. This progress was briefly interrupted in Moscow by a four-month exhibition of paintings from the Dresden Gallery, which took up all the rooms. The precious paintings rescued by the Soviet troops and brought back to the USSR were shown to the Moscow public in the summer of 1955 before being returned to the German Democratic Republic. In the summer of 1956, an exhibition of *French Painting of the Nineteenth Century* from the collections of French museums was held at the Pushkin Museum. It included, among other items, works by French Impressionists and post-Impressionists which some had forgotten, while others were seeing them for the first time.

The names of Matisse and Picasso could again be mentioned openly, but those of the art collectors who had brought the paintings of French artists to Russia at the beginning of the twentieth century were still too great a risk. Within a few more years the Moscow collectors had been completely forgotten. Then, gradually, the name of Sergei Shchukin was rehabilitated and, in the twenty-first century, his collection of artworks has attracted vast audiences from around the world. The time is now ripe to celebrate and restore to its rightful place in history the name and collection of Ivan Morozov.

27  Pavel Pavlinov's engraving depicting Morozov, *Sredi kollektsionerov* (Among Collectors) magazine, 1921.

# ENDNOTES

## Chapter I: Sketches for a Portrait

1. [Félix Fénéon], 'Les grands collectionneurs. III. M. Ivan Morosoff', *Le Bulletin de la vie artistique* (Paris: Galerie Bernheim-Jeune), vol. 1, no. 12 (15 May 1920), pp. 326–32. Our translation.
2. Fénéon's statistics are inaccurate: the collection contained 308 works by Russian artists and 188 foreign works.
3. The reality was that it had been extremely difficult to gain admission. It was only in the last few years before the revolution that Morozov made it easier for the collection to be viewed. It is this privacy which explains the paucity of memoir testimony of the details of his hanging scheme. For further details, see Chapter XII, 'A Place in History'.
4. This is an error in the text: the collection included not eight but eighteen works by Paul Cézanne.
5. Sof'ia Dymshits-Tolstaia (1889–1963) was a painter; Vladimir Tatlin (1885–1953) was an artist, and in 1918–19 was director of the Moscow Arts Board of the Fine Arts Department of the People's Commissariat for Enlightenment. Dymshits-Tolstaia was a member of the department and assistant of Tatlin in the State Free Arts Workshops (GSKhM).
6. Natal'ia Trotskaia-Sedova (1882–1962) was the civil wife of Leon Trotsky. Between 1918 and 1928 she was head of the Department of Museums and Preservation of Monuments of Art and Antiquities of the People's Commissariat for Enlightenment.
7. In August 1917, by order of the Provisional Government, palace property was evacuated from Petrograd to Moscow together with part of the collections of the Hermitage and of a number of private art galleries.
8. There is an error in the text: Sergei is confused with Pavel and vice versa.
9. The painting *In the Café-cabaret of Reichshoffen* (1878) has survived in two fragments: *Coin de café-concert* (National Gallery, London) and *Au café* (Oskar Reinhart Museum, Winterthur).
10. This is an error in the text. Mikhail Morozov died in 1903.
11. A. Efros, 'Chelovek s popravkoi. Pamiati I. A. Morozova' [The Man Who Tweaked: In Memoriam, I. A. Morozov], *Sredi kollektsionerov*, no. 10 (1921), p. 2.

12. The Morozovs bought their freedom in 1820. Together with Savva (1770–1860) and Uliana (1778–1861), their sons were freed: Yelisei (1798–1868), Zakhar (1802–57), Abram (1806–56) and Ivan (1812–64).

13. I have taken information about the development of the Morozov business from a study by Irina Potkina, the leading expert on Russian business history, based on all presently known documentation about the firm. See I. V. Potkina, *Na Olimpe delovogo uspekha. Nikol'skaia manufaktura Morozovykh. 1797–1917* [On the Olympus of Business Success: The Morozovs' Nikol'skoe Factory, 1797–1917] (Moscow: Glavarkhiv, 2004).

14. In 1855 Savva's son Zakhar established the Bogorodsk-Glukhovo Factory.

15. During the third division of the firm of Savva Morozov's Son and Co., the Tver factory became, by the drawing of lots, the property of Abram and David, grandchildren of Savva the First and the heirs of Savva's son Abram.

16. In 1873 Savva the First's son, Timofei, established the Nikol'skoe Factory of Savva Morozov's Son and Co.

## Chapter II: Varvara Khludova

1. Varvara Khludova's diary first appeared in a two-volume edition published by the Ivan Turgenev Library and Reading Room. This includes all the documents known at the present date which relate to Madame Morozova and her family. *Varvara Alekseevna Morozova. Na blago prosveshchenii Moskvy* [Varvara Alekseevna Morozova: For the Enlightenment of Moscow], eds N. A. Kruglianskaia and V. P. Aseyev, 2 vols (Moscow: Russkii put', 2008). Hereafter cited as *Na blago prosveshchenii*; vol. 1, pp. 19–140.

2. Ibid, vol. 1, p. 41.

3. Ibid, vol. 1, p. 42.

4. *Sovremennik* [The Contemporary], a journal of literary, art and social affairs, was founded by Alexander Pushkin and published between 1836 and 1866 in St Petersburg.

5. *Na blago prosveshchenii*, vol. 1, p. 87. Vissarion Belinskii, literary critic (1811–48).

6. Ibid, vol. 1, pp. 42, 140.

7. In 1842 England repealed a law prohibiting the export of spinning and weaving machinery. The Russian government permitted it to be imported duty-free.

8. The quotation is from Alexander Ostrovsky's comedy, *The Ardent Heart* [*Goriachee serdtse*], 1868. Our translation.

9. N. A. Varentsov, 'Khludovy' [The Khludovs], *Moskovskii al'bom. Vospominaniia o Moskve i moskvichakh XIX–XX vekov* [An Album of Moscow: Memories of Moscow and Muscovites of the Nineteenth–Twentieth Centuries] (Moscow: Nashe nasledie, 1997), pp. 118–19.

10. *Na blago prosveshchenii*, vol. 1, p. 114.

11. Édouard René Lefèbvre de Laboulaye (1811–83). A French writer, scholar, lawyer, educationist, journalist and politician.

12. *Na blago prosveshchenii*, vol. 1, p. 57.

13. Ibid, vol. 1, p. 167.

14. Ibid, vol. 1, pp. 242–3.

15. Nikolai Bukharin (1888–1938) was responsible for the work of party groups at the Prechistenska college. He was a Bolshevik revolutionary and close associate of Joseph Stalin, who later had him shot.

16. The Craft Museum in Moscow was founded in 1885, and from 1890 its director was Sergei Morozov, Abram's cousin. He acquired a separate building for it at 7 Leontiev Lane.

17. The Ivan Turgenev Reading Room and Library was designed by architect D. N. Chichagov and built in 1884. It was demolished in the late 1970s.

18. Abram had acquired the house in Bolshaya Alekseevskaya Street (now 27 Alexandr Solzhenitsyn Street) in 1860.

19. Vladimir Mikhnevich, *Nashi znakomye* [People We Know] (St Petersburg: Goppe, 1884), p. 151.

20. *Russkiye vedomosti*, one of the major Russian newspapers (1863–1918). From the 1870s it was a leading liberal publication whose contributors were professors at Moscow University. In 1905 the newspaper was taken over by the Constitutional Democrat Party. It was closed down by the Bolsheviks in January 1918. Besides the newspaper, V. M. Sobolevskii published the journal *Russkoe bogatstvo* [Wealth of Russia].

21. V. N. Aseyev compiled a table of expenses for the maintenance of houses, estates and housekeeping of Varvara Morozova and the members of her family. See *Na blago prosveshcheniia*, vol. 2, pp. 455–85.

22. M. K. Morozova, 'Moi vospominaniia' [My Memories], *Nashe nasledie*, no. 6, 1991, pp. 89–109. Hereafter referred to as Morozova, *Moi vospominaniia*.

23. *Na blago prosveshcheniia*, vol. 2, pp. 289–92.

### Chapter III: Mikhail Morozov

1. T. A. Aksakova-Sivers, *Semeinaia khronika* [A Family Chronicle], vol. 1 (Paris: Atheneum, 1988), pp. 89–90.

2. Morozova, *Moi vospominaniia*, p. 91.

3. Vera Nikolaevna Tret'iakova (1844–99), née Mamontova, wife of Pavel Tret'iakov and sister of Kirill Mamontov (1848–79); Ivan Nikolaevich Mamontov (1846–99), factory owner, candidate of law, magistrate.

4. Morozova, *Moi vospominaniia*, p. 94.

5. Ekaterina Dolgorukova (1847–1922); from 1880, Her Grace Princess Iur'evskaia. The morganatic wife of Tsar Alexander II.

6. Mikhail Abramovich Morozov bought the house in 1891, before his marriage. His son, Mikhail Mikhailovich Morozov, recalled much later that the mansion was said to have been built on the foundations of an earlier building, which had been an exact replica of the palace of the princes Gagarin on Novin Boulevard. It had supposedly had a hidden corridor in the basement which was decorated with Masonic emblems.

7. By an extraordinary coincidence, Mikhail's half-sister, Nataliia Vasil'evna Morozova (1887–1971), married Nikolai, the adopted son of Konstantin Popov, in 1910. Nikolai (b. 1887; shot 1938) was a chemical engineer and, before the 1917 Bolshevik coup, co-owner of the Popovs' tea trading company.

8. Morozova, *Moi vospominaniia*, p. 96.

9. Ibid.

10. Vasilii Perepletchikov (1863–1918) was a painter whose works were in the collections of Mikhail and Ivan Morozov. Mikhail Sizov (1884–1956), translator, literary critic; Nikolai Chechelev (1857–after 1917), artist, teacher at Stroganov College.

11. Petr Ivanovich Shchukin (1853–1912) was the brother of art collector Sergei Shchukin. He assembled a Museum of Russian Antiquities and, to house it, constructed a complex of buildings in the Russian Style on Bol'shaia Gruzinskaia Street. In 1905 he donated his collection of over 100,000 items to the city of Moscow and it became a branch of the Russian History Museum.

12. Vasilii Perepletchikov, *Dnevnik khudozhnika. Ocherki. 1886–1915* [An Artist's Diary: Essays, 1886–1915] (Moscow: Soyuzdezign, 2012), pp. 151–2. Hereafter referred to as Perepletchikov, *Dnevnik*.

13. The sarcophagus is now on display in the Ancient Egypt section of the Pushkin Museum. Its provenance from the Morozov Collection was only recently revealed by Alina Pushkareva, who has shared her discovery with the author.

14. Valentin Serov, *Portrait of Mikhail Morozov* (1902).

15. Morozova, *Moi vospominaniia*, pp. 99–100.

16. Sergei Vinogradov, *Prezhniaia Moskva. Vospominaniia* [Bygone Moscow: Memories], ed. N. Lapidus (Riga: MultiCentrs, 2001), p. 112. Fragments of these memoirs were published in the Latvian Russian-language newspaper *Segodnia* between 1934 and 1936. Hereafter referred to as Vinogradov, *Vospominaniia*.

17. Ibid.
18. Morozova, *Moi vospominaniia*, p. 96.

### Chapter IV: 'A Russian Rough Diamond, Polished by Civilization'

1. Vinogradov, *Vospominaniia*, p. 109.
2. Alexander Iuzhin (Prince Sumbatov, 1857–1927), actor and playwright.
3. Boris Akunin is the pseudonym of the author of a series of detective novels about Erast Fandorin. The writer, Grigorii Chkhartishvili (b. 1956), now lives in England.
4. Vladimir Ivanovich Nemirovich-Danchenko (1858–1943), theatre director and co-founder with Konstantin Stanislavski of the Moscow Art Theatre.
5. The title of Sumbatov-Iuzhin's play is taken from one of the protagonist's lines: 'A chap needs to have character and be, first and foremost, a gentleman.'
6. G. G. Elizavetina and M. P. Gromov, eds, *Perepiska A. P. Chekhova v dvukh tomakh* [Correspondence of A. P. Chekhov in two volumes] (Moscow: Khudozhestvennaia literatura, 1984), vol. 2, p. 112.
7. 'Kn. A. I. Sumbatov o "Dzhentl'mene" (Pis'mo v redaktsiiu)' [Prince A. I. Sumbatov on 'The Gentleman' (Letter to the Editor)], *Russkoe slovo*, no. 37 (14 February), 1914.
8. Perepletchikov, *Dnevnik*, p. 76.
9. M. Iur'ev, *Moi pisma (4-go dekabria 1893 goda–15 maia 1894 goda)* [My Letters (4 December 1893–15 May 1894)] (Moscow: Grosman and Knebel, 1895), p. 256.
10. Ibid, p. 17.
11. Ibid, p. 259.
12. Perepletchikov, *Dnevnik*, p. 76.
13. It was shortly after Mikhail Morozov's death that Fedor Plevako (1842–1908), a famously devout lawyer, became warden.
14. Elisei Savvich Morozov (1798–1868), who wrote a lengthy treatise on the Antichrist, and 'preferred religious devotions to the textile business', which he delegated to his sons.
15. Abram Abramovich Morozov was a member of the United Faith (*Edinoverie*) community, which consisted of Old Believers of the Rogozha Necropolis, a sect that sought to attract Orthodox priests. His sons, Mikhail, Ivan and Arseniy, were baptized in the United Faith Trinity Isagogic Church at Saltykov Bridge.
16. Morozova, *Moi vospominaniia*, p. 97.
17. As the trustee of a number of charitable societies, Mikhail Morozov was awarded ranks by the Empress Mariia Department of Institutions (a department administering charities, named after the wife of Tsar Paul I).
18. Morozova, *Moi vospominaniia*, p. 97.
19. N. R[akshan]in, 'Iz obydennoi zhizni' [From Everyday Life], *Moskovskii listok*, 14 October 1903 (no. 286).
20. Nikolai Martynov (1842–1913), artist and teacher. He taught painting in many prominent families of the nobility in Moscow.
21. It is difficult to regard Konstantin Korovin's memoirs as objective reminiscence. He does not write specifically about the character of Ivan Morozov, even though the latter bought over forty of his works.
22. Letter from E. M. Khruslov to V. A. Likin, dated 11 July 1890. Manuscript Department of the Tret'iakov Gallery, *fond* 9, *ed. khr.* 1051.
23. Manuscript Department of the State Tret'iakov Gallery, *fond* 9, *ed. khr.* 871. Petr Levchenko (1856–1917) was a landscape painter.
24. Perepletchikov, *Dnevnik*, pp. 140–1.
25. White-lining students were smart dressers whose uniforms had a white lining.
26. Vinogradov, *Vospominaniia*, p. 110.
27. Perepletchikov, *Dnevnik*, p. 142. The diary entries quoted above, and an inventory of the collection which lists old school paintings, are the only documentary evidence that M. A. Morozov ever acquired Western old masters.

28. S. Diagilev, 'M. A. Morozov. Nekrolog' [M. A. Morozov. An Obituary], *Mir iskusstva* [World of Art], no. 9, 1903, p. 141.

29. Vrubel's painting of the picture was inspired by N. A. Rimskii-Korsakov's opera *The Tale of Tsar Saltan*. This was staged in Savva Mamontov's Private Opera, for which Vrubel provided sketches for the sets and costumes. The role of the Swan Princess was performed by Vrubel's wife.

30. Paul Durand-Ruel (1831–1922), a French art dealer and gallery owner whose clients included the Morozov brothers.

31. Paul-Albert Besnard (1849–1934), a French artist.

32. S. V. Giatsintova, *S pamiat'iu naedine* [Alone with My Memory] (Moscow: Iskusstvo, 1985), p. 413.

33. The painting was bought for Mikhail Morozov by the Durand-Ruel Gallery in 1901 for 15,000 francs. In 1907 it was sold by Ivan Morozov on behalf of Mikhail's widow through the Bernheim-Jeune Gallery for 16,000 francs. Detail established by the author from documents in the archive of the Durand-Ruel Gallery. In 1912 *Féerie intime* was shown at the exhibition *One Hundred Years of French Painting (1812–1912)*, organized in St Petersburg by the journal *Apollon*, as the property of journalist and politician Joseph Reinach. Today it is in the collection of Lucile Audouy, Paris.

34. The insurance valuation of Besnard's painting was 6,000 rubles, and of the Renoir 10,000 rubles (1 franc was equal to 37.5 kopecks).

35. Vinogradov, *Vospominaniia*, p. 124.

36. 500 francs was equal to 187 rubles and 50 kopecks.

37. *Konstantin Korovin vspominaet . . .* [Konstantin Korovin Reminisces] (Moscow: Izobrazitel'noe iskusstvo, 1990), pp. 605–6.

38. There were six works by K. A. Korovin in the collection of Mikhail Morozov.

39. Rue Jouffroy d'Abbans is located near Avenue de Wagram, where the apartment of the youngest of the Shchukin brothers, Ivan Ivanovich (1869–1908), was located; from 1895, he lived permanently in Paris.

40. See Théodore Duret, *Histoire d'Édouard Manet et de son œuvre* (Paris, 1902), p. 268. E. Manet, *Kabachok* [In the Bar] (1878–9). The painting's provenance was clarified by the author from documents in the archive of the Durand-Ruel Gallery.

41. Perepletchikov, *Dnevnik*, p. 150.

42. Toulouse-Lautrec had donated the portrait to art critic Arsène Alexandre (1859–1937), one of the founders of the satirical magazine *Le Rire*, for which Toulouse-Lautrec provided illustrations. It was this magazine which commissioned a portrait of Yvette Guilbert (1867–1944), one of Lautrec's favourite models at the time. When the star of the Moulin Rouge and Folies Bergères learned he had promised to paint her portrait for the magazine, she sang him a chorus of the then popular English song 'Linger Longer, Loo'.

43. Stefan Bakałowicz (1857–1947) was a Polish artist, a salon academic painter mainly of themes of Ancient Rome. In summer 1903 Durand-Ruel acquired an early painting, *The Mistress of the Castle* (1875, whereabouts unknown) for Morozov at auction. The paintings by Corot and Millet were not bought. Clarification by the author from documents in the archive of the Durand-Ruel Gallery.

44. Perepletchikov, *Dnevnik*, p. 151.

45. Morozova, *Vospominaniia*, p. 99.

46. Perepletchikov, *Dnevnik*, p. 140.

47. Ibid, pp. 141–2.

48. Morozova, *Vospominaniia*, p. 99.

### Chapter V: To Moscow! To Prechistenka!

1. Ivan Morozov matriculated at Zurich Polytechnic in October 1891 and graduated on 16 March 1895. His personal file is in the Hochschularchiv der ETH Zürich, EZ-REK1-1-7383.

2. N. A. Varentsov, *Slyshannoe. Vidennoe. Peredumannoe. Perezhitoe* [Heard. Seen. Thought and Lived Through] (Moscow: Novoe literaturnoe obozrenie, 1999), p. 679.

3. I. E. Bondarenko, *Zapiski khudozhnika-arkhitektora. Trudy, vstrechi, vpechatleniia* [Notes of an Artish-Architect. Works, Meetings, Impressions], ed. M. V. Nashchokina, vol. 2 (Moscow: Progress-traditsiia, 2018), p. 218.

4. Iu. A. Bakhrushin, *Vospominaniia* [Memoirs] (Moscow: Khudozhestvennaia literatura, 1994), p. 281. Hereafter referred to as Bakhrushin, *Vospominaniia*.

5. Letter from I. S. Ostroukhov to A. P. Botkina, dated 4 January 1905. Tret'iakov Gallery, *fond* 48, *ed. khr.* 378.

6. Bakhrushin, *Vospominaniia*, p. 281.

7. Joaquín Sorolla y Bastida (1863–1923), Spanish Impressionist painter. The collection had just one painting by the artist, *Preparing Raisins* (1901).

8. The *Bande noire* (The Nubians) was a group of French artists (Charles Cottet, Lucien Simon, et al.), so named because of their bias in favour of dark colours. The collection included *A Gust of Wind* (1890s) by Lucien Simon (1861–1945).

9. Louis Legrand (1863–1951), *The Supper of the Apache* (c.1901). According to the latest research in the Duran Ruel archive, the first purchases were done already in 1901.

10. Ignacio Zuloaga (Zuloaga y Zabaleto) (1870–1945), Spanish artist. *Preparation for a Bullfight* (1903), reproduced in the journal *Mir iskusstva* [The World of Art], no. 11, 1903.

11. A receipt from the Durand-Ruel Gallery for payment for M. Dethomas' drawing (no. 22 in the exhibition catalogue) is extant. Manuscript Department of the State Museum of Fine Arts (Pushkin Museum), *kollektsiia* 12, *razdel* 1, *ed. khr.* 1, *list* 1.

12. Albert Lebourg (1849–1928), *By the River (May in Meudon)* (before 1903).

13. Letter from Paul Durand-Ruel to I. A. Morozov, dated 22 June 1903. Manuscript Department of the Pushkin Museum, *koll.* 12, *razdel* 1, *ed. khr.* 1, *list* 43. Paul Durand-Ruel organized the first solo exhibition of Alfred Sisley in 1883. For 9,300 francs he acquired *Frost in Louveciennes* in 1902 at the sale of the collection of Jules Strauss at the Hôtel Drouot.

14. Quoted from Lionello Venturi, *Impressionists and Symbolists: Manet, Degas, Monet, Pissarro, Sisley, Renoir, Cézanne, Seurat, Gauguin, Van Gogh, Toulouse-Lautrec*, trans. Francis Steegmuller (London–New York: Scribner, 1950), p. 88. The author is quoting an article by Octave Mirbeau published in *Le Figaro* in 1892.

15. Notes made in the margins of catalogues belonging to I. A. Morozov were discovered in the Research (*Nauchnaia*) Library of the Pushkin Museum of Fine Arts by K. I. Panas and deciphered by A. V. Petukhov, curator of the Morozov collection, who kindly shared his findings with me.

16. The Durand-Ruel Gallery acquired the portrait in 1903 at the sale of property of the actress's husband, Paul Lagarde. Morozov purchased it for 25,000 francs.

17. Georges Viau (1855–1939), a Parisian dental surgeon and art collector. See *Catalogue des tableaux modernes, pastels, et aquarelles . . . composant la collection de G. Viau, et dont la vente aura lieu à Paris, Galeries Durand-Ruel . . . le . . . 4 mars 1907* ([Paris:] Berger, 1907).

18. Renoir's *La Loge* was first shown in Paris in 1874 and later that year in London at an exhibition arranged by Durand-Ruel, making it one of the first major Impressionist paintings to be shown in this country. In 1925 the painting was acquired by the English industrialist and art collector Samuel Courtauld for £22,600. It was his most expensive acquisition.

19. The telegram is in the archive of the Durand-Ruel Gallery.

20. Ambroise Vollard, *Recollections of a Picture Dealer*, trans. Violet M. Macdonald (Mineola, New York: Dover, 2002), p. 20.

**Chapter VI:** *Chevalier de la Légion d'honneur*

1. Bakhrushin, *Vospominaniia*, p. 281.

2. Boris Ternovets (1884–1941), sculptor, art historian, critic, museum curator. For further details, see Chapter XV, 'Citizen Morozov'.

3. The insurance valuation of the 107 most valuable paintings by West European artists was 255,000 rubles; of those by Russian artists, 25,000 rubles. After the outbreak of the First World War a revaluation doubled the insurance sums. At 3 January 1917, the value was put at 560,000 rubles.

4. Bakhrushin, *Vospominaniia*, p. 281.

5. Vinogradov, *Vospominaniia*, p. 108.

6. Ibid, pp. 107–8.

7. B. N. Ternovets, *Pis'ma. Dnevniki. Stat'i* [Letters, Diaries, Articles], eds L. S. Aleshina and N. V. Iavorskaia (Moscow: Sovetskii khudozhnik, 1977), p. 100.

8. Auguste Renoir, *Portrait of a Young Woman* (1876, Neue Pinakothek, Munich).

9. John Rewald, *The History of Impressionism*, 4th rev. ed. (London: Secker and Warburg, 1973).

10. The World of Art was the name both of an art association and the magazine it published – *Mir iskusstva* (St Petersburg, 1898–1904). The exhibitions (1899–1903) bore the same name, and the soul and driving force behind it all was Sergei Diaghilev.

11. The artist Léon Bakst (1866–1924) designed the exhibition hall. The oriental vividness and European sophistication of his art was soon to conquer Europe and America.

12. Baron Jean-Marie-Denys Cochin (1851–1922) was the scion of a famous family of the French intellectual and political elite. His first commission for Maurice Denis was a stained-glass window, a Symbolist landscape *The Road of Life* (1895). Cochin next commissioned from Denis *The Legend of St Hubert* (1897–8), a mural for his study in the mansion at 51 rue de Babylone. See Maurice Denis, *La Légende de Saint Hubert, 1896–1897* (Paris: Somogy, 1999).

13. *Polyphemus*, exhibited at the Salon des Indépendants in 1906, was last shown in 2000 at the exhibition *Light of the Desert, the Beaches of Maurice Denis*, Valence Museum, property of Alain Lesieutre. This information has been kindly provided by Marie-Claire Rodriguez, who is compiling a catalogue raisonné of the works of Maurice Denis.

## Chapter VII: 'Cézanne Season'

1. Vladimir Maiakovskii, *Sezann i Verlen* (1924–5). '*Бывало – сезон,/ наш бог – Ван-Гог,/ другой сезон – Сезан.*'

2. S. I. Shchukin, interview with a correspondent of *Russkoe slovo*, 22 September 1911. Quoted in Al'bert Kostenevich and Nataliia Semenova, *Collecting Matisse* (Paris: Flammarion, 1993), p. 22.

3. Note by S. A. Vinogradov in the margin of the catalogue, Research Library of the Pushkin Museum. In the Salon d'Automne of 1904, thirty-three works were exhibited in the Cézanne Room.

4. The Cézanne retrospective in the Salon d'Automne of 1907 comprised fifty-nine paintings.

5. Letters from C. Pissarro to L. Pissarro, dated 21 and 22 November 1895. Quoted from *Pol' Sezann. Perepiska. Vospominaniia sovremennikov* [Paul Cézanne: Correspondence, Reminiscences by Contemporaries], ed. N. V. Iavorskaia (Moscow: Iskusstvo, 1972), p. 167.

6. In 1912 Louisine Havemeyer bought Degas' *Dancers Practising at the Barre* at the Henri Rouart auction for 478,000 francs ($95,700), a record at the time for the work of a living artist.

7. Letter from I. A. Morozov to I. S. Ostroukhov, dated 11/24 September 1908. Manuscript Department of the Tret'iakov Gallery, *fond* 10, *ed. khr.* 4325.

8. Louisine W. Havemeyer, *Sixteen to Sixty: Memoirs of a Collector* (New York: Ursus Press, 1993), p. 8.

9. In 1894 the New York branch of the Durand-Ruel Gallery (which opened in 1888) was located in a building belonging to Havemeyer. See Frances Weitzenhoffer, *The Havemeyers: Impressionism Comes to America* (New York: Abrams, 1986), p. 94.

10. Ibid., p. 119.

11. Louisine Havemeyer was paid $3,000 (15,000 francs). In the Durand-Ruel Gallery's ledgers a price of 30,000 francs for the two works is shown. In the Morozov-Ternovets account, the price of *Self-portrait in a Cap* is given as 12,000 francs, and of *The Banks of the Marne (Villa on the Bank of a River)* as 18,000 francs.

12. We only have a view of the Cézanne Room photographed in 1923. From the memoirs of Ternovets it would seem that neither Cézanne nor Gauguin had previously had a separate room. Not one of the paintings retained its previous place in the rehanging he undertook. Ternovets, *Pis'ma*, p. 124.

13. S. Makovskii, 'Frantsuzskie khudozhniki iz sobraniia I. A. Morozova' [French Artists in the Collection of I. A. Morozov], *Apollon*, nos 3–4, 1912, p. 6.

14. Auguste Pellerin (1853–1929), collector of Impressionist paintings, owner of the best collections of Édouard Manet and Paul Cézanne, whose first painting he acquired from Vollard in 1898. In the Cézanne retrospective at the Salon d'Automne of 1907, half the works exhibited belonged to Pellerin (twenty-five items). Two paintings from this renowned collection, *Bridge over a Pond* and *The Banks of the Marne*, were acquired by Ivan Morozov.

15. Makovskii, 'Frantsuzskie khudozhniki', p. 7.

### Chapter VIII: 'A Russian Who Doesn't Haggle?'

1. Vollard, *Recollections of a Picture Dealer*, p. 142.

2. If we compare the prices we know for Russian paintings bought by Ivan Morozov, one of the cheapest is Konstantin Somov's *In an Old Park* (1907, 100 rubles), while the most expensive are works by Aleksandr Golovin and Konstantin Korovin (from 800 rubles).

3. Letter from I. A. Morozov to I. S. Ostroukhov, dated 11/24 September 1908. Manuscript Department of the Tret'iakov Gallery, *fond* 48, *ed khr*. 4324.

4. Letter from the gallery of Paul Cassirer to I. A. Morozov, dated 28 August 1908 (in German), Manuscript Department of the Pushkin Museum, *koll*. 12, *razdel* 1, *ed. khr*. 63. Munch's painting *The Port in Lübeck* (Hafen von Lübeck, 1907), which Ivan Morozov refused to buy, is now property of Kunsthaus Zürich. The exchange rate of the mark and franc in 1907 was almost one to one. Mikhail Morozov acquired *The Girls on the Bridge* by Edvard Munch in 1903 for 500 francs.

5. In 1907–10 Ivan Morozov bought eleven canvases by Paul Gauguin for 107,000 francs. Sergei Shchukin paid roughly the same for sixteen.

6. Iakov Tugendkhol'd's graphic description.

7. Emil' Verkharn (Émile Verhaeren), 'Moskovskie vospominaniia' [Moscow Memories], *Russkie vedomosti*, nos 3 and 5, 1914.

8. Alfred H. Barr, Jr, 'Russian Diary 1927–28', *October* (MIT), vol. 7 (Winter, 1978): 'Soviet Revolutionary Culture', pp. 10–51. Alfred H. Barr (1902–81) was an American art historian and the first director of the Museum of Modern Art in New York (1929–43). He transformed MoMA into the world's largest collection of twentieth-century painting and sculpture.

9. In 1928 the existence of two overlapping sections was considered inexpedient and economically unjustified. By order of Glavnauka (the Main Committee for Science), dated 24 October 1928, the collections of Sections 1 and 2 of the State Museum of New Western Art (GMNZI) were merged into a single museum. The entire Shchukin Collection was transferred to the former mansion of Ivan Morozov on what by now had been renamed Kropotkin Street.

10. At the 1906 posthumous Gauguin exhibition in the Salon d'Automne, 227 works were exhibited.

11. Memoirs of N. P. Vishniakova. TsGIA g. Moskvy [Central State History Archive of Moscow], *fond* 1334, *opis'* 1, *ed. khr*. 10, *chast'* 6, p. 115 *ob*., 117.

12. Boris Ternovets notes that Morozov first saw Gauguin 'in the dimly lit rooms of the ground floor'. Shchukin didn't immediately have the courage to hang his Gauguins in the principal reception rooms. This may have been around 1904, when Sergei Shchukin brought two paintings to Moscow: *Her Name Is Vairumati* and *Women on the Seashore: Motherhood*, not around 1900, as Ternovets suggests (Ternovets, *Pis'ma*, p. 106).

13. Sergei Makovskii, *Stranitsy khudozhestvennoi kritiki* [Some Pages of Art Criticism] (St Petersburg-Apollon: Panteon, 1913), pp. 178–9.

14. Ibid.

15. Roseline Bacou, 'Paul Gauguin et Gustave Fayet', *Actes du colloque Gauguin 11–13 janvier 1989* (École du Louvre, Paris, Documentation française: 1989), p. 29. After buying the Fontfroide Abbey in January 1908, Gustave Fayet undertook restoration and renovation of the building. The work continued for ten years. See Stéphane Guibourgé et al., *Gustave Fayet: L'œil souverain* (Paris: Éditions du Regard, 2015).

16. Morozov paid Vollard 20,000 francs for *The Great Buddha*, which really does seem excessive, as has been pointed out by Marie Joseph Lesure in her assessment of the purchases, and who kindly made her materials available to the author.

17. Invoice for the purchase of the painting, Manuscript Department of the Pushkin Museum, *koll.* 12, *opis'* 1, *ed. khr.* 14, *list* 7.

18. Nikolai Riabushinskii (1876–1951), philanthropist and art collector.

19. Martiros Sar'ian (1880–1972), painter.

20. Quoted from *Gogen. Vzgliad iz Rossii* [Gauguin: the View from Russia] (Moscow: Sovetskii khudozhnik, 1989), p. 114.

21. Ibid.

22. Osip Mandel'shtam et al., *Shum vremeni. Memuarnaia proza. Pis'ma. Zapisnye knizhki* [The Sound of Time: Memoir Prose, Letters, Notebooks] (Moscow: Olma-Press, 2003), p. 101.

23. *The Complete Letters of Vincent Van Gogh*, 3 vols, trans. J. van Gogh-Bonger and C. de Dood (London: Thames and Hudson, 1958), vol. 3, p. 101, letter no. 559.

24. Alexandre Louis Philippe Marie Berthier, Fourth Prince of Wagram (1883–1918), inherited his title from his grandfather, Marshal Napoléon, who was awarded it after the battle of Wagram. He began collecting art at the age of twenty-two and assembled a first-class collection which included thirty paintings by Courbet, fifty by Renoir, forty-seven by Van Gogh, twenty-eight by Cézanne, forty by Monet, twenty-six by Sisley, twenty by Pissarro, ten by Puvis de Chavannes, eleven by Degas and twelve by Manet.

25. *Thatched Cottages and Houses* was bought by Druet for Morozov at a sale of paintings by contemporary artists at the Hôtel Drouot in May 1908 for 5,865 francs.

26. Letter from E. Druet to I. A. Morozov, dated 20 September 1909. Manuscript Department of the Pushkin Museum, *koll.* 12, *razdel* 1, *ed. khr.* 37.

27. Letter from E. Druet to I. A. Morozov, dated 28 September 1909. Ibid, *ed. khr.* 38.

28. *Cinquante tableaux de Vincent van Gogh: [exposition], Galérie E. Druet, du 8 au 20 novembre 1909.* Ibid, *ed. khr.* 44. Letter from E. Druet, dated 23 October 1909, about his intention to send the paintings when the exhibition ended.

## Chapter IX: Cupid and Psyche

1. Two other rooms, adjacent to the Music Salon, had natural light.

2. Ivan Morozov subsequently acquired the sketches by Mikhail Vrubel for panels for the mansion of Sergei Morozov at 17 Spiridonovka Street.

3. The present name of the illustrious restaurant at Gare de Lyon, to which François Flameng contributed mural paintings in 1900, is Le Train Bleu.

4. See M. B. Aksenenko, 'Monumental'nyi ansambl' M. Deni i A. Maiolia v moskovskom osobniake I. A. Morozova' [The Monumental Ensemble of M. Denis and A. Maillol in the Moscow Mansion of I. A. Morozov], *Sovetskoe iskusstvoznanie*, issue 27 (1991), pp. 423–8.

5. In the exhibition, held from 8 to 20 April 1907 at the Bernheim-Jeune Gallery, forty-five paintings and twenty drawings were exhibited. See *Maurice Denis. Exposition particulière à la Galérie Bernheim-Jeune. 8–20 Avril 1907.*

6. Letter from M. Denis to I. A. Morozov, dated 6 April 1907, Manuscript Department of the Pushkin Museum, *koll.* 12, *razdel* 1, *ed. khr.* 28, *listy* 1–2.

7. Maurice Denis wrote an introduction to the catalogue of Cross' exhibition, held at the Bernheim-Jeune Gallery from 22 April to 8 May, and it was probably at his instigation that Morozov acquired *Around My House (Near the House)* for 2,000 francs. Paul Signac's *The Harbour at Marseille*, exhibited at the Salon des Indépendants, was also purchased at the Bernheim-Jeune Gallery.

8. Neo-Impressionism is a movement that appeared around 1885. It attempted to bring scientific rigour to the breaking down of complex colours into primary colours, and also to the use of different brushstrokes as painting techniques. Its main representatives were Georges Seurat and Paul Signac.

9. Denis exhibited *Bacchus and Ariadne* in 1907 at the Salon of the Société Nationale des Beaux-Arts (No. 376), and indicated in the catalogue that it belonged to 'M. Morosoff'.

10. Letter from M. Denis to I.A. Morozov, dated 21 July 1907, Manuscript Department of the Pushkin Museum, *koll.* 12, *razdel* 1, *ed. khr.* 29. There is a note on the letter: 'Replied 14/27 July'.

11. From a Russian ballad, *'Ei, iamshchik goni-ka k Iaru'* ('Hey, coachman, take me to Yar'). The ballad became famous abroad after Deanna Durbin sang it in *His Butler's Sister* (1943).

12. Evdokia Sergeevna Morozova (née Kladovshchikova), 1885–1959. In the Russian Empire the estate to which a person belonged was invariably shown in marriage certificates.

13. In 1913 A. A. Bakhrushin donated his museum to the Academy of Sciences.

14. I. E. Bondarenko, 'Zapiski kollektsionera' [Jottings of a Collector], *Pamiatniki Otechestva* [Historic Artefacts of the Fatherland], no. 29 (1993), p. 32. Ilya Bondarenko (1870–1947), architect, designer of civil and church buildings in the neo-Russian style.

15. Bakhrushin, *Vospominaniia*, p. 35.

16. Ibid, p. 153.

17. Ibid, p. 284.

## Chapter X: Maurice Denis, or the French Occupy Moscow

1. As a result, Denis missed Morozov, who arrived in Paris in late September after his holiday in Biarritz. See the letter from M. Denis to I. A. Morozov, dated 14 September 1907. Manuscript Department of the Pushkin Museum, *koll.* 12, *razdel* 1, *ed. khr.* 30.

2. Maurice Denis, *Journal*, 3 vols (Paris: Éditions du Vieux Colombier, 1957–9), vol. 2: 1905–20, p. 89.

3. Murals by Giulio Romano in the Palazzo Te, a suburban villa of the Marquis of Mantua, Federico II Gonzaga, built by Romano in 1524–5 and then painted by him and his students. See Giorgio Vasari, *Lives of the Artists*, trans. George Bull (London: Chatto and Windus, 1908), vol. 2, s.v. 'Giulio Romano'.

4. Denis, *Journal*, p. 80.

5. At the exhibition, held at the Druet Gallery from 23 November to 5 December 1908, seventy paintings and twenty drawings, as well as ceramic vases, were exhibited. In 1904 Druet was the first person to give Maurice Denis a solo exhibition. André Gide wrote the foreword to the catalogue.

6. Denis, *Journal*, p. 94.

7. Ibid, p. 95. Letter from Maurice Denis to Madame de la Laurencie, dated 2 August 1908. Berthe de la Laurencie (1876–1913) was the daughter of composer Vincent d'Indy. Denis painted a portrait of her and her children in 1904.

8. Ibid, p. 95. Letter from Maurice Denis to Madame de la Laurencie, dated 26 September 1908.

9. Letter from I. A. Morozov to M. Denis, dated 6 October 1908. Archive of Maurice Denis, Saint-Germain-en-Laye. Copy in the author's archive.

10. Ostroukhov assisted in resolving the issue of how to install the panels on the walls of the Music Salon. Each panel was framed with cloth-of-gold ribbons. See a letter from I. A. Morozov to I. S. Ostroukhov, dated 6/19 November 1908. Manuscript Department of the Tret'iakov Gallery, *fond* 10, *ed. khr.* 4325.

11. Denis, *Journal*, pp. 99–100.

12. Sergei Shcherbatov (1874–1962), prince, art collector and public figure. Vladimir von Meck (1877–1932), art collector and patron, amateur artist.

13. Pavel Kuznetsov (1878–1968), artist. There were Symbolist works by him in Ivan Morozov's collection: *Birth* and *Garden in Bloom in Bakhchisarai* (both in the Tret'iakov Gallery). In Denis' diary, Sar'ian is mistakenly called Servian.

14. Denis, *Journal*, pp. 99–100.
15. Ibid, p. 108. On Petr Shchukin, see note 11 to Chapter III.
16. Ibid, p. 102.
17. The reference is to *The Virgin of Verneuil* by Camille Corot (Pushkin Museum). The location of the panel *Faust and Margarita* by Vrubel is not known.
18. Vladimir Girshman (1867–1936), entrepreneur, patron of the arts, collector of Russian painting. He supported the Free Aesthetics society (1906–7), which held its meetings in his mansion.
19. Denis, *Journal*, p. 99. Wanda Landowska (1879–1959), Polish pianist and harpsichord player.
20. Filipp Maliavin (1869–1940), painter; *The Whore* (1903).
21. There were some thirty works by Levitan in the collection, mainly small studies but ranging from his earliest to his last works. The only large, finished work was the landscape *Silence* (1898).
22. Denis apparently had in mind Cézanne's *Great Pine at Aix*.
23. Denis, *Journal*, p. 100.
24. Ibid, p. 101.
25. Ibid, p. 100.
26. Ibid, p. 98. Théo van Rysselberghe (1862–1926), a Belgian Neo-Impressionist painter.
27. By autumn the additional panels were finished. 'This week I exhibited two ... of your panels by Maurice Denis ... They were a great success. I have sent them over to be packed up. You will receive them shortly,' Émile Druet advised Morozov on 23 October 1909. Manuscript Department of the Pushkin Museum, *koll.* 12, *razdel* 1, *ed. khr.* 39.
28. In a letter dated 15 October 1909, Ivan Morozov informed Maurice Denis that he had sent a parcel with a sample of the fabric which was to be used for upholstering the furniture. Archive of Maurice Denis.
29. For each statue, Aristide Maillol was paid 14,000 francs. He was to make only one cast of the bust of each figure, but later violated this condition.
30. Initially the urns were placed on rotating pedestals in the corners of the salon, but these were later replaced by sculptures. The lighting in the Music Salon proved ill-suited for bronze statues, and in the 1920s they were transferred to the next room, which had paintings by Monet and the Impressionists.
31. Alexander Benois, *Moi vospominaniia* [My Memoirs] (Moscow: Nauka, 1990), vol. 2, p. 151.
32. Ivan Morozov paid Maurice Denis a total of 70,000 francs for seven large panels, four narrow panels and two borders. After this, Denis began negotiating to buy a house in Saint-Germain-en-Laye, and in the summer of 1914 acquired the estate. Today it is a museum dedicated to Denis and Symbolist and Nabis painters. The Nabi group of French painters (from the Arabic *nabi* – a prophet) included Denis, Vuillard, Bonnard and Roussel, and the trend emerged around 1888, ending in 1905. These artists were much influenced by the discoveries of post-Impressionism and the painting of Paul Gauguin.
33. Émile Verhaeren, 'Moskovskie vospominaniia'.

#### Chapter XI: The Mediterranean–Moroccan Suite

1. Letter from Ivan Morozov to Maurice Denis, dated 14 February 1910. Archive of Maurice Denis. Copy in the author's archive.
2. In November 1909 Durand-Ruel offered Morozov an early work by Maurice Denis, but this was ignored. The letter and a photograph of *The Annunciation* (1894) were discovered by the author in the Durand-Ruel Gallery archive.
3. The painting was Bonnard's *Landscape: Goods Train and Barges* (1895), which Sergei Shchukin returned almost immediately to the dealer.
4. Benois, *Moi vospominaniia*, vol. 2, pp. 154–5.

5. The paintings are *Morning in Paris* and *Evening in Paris* (1911), commissioned in January 1910 through the Bernheim-Jeune Gallery at the same time as the triptych. The paintings were bought in 1912 for 5,000 francs, and the triptych in 1911 for 25,000 francs.

6. Letter from Pierre Bonnard to his mother, September 1910. Quoted by N. V. Iavorskaia, *Pierre Bonnard* (Moscow: Iskusstvo, 1972), p. 72.

7. In a 1923 catalogue, Boris Ternovets calls them '*The Mediterranean*: decoration additional to the central panel of the triptych *On the Mediterranean*'. Bonnard exhibited the triptych, commissioned from him in May 1911, under the title of *The Mediterranean: Panels Between Pillars* in the Salon d'Automne of 1912.

8. Manuscript Department of the Pushkin Museum, *koll.* 12, *razdel* 1, *ed. khr.* 19.

9. Manuscript Department of the Pushkin Museum, *koll.* 12, *razdel* 1, *ed. khr.* 66.

10. Letter from Sergei Shchukin to Henri Matisse, dated 10 January 1913. See Kostenevich and Semenova, *Collecting Matisse*, p. 173. The reference is to Bonnard's painting *Summer: Dance* (1912).

11. The contract Matisse signed on 18 September 1909 with Bernheim-Jeune reads, 'All the pictures which Monsieur Henri Matisse will paint before 15 September 1912 he undertakes to provide to the company, which undertakes to buy them from him, whatever their subject matter.' The price was to be calculated on the basis of the formats customary in France. There were ten of these, the largest being Format 50 (116 x 189 cm).

12. Ivan Morozov was seventeen years younger than Sergei Shchukin. The words quoted are from an interview Matisse gave in 1944. E. Tériade, 'Matisse Speaks', *Art News Annual*, 21 (1952), pp. 40–77. Repr. Jack D. Flam, ed., *Matisse on Art* (New York: E. P. Dutton, 1978), p. 39.

13. Henri Matisse, 'Notes d'un peintre', *La Grande Revue*, no. 52 (25 December 1908) pp. 731–45. Flam, *Matisse on Art*, p. 36.

14. Evdokia the Younger was born on 24 July 1903 in Moscow. Her parents married four years later. In the extant pre-revolutionary documents Ivan Morozov invariably indicated that he had an adopted daughter.

15. Letter from Ivan Morozov to Henri Matisse, dated 23 March 1910. See Kostenevich and Semenova, *Collecting Matisse*, p. 181.

16. I. S. Zil'bershtein and V. A. Samkov, eds, *Valentin Serov v perepiske, dokumentakh i interv'iu* [Valentin Serov in Correspondence, Documents and Interviews], 2 vols (Leningrad: Khudozhnik RSFSR, 1971), vol. 2, p. 236.

17. Efros, 'Chelovek s popravkoi', p. 2. The reference is to *Portrait of I. A. Morozov* (1910).

18. Quoted from Kostenevich and Semenova, *Collecting Matisse*, p. 23.

19. Letter from Henri Matisse to Ivan Morozov, dated 29 September 1912. Quoted from ibid, pp. 182–3.

20. The reference is to *Bottle of Schiedam* (1896).

21. Letter from Henri Matisse to Ivan Morozov, dated 19 September 1911. Quoted from Kostenevich and Semenova, *Collecting Matisse*, p. 181.

22. Letter from Henri Matisse to Amélie Matisse, dated 1 April 1912. Quoted from ibid, p. 141.

23. Letter from Henri Matisse to Ivan Morozov, dated 29 September 1912. Quoted from ibid, p. 183.

24. Letter from Henri Matisse to Ivan Morozov, dated 19 April 1913. Quoted from ibid, p. 183.

25. *Exposition Henri Matisse. Tableaux du Maroc et sculpture. Chez MM. Bernheim-Jeune & Cie. 14–19 avril* (Paris, 1913).

26. In 1948, during the dividing up of works of art between the Pushkin Museum and the State Hermitage, the Moroccan triptych was split: *Zorah on the Terrace* and *Window at Tangier* remained in Moscow, while *Entrance to the Kasbah* was sent to the Hermitage in Leningrad. Only in 1968 was the right-hand section of the triptych returned to Moscow.

27. Kostenevich and Semenova, *Collecting Matisse*, p. 175.

28. This refers to the huge *Seated Rifian* against a red, yellow and green background. It was acquired by the Danish collector, Christian Tetzen-Lund, in 1918, who in 1925 sold the painting to Alfred Barnes (now at the Barnes Foundation, Philadelphia). The Rifs inhabit a mountainous region of northern Morocco.

29. Letter from Henri Matisse to Ivan Morozov, dated 25 May 1913. Quoted from Kostenevich and Semenova, *Matiss v Rossii*, p. 184.

## Chapter XII: A Place in History

1. Ternovets, *Pis'ma*, p. 119.
2. Arsenii Abramovich Morozov died on 24 December 1908 at his estate.
3. Nina Konshina (née Okromchedlova, 1871–1952).
4. See 'Delo o zaveshchanii A.A. Morozova' [The Case of the Will of A.A. Morozov], *Russkie vedomosti*, no. 239 (18 October) 1909. The will was declared null and void only in 1913 after a lawsuit brought by I. A. Morozov and M. K Morozova, but the mansion was awarded to N. A. Konshina-Okromchedlova. The lawful wife and heiress of Arsenii Morozov was Vera Sergeevna Morozova (née Fedotova, in her second marriage, Naval', 1883–1944, Vienna). She was the niece of a famous actress, Glikeriia Fedotova.
5. 'Delo o zaveshchanii A. A. Morozova'.
6. The reference is to the *Portrait of Mika Morozov* (1901). In Ivan Morozov's collection there were, in addition to two portraits painted by Valentin Serov, three of his other works: *Sheds, Hall of the Old House*, and *Pushkin in Mikhailovskoe Park*.
7. There was so much talk about the Morozov lectures in the city that revolutionary 'illegals' began turning up and, instead of listening to the lectures, argued with each other and created a disturbance. At a fund-raising evening for the Bund (the General Jewish Workers' Union in Lithuania, Poland and Russia) there was an uproar, and the mayor of Moscow, A. A. Kozlov, banned the crowded meetings. They continued on a more intimate scale.
8. Stepan Fortunatov (1850–1918), historian and publicist.
9. Ekaterina Breshko-Breshkovskaia (1844–1934) was one of the founders and leaders of the SRs (Socialist Revolutionaries) and their Combat Organization. She spent many years in exile, and did not accept the legitimacy of the Soviet regime.
10. The All-Russian Congress of Zemstvo Representatives was held in the Morozov mansion on Smolensk Boulevard. Margarita Morozova appealed to A. A. Kozlov, whom she considered her guardian, and the mayor granted permission for it.
11. Fedor Stepun, *Byvshee i nesbyvsheesia* [The Past, and a Future that Never Came] (Moscow: Aleteya, 1995), pp. 198–204.
12. Andrei Belyi, *Nachalo veka. Vospominaniia* [How the Century Began. Memories], vol. 2 (Moscow: Khudozhestvennaia literatura, 1990), p. 504.
13. A. V. Lavrov and John Malmstad, eds, *'Vash rytsar''. Andrei Belyi. Pis'ma k M.K. Morozovoy. 1901–1928* ['Your Knight.' Andrey Bely. Letters to M. K. Morozova. 1901–1928] (Moscow: Progress-Pleiada, 2006), p. 117. At that time Andrei Belyi, who had become a follower of Rudolf Steiner, was living in Dornach, an 'anthroposophical citadel near Basel'.
14. Manuscript Department of the Russian State Library, *fond* 171, *k.* 3, *ed. khr.* 18, *list* 1, 1 *ob.* The declaration was accompanied by a list of paintings M. K. Morozova was retaining for her lifetime (*listy* 4–6). First published in *Na blago prosveshcheniia*, vol. 2, p. 342. See also *Gosudarstvennaia Tret'iakovskaia galereia. Ocherki istorii. 1856–1917* [The State Tret'iakov Gallery: Essays on Its History, 1856–1917] (Leningrad: Khudozhnik RSFSR, 1981), pp. 212–13, illustrations. An initial estimate suggests the value of the collection of foreign painters donated to the gallery was some 185,000 francs, and of Russian painters, 51,000 rubles.
15. Morozova, *Moi vospominaniia*, p. 94.
16. Ibid.
17. Sergei Tret'iakov (1834–92). Access to his collection of West European paintings of the mid-nineteenth century was, from 1881, open to anyone 'on recommendation'. In 1892 his collection of eighty-four works was merged with his brother's gallery of Russian artists and named 'The Municipal Art Gallery of Pavel and Sergei Mikhailovich Tret'iakov'.
18. Letter from I. S. Ostroukhov to Baron N. N. Wrangel, dated 6/19 June 1911. Manuscript Department of the Tret'iakov Gallery, *fond* 10, *ed. khr.* 136.

19. Evgenii Trubetskoi (1863–1920), Orthodox philosopher, legal scholar and public figure. Author of *Voina i mirovaia zadacha Rossii* [The War and Russia's Global Mission], *Rossiia v ee ikone* [Russia in its Icon], *Umozrenie v kraskakh* [Philosophical Speculation in Paint], etc.

20. "'Nasha liubov' nuzhna Rossii . . .". Perepiska E. N. Trubetskogo i M. K. Morozovoi' ['Russia Needs Our Love . . .': the Correspondence of E. N. Trubetskoi and M. K. Morozova], ed. A. A. Nosov, *Novyi mir*, no. 9, 1993, pp. 172–229; no. 10, 1993, pp. 174–215.

21. V. I. Keidan, ed., *Vzyskuiushchie grada: khronika russkoi religiozno-filosofskoi i obshchestvennoi zhizni pervoi chetverti XX veka v pis'makh i dnevnikakh sovremennikov* [Seekers After the City: A Chronicle of Russian Religious, Philosophical and Social Life in the First Quarter of the Twentieth Century in the Letters and Diaries of Contemporaries] (Moscow: Shkola 'Iazyki russkoi kul'tury', 1997), pp. 268, 275.

22. The publishing house survived until 1919 and published some fifty volumes, principally on religious and philosophical topics. Margarita Morozova also paid for publication of the journal *Voprosy filosofii i psikhologii* [Issues of Philosophy and Psychology] and the socio-political newspaper *Moskovskii ezhenedel'nik* [Moscow Weekly].

23. Stepun, *Byvshee i nesbyvsheesia*. Morozova was one of the founders and active participants of the Vladimir Solov'ev Memorial Moscow Religious and Philosophical Society, whose members were the major Russian philosophers of the time.

24. Sergei Makovskii (1877–1962), son of the artist Konstantin Makovskii; art critic, editor and publisher of the magazine *Apollon* (1909–17).

25. S. Makovskii, 'Frantsuzskie khudozhniki iz sobraniia I. A. Morozova' [French Artists in the Collection of I. A. Morozov', *Apollon*, nos 3–4, 1912, p. 5. The 'Morozov issue' of *Apollon*, which included a complete catalogue of his paintings by French artists, appeared in spring 1912. Not later than the end of 1913, Morozov twice entered new purchases in his copy of the catalogue, which is today preserved in the Research Library of the Pushkin Museum. See *Katalog kartin frantsuzskikh khudozhnikov iz sobraniia I. A. Morozova v Moskve* [Catalogue of the Paintings by French Artists in the Collection of I. A. Morozov in Moscow], ibid, pp. 18–25.

### Chapter XIII: Elusive Manet

1. On the purchase of *In the Bar 'Le Bouchon'*, see note 40 to Chapter IV. The *Portrait of Antonin Proust* was purchased from Vollard by Ivan Shchukin, the brother of Sergei, who became obsessed with collecting Spanish old masters and sold it to Ilya Ostroukhov for 2,000 francs in 1898.

2. According to Ternovets, *The Lion Hunter*, a huge canvas (150 × 170 cm) by Édouard Manet (1881), was rejected because of the 'artificiality of the general concept'. Ternovets, *Pis'ma*, p. 115.

3. Letter from Igor Grabar to Ivan Morozov, dated 12/25 July 1909. Quoted from Ternovets, *Pis'ma*, p. 115. In the same letter, Grabar writes '*The Turkeys* by Claude Monet (40,000 – the same size as your landscape with flowers [the reference is to *Corner of the Garden at Montgeron*], and *Luncheon* (40,000), also by Monet, are both still available, but both works are inferior to *The Hunter*.'

4. In 1909, Pellerin (on whom see note 14 in Chapter VII), focusing on acquiring works by Cézanne, decided to sell off his dazzling collection of Manet and Impressionists, putting it in the hands of a consortium of leading French and German dealers which included Durand-Ruel, Vollard and Cassirer.

5. Letter from Ambroise Vollard to Ivan Morozov, dated 4 October 1909. Manuscript Department of the Pushkin Museum, *koll.* 12, *razdel* 1, *ed. khr.* 23. Quoted from Ternovets, *Pis'ma*, p. 116. The work, as Vollard emphasized, was undoubtedly 'one of the rarest paintings in Manet's entire oeuvre' and was 'entirely free of the influence of the old masters'.

6. Letter from Valentin Serov to Ivan Morozov, dated 10 December 1909. Quoted from I. S. Zil'bershtein and V. A. Samkov, eds, *Valentin Serov v perepiske, dokumentakh i interv'iu* [Valentin Serov in Correspondence, Documents and Interviews], vol. 2 (Leningrad: Khudozhnik RSFSR, 1989), p. 186.

7. The painting is today in the J. Paul Getty Museum in Los Angeles, California.
8. Hippolyte Lejosne (1814–84), army officer, cousin of the artist Frédéric Bazille, art collector. Manuscript Department of the Pushkin Museum, *koll.* 12, *razdel* 1, *ed. khr.* 67. Letter quoted from Ternovets, *Pisma*, p. 117.
9. Manet presented a version of *Le Déjeuner* (90 × 117 cm) to his friend Hippolyte Lejosne, whose family sold the painting in 1924. In 1928 it was acquired by Samuel Courtauld for £10,000. The large painting (207 × 265 cm) was donated in 1906 to the Louvre, and is now in the Musée d'Orsay.
10. L. V. Rozental, *Neprimechatel'nye dostovernosti* [Unremarkable Truths] (Moscow: Novoe literaturnoe obozrenie, 2010), p. 27.
11. Letter from Sergei Makovskii to Ivan Morozov, dated 8 March 1912. Manuscript Department of the Pushkin Museum, *koll.* 12, *razdel* 1, *ed. khr.* 49. Twenty-one works by Courbet were shown at the exhibition, from both Russian and Paris collections.
12. Constantin Guys (1802–92), French painter and graphic artist.
13. Efros, 'Chelovek s popravkoi', p. 3.
14. This idea was formulated by the St Petersburg art historian Ilya Doronchenkov.
15. L. Vauxcelles, 'Le Salon d'automne', *Gil Blas*, 17 October 1905.

## Chapter XIV: Last Acquisitions

1. Vollard, *Recollections of a Picture Dealer*, p. 99.
2. Pavel Tret'iakov had created the gallery as a museum of Russian art. After his death in 1892, his brother Sergei's collection of West European paintings was merged with it. In his will Pavel Tret'iakov stipulated how the collection should grow, noting specifically that purchasing works by foreign artists was to be avoided.
3. Letter from Igor Ostroukhov to Baron N. N. Wrangel, dated 6/19 June 1911. Manuscript Department of the Tret'iakov Gallery, 10/136.
4. Gertrude Stein (1874–1946), American writer; Leo Stein (1872–1947), her brother.
5. For Picasso's *Young Acrobat with Ball*, *Three Women* and *Nude with Towel*, Gertrude Stein received 20,000 francs and one of Picasso's latest works, *The Old Guitarist*.
6. A Kahnweiler Gallery invoice dated 12 November 1913, for 18,500 francs, has been preserved, of which Morozov paid 16,000 francs for *Young Acrobat with Ball* and 2,500 francs for André Derain's *Tree Trunks*.
7. Clovis Sagot (d. 1913), an art dealer whose gallery was located at 46 rue Laffitte.
8. Vollard, *Recollections of a Picture Dealer*, p. 232.

## Chapter XV: Citizen Morozov

1. Vladimir Ipat'ev (1867–1952) was a Russian-American chemist.
2. A. A. Romanov, 'Razvitie promyshlennogo potentsiala Moskvy i Moskovskoi gubernii v gody pervoi mirovoi voiny' [Development of the Industrial Potential of Moscow and Moscow Province During the First World War]. https://cyberleninka.ru/article/n/razvitie-promyshlennogo-potentsiala-moskvy-i-moskovskoy-gubernii-v-gody-pervoy-mirovoy-voyny (accessed 11 May 2020).
3. S. Glagol', 'Moskovskie khudozhestva (kartinnye vystavki)' [The Moscow Art Scene (Art Exhibitions)], *Russkaia volia*, no. 4 (5 January) 1917.
4. The building is currently occupied by a section of the Administrative Department of the Presidential Administration.
5. Konstantin Paustovsky, *Story of a Life*, 5 vols, trans. Manya Harari and Michael Duncan (London: Harvill, 1967), vol. 2: 'In That Dawn', p. 82.
6. The collection of Aleksey Vikulovich Morozov, containing almost 10,000 items (icons, engravings, silver, miniatures, porcelain) was opened to the public on 4 December 1919 as the Museum and Exhibition of Artistic Antiquities, and later transformed into the Museum of Porcelain. In 1928 the porcelain collection was transferred to the mansion of Sergei

Shchukin, and in 1932 removed to Kuskovo, the former estate of the prince Sheremetev, where it remains to this day. A. V. Morozov died in 1934, having been the reluctant witness of the gradual destruction of his beloved collection, which was dispersed between a number of museums.

7. Morozova, *Vospominaniia*, p. 100. The mansion in Vvedenskii (Podsosenskii) Lane (1869, architect D. N. Chichagov) had been specially adapted to store the collections. Mikhail Vrubel painted panels for the reception room and study, which was designed in a Gothic style by F. P. Shekhtel. The architect I. E. Bondarenko designed an extension to the mansion to house a collection of over 200 icons dating from the thirteenth to the seventeenth centuries.

8. In the 1920s an appropriate use was found for the pantry: it was adapted for the storage of Leo Tolstoy's manuscripts.

9. Pavel Buryshkin claimed that in summer 1917 Morozov packaged his paintings, saying that he was going to move the collection out of Moscow. See P. A. Buryshkin, *Moskva kupecheskaia* [Moscow of the Merchants] (Moscow: Vysshaia shkola, 1991), p. 147. Pavel Buryshkin (1887–1955) was a major Moscow factory owner, descended from a merchant family. In exile he wrote his memoirs, which were first published in New York in 1954.

10. The Iusupovs succeeded in taking out a small quantity of jewellery and a few valuable paintings, including Rembrandt's *Portrait of a Gentleman with a Tall Hat and Gloves* and *Portrait of a Lady with an Ostrich-Feather Fan*, which had been part of the Arkhangelskoye Estate collection. Both paintings were sold in August 1921 and are now in the National Gallery of Art, Washington, D.C.

11. 'Preservation orders' were issued in 1918 to the owners of art and scientific collections. 'Consolidation' (*Uplotnenie*) was the confiscation of 'surplus housing space', generally in favour of people of proletarian social origin, following the decree of 20 August 1918 on 'Abolition of the right of private ownership of accommodation in cities'. It led to the appearance of communal apartments in the USSR.

12. *Vospominaniia L. V. Gol'd. Vesna 1911 goda* [Reminiscences of L. V. Gol'd: Spring 1911], private collection, Moscow. Sergei Konyonkov's rambling monologue was recorded by one of his models from the account of an eyewitness to the episode in the mansion.

13. In 1922 Konyonkov left Soviet Russia, but returned in 1945. Upon his return from America, not only was he not despatched to the forced labour camps and sent far out to the wilds of Russia, but he was awarded the title of People's Artist of the USSR and presented with a very large studio right in the centre of Moscow. Konyonkov owed both the studio and the steamer, chartered by order of Stalin to transport his work, to his wife Margarita, who was 'friends' with Einstein and obtained nuclear secrets at the behest of the NKVD.

14. Paustovsky, *Story of a Life*, p. 36.

15. I. E. Grabar', *Pis'ma: 1917–1941* [Letters: 1917–41], eds N. A. Evsina and T. P. Kazhdan (Moscow: Nauka, 1977), vol. 2, p. 20.

16. The Department for Museums and the Preservation of Works of Art and Antiquities was established within the People's Commissariat for Enlightenment on 28 May 1918. A month earlier, on 27 April, a decree of the Council of People's Commissars was published abolishing the right of inheritance.

17. Oleksa Hryshchenko, *Moï zustrichi i rozmovy z frantsuz'kymy mysttsiamy* [My Encounters and Discussions with French Artists] (New York: O. Hryshchenko Foundation, 1962), p. 83. Oleksa Hryshchenko (1883–1977), Ukrainian artist.

18. The reference is to *Chelovek s ruzh'em* [Man with a Gun], 1938, dir. Sergei Iutkevich.

19. Fragments from the diary and memoirs of the painter T. A. Lebedeva (1906–80) were published in: 'T. A. Lebedeva, "Kartiny i khudozhniki. Nabroski vospominanii"' [Paintings and Painters. Sketches for Memoirs], publ. Iu. A. Molok, *Panorama iskusstv*, o. 5 (Moscow: Sovetskii khudozhnik, 1982), pp. 186–7.

20. Heinrich Wölfflin (1864–1945), Swiss theorist and art historian.

21. Vera Mukhina (1889–1953), sculptor. Her sculptural group *The Worker and Collective Farm Woman* crowned the Soviet pavilion at the 1937 World Exhibition in Paris and became a symbol of the USSR.

## Chapter XVI: Emigration

1. Muir and Merrilees was the largest department store in Moscow in the early twentieth century. It is now the Central Department Store (TsUM).
2. Ternovets, *Pis'ma*, p. 123.
3. It was intended that Museums of Painting (Muzei zhivopisnoi kul'ltury), unlike any other museum in the world, should bring together Russian and Western exhibits. Such a museum was organized in 1919 in Moscow (from 1924 it was a branch of the State Tret'iakov Gallery and it was abolished in December 1928); and in Petrograd (abolished in 1926).
4. Ternovets, *Pis'ma*, p. 123.
5. The physicist and philosopher Sergei Khoruzhii coined the term 'a steamship for philosophers' for the campaign to deport independently minded intellectuals from Soviet Russia or exile them to remote regions.
6. Diary of Nicholas Isnard (1851–1932), an engineer and public figure. See 'The Nicholas Isnard Diaries and Correspondence', Bakhmeteff Archive, Rare Book and Manuscript Library, Columbia University. I am grateful to Tat'iana Chebotareva, curator of the archive, who acquainted me with these documents.
7. Ibid.
8. Varentsov, *Slyshannoe. Vidennoe. Peredumannoe. Perezhitoe*, p. 680.
9. Nikolai Varentsov (1862–1947), director of the Moscow Trade and Industry Company and chairman of the board of the Great Kineshma Manufacturing Company. In 1918 he was arrested, but released thanks to the workers of his former factory. He got by on casual earnings but lost his entire family. His memoirs were written in the 1930s. Fragments were published in *Nashe nasledie*, nos 43–4, 1997, published as a book in 1999.
10. This 'fact', with a reference to N. A. Varentsov's memoir, is repeated in the introduction to the catalogue raisonné of the Pushkin Museum. See *Gosudarstvennyi muzei izobrazitel'nykh iskusstv imeni A.S. Pushkina, Frantsiia. Vtoraia polovina XIX veka–XX vek: Sobranie zhivopisi. Katalog* [A. S. Pushkin State Museum of Fine Arts, 'France: The Second Half of the Nineteenth Century–Twentieth Century: Collection of paintings'. Catalogue] (Moscow: Krasnaia Ploshchad', 2005), p. 12.
11. Archive of Pierre Konowaloff, Paris.
12. The death certificate was discovered by the family of the great-grandson of I. A. Morozov. They also managed to find the last will and testament of his great-grandfather in the archives.
13. B. N. Ternovets got the date of death wrong, writing 22 June instead of 22 July. This error was then regularly repeated. He did, however, indicate the place of death correctly as Carlsbad (Karlovy Vary). The issue of *Sredi kollektsionerov* appeared in November 1921.

## Chapter XVII: The Palace on Kropotkin Street

1. The Moscow Offloading Commission was created in January 1921 in connection with the redeployment of institutions and enterprises from Petrograd to Moscow and the removal of surplus institutions from the new capital.
2. According to the inventory, the Russian part of the collection comprised 318 items, including six sculptures.
3. Manuscript Department of the Tret'iakov Gallery, *fond* 8 / IV, *opis'* 1, *ed. khr.* 50. *list* 46. The paintings by Russian artists remained in the Tret'iakov Gallery, while the foreign masterpieces were moved in 1925 back to the former mansion of Ivan Morozov, which was now the Second (Morozov) Section of the Museum of New Western Art.
4. Efros, 'Chelovek s popravkoi', p. 3.
5. Vinogradov, *Vospominaniia*, p. 116.
6. Oleksa Hryshchenko, *Moï zustrichi i rozmovy z frantsuz'kymy mysttsiamy* [My Encounters and Discussions with French Artists] (New York: O. Hryshchenko Foundation, 1962), p. 42.

7. Letter from I. S. Ostroukhov to A. P. Botkina, dated 6 January 1905. Tret'iakov Gallery, *fond* 48, *ed. khr.* 379.
8. Efros, 'Chelovek s popravkoi', p. 3.
9. Ia. Tugendkhol'd, 'Novyi talant' [A New Talent], *Russkie vedomosti*, no. 71 (29 March) 1915.
10. David Burliuk, *Filonov. Povest'* [Filonov. A Tale] (Moscow: Gileia, 2017), pp. 82–3.
11. Mikhail Larionov's *Ugolok provintsii (Etiud dvora)* [A Provincial Nook (Study of a Courtyard)] (1907) was stolen from the dacha of his cousin, Alexei Vikulovich Morozov, in Polushkino, Moscow province, in summer 1918.
12. Ia. Tugendkhol'd, 'Mark Shagal' [Marc Chagall], *Apollon*, no. 2, 1916, p. 20. *Parikmakherskaia* [The Barber's Shop] (1914).
13. Iakov Kagan-Shabshai (1877–1939). For further information, see Ia. Bruk, *Iakov Kagan-Shabshai i ego Evreiskaia khudozhestvennaia galereia* [Iakov Kagan-Shabshai and his Jewish Art Gallery] (Moscow: Tri kvadrata, 2015).
14. Tugendkhol'd, 'Mark Shagal', p. 20.
15. A. Benua [Alexander Benois], 'Dnevnik khudozhnika' [An Artist's Diary], *Rech'*, 21 October 1913.
16. Efros, 'Chelovek s popravkoi', p. 4.
17. According to the GMNZI report for 1922–3, the French section of the Morozov Department by then consisted of 252 items: 202 paintings, 39 sculptures and 11 ceramic works.
18. Manuscript Department of the Pushkin Museum, *fond* 13, *opis'* 1, *ed. khr.* 127. Typescript. Extract from Minutes No. 20 of the meeting of the Academic Council of GMNZI, 5 November 1925. Communication by B. N. Ternovets regarding transference to the Tret'iakov Gallery of the Russian painting collection from the Second Section of the Museum. Request to the Museums Department to leave the paintings of Marc Chagall in the Museum of New Western Art.
19. See M. B. Aksenenko, 'Kak zakryvali Sezanna i Matissa' [Hiding Away Cézanne and Matisse], *Mir muzeia*, nos 6–7, 1998, pp. 42–8.
20. Magnitostroi, the Magnitogorsk Iron and Steel Works in Siberia, one of the largest construction projects of the First Five-Year Plan.
21. The first batch of paintings sent to the Hermitage was the largest, comprising forty-three works. There were slightly fewer in the second batch – thirty-six. One might have imagined the Hermitage would have greeted such an influx of works with delight and gratitude, but that was far from the case. GMNZI was accused of supplying 'low-quality' paintings. The Muscovites parted with Morozov's paintings *Bank of the Pond at Montgeron* and *Waterloo Bridge* by Monet, Renoir's *Girl with a Fan*, Marquet's *Louvre Embankment and the New Bridge* and *Rainy Day in Paris*, *Vase with Two Handles* (*Bouquet*) by Matisse, Bonnard's *Landscape with Goods Train* and Gauguin's *Sacred Spring, Sweet Dreams*. All these paintings the Hermitage dismissed as second-rate.

### Chapter XVIII: The End of the Museum

1. Nina Iavorskaia (1902–92) was an art critic, museum specialist and from 1923 until 1948 worked at GMNZI.
2. N. V. Iavorskaia, *Istoriia Gosudarstvennogo muzeia novogo zapadnogo iskusstva (Moskva) 1918–1948* [A History of the State Museum of New Western Art, Moscow, 1918–48] (Moscow: State Pushkin Museum, 2012), p. 395.
3. M. Belkina, *Skreshchenie sudeb* [A Crossing of Destinies] (Moscow: Kniga, 1988), pp. 289–90.
4. From 1932 until 1991 a special institute for registering a place of abode existed in the USSR. All those living in cities who had internal passports (peasants did not have even these) were required to have a residence permit (*propiska*). In major cities, and especially in Moscow and Leningrad, obtaining such a permit was extremely difficult.

5. 'Pis'ma A. K. Gladkova k bratu' [Letters of A. K. Gladkov to his brother], *Vstrechi s proshlym* (Moscow), issue 4, 1982, p. 412.

6. The Museum of Oriental Cultures (State Museum of the East) was situated in the former church of Elijah the Prophet on Vorontsov Field Street (from 1935 to 1992, called Obukh Street), where it now has its storage depository and restoration workshops.

7. Iavorskaia, *Istoriia Gosudarstvennogo muzeia*, pp. 408–10.

8. In its broad sense, 'formalism' is an artist's giving priority to form over subject matter. From the late 1920s, however, when theme and subject matter were given priority during the period of Socialist Realism, which dominated Soviet art in the 1930s, the term acquired a negative connotation. Artists for whom context and content were less important than the formal aspects of colour, line, texture, and so on, were publicly condemned. Until the early 1960s, all artists whose practice did not conform to the official doctrine were branded 'Formalists'.

9. The 'anti-cosmopolitan' campaign conducted in the USSR between 1948 and 1953 targeted individual members of the intelligentsia who adhered to Western trends. It had, among other things, strong overtones of anti-Semitism.

10. State Archive of the Russian Federation, *fond Soveta Ministrov*, R-5446, *opis'* 1, *delo* 327. The decree is published in full in Iavorskaia, *Istoriia Gosudarstvennogo muzeia*, pp. 430–1.

11. Gerasimov immortalized 'The First Red Officer' in a famous painting of *J. V. Stalin and K. E. Voroshilov in the Kremlin* (1938).

12. Memoirs of A.A. Labas, Archive of O. M. Beskina-Labas, Moscow.

13. Polikarp Lebedev (1904–81), from 1938 to 1941 and 1954 to 1979 director of the Tret'iakov Gallery. Petr Sysoev (1906–89), between 1958 and 1988 academic secretary of the Presidium of the Academy of Arts.

14. From 13 to 20 March 1948, 635 paintings, 122 sculptures, 23 ceramics, 1 tapestry, 5,006 drawings and 2,273 reproductions were transferred to the premises of the Pushkin Museum.

15. N. Iavorskaia, 'Rasskaz ochevidtsa o tom, kak byl zakryt Muzei novogo zapadnogo iskusstva' [An Eyewitness Account of the Shutting Down of the Museum of New Western Art], *Dekorativnoe iskusstvo SSSR*, no. 7, 1988, pp. 12–13.

16. All thirty-seven staff of the GMNZI were made redundant. The Pushkin Museum was allowed to take on only 'specialist personnel, five items'.

17. Iavorskaia, *Istoriia Gosudarstvennogo muzeia*, p. 426.

18. Andrei Chegodaev (1905–94), art historian. Between 1945 and 1950 he was the head curator of the collection of paintings and sculptures of the Dresden Gallery, which had been removed from Germany and housed in the premises of the Pushkin Museum.

19. Manuscript Department of the Tret'iakov Gallery, *fond* 236, *opis'* 1, *ed. khr.* 17, *list* 66. Between 1944 and 1949 Alexander Lopukhin (1897–1985) was the principal artist of the Pushkin Museum. His diary, discovered in the Manuscript Department of the Tret'iakov Gallery by Nataliia Aleksandrova, senior researcher at the Pushkin Museum's manuscript department, who kindly shared the document with me, remains the sole documentation of the process of dividing up the collection.

20. Manuscript Department of the Tret'iakov Gallery, *listy* 66 *ob.*–67.

# SELECT BIBLIOGRAPHY

Bacou, Roseline, 'Paul Gauguin et Gustave Fayet', *Actes du colloque Gauguin 11–13 janvier 1989* (École du Louvre, Paris, Documentation française: 1989).

Barskaia, Anna G. and Kostenevich, Albert G., *French Painting: Mid-Nineteenth to Twentieth Centuries (the Hermitage Catalogue of Western European Painting, vol. 12)* (Moscow: Iskusstvo/Florence: Giunti, 1991).

Denis, Maurice, *Journal*, vol. 2: 1905–1920 (Paris: Éditions du Vieux Colombier), 1957.

Fénéon, Félix, 'Les grands collectionneurs. III. M. Ivan Morosoff', *Le Bulletin de la vie artistique* (Paris: Galerie Bernheim-Jeune), vol. 1, no. 12 (15 May 1920), pp. 326–32.

Havemeyer, Louisine W., *Sixteen to Sixty: Memoirs of a Collector*, eds Susan Stein and Gary Tinterow (New York: Ursus Press, 1993).

Kean, Beverly W., *All the Empty Palaces: The Merchant Patrons of Modern Art in Pre-Revolutionary Russia* (New York: Universe, 1983).

Kostenevich, Albert, Semenova, Natalya, *Collecting Matisse* (Paris: Flammarion, 1993).

Meyerson, Åke, 'Van Gogh and the School of Pont-Aven', *Konsthistorisk Tidskrift/Journal of Art History*, Stockholm, issue 3–4, vol. 15 (1946), pp. 135–49.

Rewald, John, *The History of Impressionism* (New York: Museum of Modern Art, 1946).

—, *Post-Impressionism, from Van Gogh to Gauguin* (New York: Museum of Modern Art, 1956).

Semyonova, Natalya and Iljine, Nicolas V., *Selling Russia's Treasures: The Soviet Trade in Nationalized Art, 1917–1938* (New York: Abbeville, 2014).

Spurling, Hilary, *The Unknown Matisse. A Life of Henri Matisse*, vol. 1: 1869–1908 (New York: Knopf, 1998).

—, *Matisse the Master. A Life of Henri Matisse*, vol. 2: 'The Conquest of Colour, 1909–1954' (London: Hamish Hamilton, 2005).

Venturi, Lionello, *De Manet à Lautrec* (Paris: Albin Michel, 1953).

Vollard, Ambroise, *Recollections of a Picture Dealer*, trans. Violet M. Macdonald (Mineola, New York: Dover, 2002).

Weitzenhoffer, Frances, *The Havemeyers: Impressionism Comes to America* (New York: Abrams, 1986).

# SELECT BIBLIOGRAPHY

## In Russian

Aksenenko, M. B., 'Istoriia Gosudarstvennogo muzeia novogo zapadnogo iskusstva', *Muzei 3, Khudozhestvennye sobraniia SSSR* [History of the State Museum of New Western Art: Museum 3, Art Collections of the USSR] (Moscow, 1982), pp. 216–25.

—, 'Monumental'nyi ansambl' M. Deni i A. Maiolia v moskovskom osobniake I. A. Morozova' [The Monumental Ensemble of M. Denis and A. Maillol in the Moscow Mansion of I. A. Morozov], *Sovetskoe iskusstvoznanie*, issue 27, 1991, pp. 423–48.

—, 'Kak zakryvali Sezanna i Matissa' [Hiding Away Cézanne and Matisse], *Mir muzeia*, nos 6–7, 1998, pp. 42–8.

Bakhrushin, Iu. A., *Vospominaniia* [Memoirs] (Moscow: Khudozhestvennaia literatura, 1994).

Belyi, A., *Nachalo veka. Vospominaniia* [How the Century Began. Memories], vol. 2 (Moscow: Khudozhestvennaia literatura, 1990).

—, 'Vash rytsar'': *Pis'ma k M. K. Morozovoi. 1901–1928* ['Your Knight': Letters to M. K. Morozova, 1901–1928], eds A. V. Lavrov and John Malmstad (Moscow: Progress-Pleiada, 2006).

Benua, A. N. [Alexander Benois], *Moi vospominaniia* [My Memories], eds N. I. Aleksandrova et al., 5 vols (Moscow: Nauka 1990).

Bernar E. [Émile Bernard], *Pol' Sezann, ego neizdannye pis'ma i vospominaniia o nem* [Paul Cézanne, His Unpublished Letters and Reminiscences About Him], trans. P. P. Konchalovskii (Moscow: Grosman and Vendel'shtein, 1912).

Bondarenko, I. E., 'Zapiski kollektsionera' [Jottings of a Collector], *Pamiatniki Otechestva* [Historic Artefacts of the Fatherland], no. 29, 1993.

Buryshkin, P. A., *Moskva kupecheskaia* [Moscow of the Merchants] (Moscow: Vysshaia shkola, 1991).

Bychkov, Iu. A., *Konenkov* (Moscow: Molodaia gvardiia, 1982).

Demskaia, A. A. and Semenova, N. Iu, *U Shchukina, na Znamenke . . .* [With Shchukin on Znamensky Lane] (Moscow: Stolichnyi Bank, 1993).

Diagilev, S. P., 'M. A. Morozov. Nekrolog' [M. A. Morozov. An Obituary] *Mir iskusstva* [World of Art], no. 9, 1903, p. 141.

—, *Sergei Diagilev i russkoe iskusstvo* [Sergei Diaghilev and Russian Art], eds I. S. Zil'bershtein and V. A. Samkov, 2 vols (Moscow: Izobrazitel'noe iskusstvo, 1982).

Dumova, N. G., *Moskovskie metsenaty* [Moscow Patrons of the Arts] (Moscow: Molodaia gvardiia, 1992).

Efros, A. M., 'Chelovek s popravkoi. Pamiati I. A. Morozova' [The Man Who Tweaked. In Memoriam, I. A. Morozov], *Sredi kollektsionerov*, no. 10, 1920, pp. 1–4.

Ernst, S., *K. A. Somov* (St Petersburg: Obshchina Sv. Evgenii, 1918).

—, *Dva veka russkogo iskusstva* [Two Centuries of Russian Art] (Moscow: Iskusstvo, 1969).

—, *Profili* [Profiles] (Moscow: Federatsiia, 1930).

Ettinger, P. D., *Stat'i. Iz perepiski. Vospominaniia sovremennikov* [Articles. From Correspondence. Reminiscences by Contemporaries], eds A. A. Demskaia and N. Iu. Semenova (Moscow: Sovetskii khudozhnik, 1989).

Filatkina, N. and Drozdov, M. S., *Morozovy: Dinastiia fabrikantov i metsenatov: Opyt rodosloviia* [The Morozovs, a Dynasty of Manufacturers and Philanthropists: An Attempt at a Genealogy] (Noginsk [Bogorodsk], 1995).

Georgievskaia, E. B., 'Moris Deni v Rossii' [Maurice Denis in Russia], *Vvedenie v khram*, ed. L. I. Akimova (Moscow: Iazyki russkoi kul'tury, 1997), pp. 441–56.

Gogen, P. [Paul Gauguin], *Pis'ma. Noa Noa. Iz knigi 'Prezhde i potom'* [Letters. Noa Noa. From Before and After] (Moscow: Iskusstvo, 1972).

—, *Vzgliad iz Rossii: Al'bom-katalog* [The View from Russia: An Illustrated Catalogue] (Moscow: Sovetskii khudozhnik, 1989).

Golovin, A. Ia., *Vstrechi i vpechatleniia* [Meetings and Impressions], ed. E. F. Gollerbakh (Leningrad–Moscow: Iskusstvo, 1940).

*Gosudarstvennaia Tret'iakovskaia galereia: Ocherki istorii. 1856–1917* [State Tretyakov Gallery: Essays on its History, 1856–1917] (Leningrad: Khudozhnik RSFSR, 1981).

# SELECT BIBLIOGRAPHY

*Gosudarstvennyi muzei izobrazitel'nykh iskusstv imeni A. S. Pushkina: Frantsiia vtoroi poloviny XIX–XX veka: Sobranie zhivopisi: Katalog* [Pushkin State Museum of Fine Arts: France. The Second Half of the Nineteenth and the Twentieth Centuries: The Collection of Paintings, Catalogue], 2 vols (Moscow: Krasnaia Ploshchad', 2005).

Grabar', I. E., *Pis'ma: 1917–1941* [Letters: 1917–41], eds N. A. Evsina and T. P. Kazhdan (Moscow: Nauka, 1974).

—, *Moia zhizn': Avtomonografiia. Etiudy o khudozhnikakh* [My Life: An Auto-monograph: Studies of Artists] (Moscow: Respublika, 2001).

Gumilev, N., 'Dva Salona' [Two Salons], *Vesy*, no. 5, 1908, pp. 103–5.

Iavorskaia, N. V., 'Rasskaz ochevidtsa o tom, kak byl zakryt Muzei novogo zapadnogo iskusstva' [An Eyewitness Account of the Shutting Down of the Museum of New Western Art], *Dekorativnoe iskusstvo SSSR*, no. 7, 1988, pp. 12–13.

—, *Istoriia Gosudarstvennogo muzeia novogo zapadnogo iskusstva (Moskva). 1918–1948* [A History of the State Museum of New Western Art, Moscow, 1918–48] (Moscow: State Pushkin Museum, 2012).

Konenkov, S. T., *Moi vek. Vospominaniia* [My Times. Memoirs] (Moscow: Politizdat, 1988).

Korovin, K., *Konstantin Korovin vspominaet . . .* [Konstantin Korovin Reminisces . . .], eds I. S. Zil'bershtein and V. A. Samkov (Moscow: Izobrazitel'noe iskusstvo, 1990).

Kostenevich A. G., *Iskusstvo Frantsii 1860–1950. Zhivopis'. Risunok. Skul'ptura* [French Art, 1860–1950: Painting, Drawing, Sculpture], 2 vols (St Petersburg: Gosudarstvennyi Ermitazh, 2008).

Kostenevich, A. G. and Semenova, N. Iu., *Collecting Matisse* (Paris: Flammarion, 1993).

Kovalevskii, M. M., *Moia zhizn': Vospominaniia* [My Life: Memoirs] (Moscow: RossPen, 2005).

Lapshin, V. P., *Soiuz russkikh khudozhnikov* [The Union of Russian Artists] (Leningrad: Khudozhnik RSFSR, 1974).

Lebedeva, T. A., *Kartiny i khudozhniki: Nabroski vospominanii* [Paintings and Artists: Draft Memoirs], eds L. P. Zusman and Iu. A. Molok, *Panorama iskusstv*, no. 5, 1982.

Makovskii, S. K., 'Frantsuzskie khudozhniki iz sobraniia I.A. Morozova' [French Artists in the Collection of I. A. Morozov], *Apollon*, nos 3–4, 1912, pp. 5–34.

—, *Stranitsy khudozhestvennoi kritiki* [Some Pages of Art Criticism], 3 vols (St Petersburg: Panteon-Apollon, 1909–13).

*Morozov i Shchukin — russkie kollektsionery: Ot Mone do Pikasso* [Morozov and Shchukin — Russian Art Collectors: From Monet to Picasso], exhibition catalogue (Cologne: DuMont, 1993).

Morozova, Margarita Kirillovna, 'Moi vospominaniia: Chetyre epokhi odnoi zhizni' [My Memories: Four Eras of a Life], postface by N. Iu. Semenova, *Nashe nasledie*, no. 6, 1991.

Morozova, Varvara Alekseevna, *Na blago prosveshcheniia Moskvy* [For the Enlightenment of Moscow], eds N. A. Kruglianskaia and V. N. Aseyev (Moscow: Russkii put', 2008).

*Moskovskii al'bom: Vospominaniia o Moskve i moskvichakh XIX–XX vekov* [A Moscow Album: Memories of Moscow and Muscovites of the Nineteenth–Twentieth Centuries] (Moscow: Nashe nasledie, 1997).

Muratov, P., 'Staroe i molodoe na poslednikh vystavkakh' [The Old and the Young at the Latest Exhibitions], *Zolotoe Runo*, no. 1, 1908, pp. 87–90.

Nashchokina, M. V., ed., *Zapiski khudozhnika-arkhitektora. Trudy, vstrechi, vpechatleniia*, vol. 2 (Moscow: Progress-traditsiia, 2018).

Nesterov, M. V., *Vospominaniia* [Memoirs], ed. A.A. Rusakova (Moscow: Sovetskii khudozhnik, 1985).

—, *Davnie dni. Vstrechi i vospominaniia* [Days of Long Ago: Meetings and Memories], ed. T. F. Prokopov (Moscow: Russkaia kniga, 2005).

Perepletchikov, V. V., *Dnevnik khudozhnika. Ocherki. 1886–1915* [An Artist's Diary. Essays, 1886–1915] (Moscow: Soyuzdezign, 2012).

Polenova, N. V., 'Otryvki iz vospominanii' [Extracts from Memoirs], *Panorama iskusstv*, no. 10, 1987, pp. 168–94.

# SELECT BIBLIOGRAPHY

Polunina, N. and Frolov, A., *Kollektsionery staroi Moskvy: Illiustrirovannyi biograficheskii slovar'* [Art Collectors of Old Moscow: An Illustrated Biographical Dictionary] (Moscow: Nezavisimaia gazeta, 1997).

R[akshan]in, N., 'Iz obydennoi zhizni' [From Everyday Life], *Moskovskii listok*, no. 286 (14 October), 1903.

Semenova, N. Iu., 'Levyi muzei' [A Left Museum], *Ermitazh*, no. 2, 2006.

—, 'Sobranie Morozova. Analiz tsen' [The Morozov Collection: A Price Analysis], *Antiq.info* (St Petersburg), no. 46 (November 2006).

—, *Zhizn' i kollektsiia Ivana Morozova* [The Life and Collection of Ivan Morozov]. Unpublished manuscript (Moscow, 2007).

—, *Moskovskie kollektsionery: S. I. Shchukin, I. A. Morozov, I. S. Ostroukhov. Tri sud'by, tri istorii uvlechenii* [The Moscow Art Collectors S. I. Shchukin, I. A. Morozov, and I. S. Ostroukhov. Three Fates, Three Tales of a Passion] (Moscow: Molodaia gvardiia, 2010, 2018).

Serov, V., *Valentin Serov v perepiske, dokumentakh i interv'iu* [Valentin Serov in Correspondence, Documents and Interviews], eds I. S. Zil'bershtein and V. A. Samkov, 2 vols (Leningrad: Khudozhnik RSFSR, 1989).

Sezann, P. [Paul Cézanne], *Perepiska. Vospominaniia sovremennikov* [Correspondence. Reminiscences by Contemporaries], ed. N. V. Iavorskaia (Moscow: Iskusstvo, 1972).

Shagal, M. Z., *Moia zhizn'* [My Life] (Moscow: Ellis Lak, 1994).

Shcherbatov, S. A., *Khudozhnik v ushedshei Rossii* [An Artist in a Bygone Russia] (Moscow: Soglasie, 2000).

Stepun, Fedor, *Byvshee i nesbyvsheesia* [The Past, and a Future that Never Came] (Moscow: Aleteya, 1995).

Sternin, G. Iu., *Russkaia khudozhestvennaia kul'tura vtoroi poloviny XIX–nachala XX veka* [Russian Artistic Culture of the Second Half of the Nineteenth–Early Twentieth Centuries] (Moscow: Sovetskii khudozhnik, 1984).

—, *Khudozhestvennaia zhizn' Rossii 1900–1910-kh godov* [The Artistic Life of Russia in the 1900–1910s] (Moscow: Iskusstvo, 1988).

Ternovets, B. N., 'Sobirateli i antikvary proshlogo' [Art Collectors and Antiquarians of the Past], *Sredi kollektsionerov*, no. 10, 1921, pp. 38–41.

—, 'Frantsuzskaia skul'ptura v Moskve' [French Sculpture in Moscow], *Sredi kollektsionerov*, no. 10, 1922.

—, *Pis'ma. Dnevniki. Stat'i* [Letters. Diaries. Articles], eds L. S. Aleshina and N. V. Iavorskaia (Moscow: Sovetskii khudozhnik, 1977).

Tugendkhol'd, Ia., *Peizazh vo frantsuzskoi zhivopisi* [The Landscape in French Painting] (St Petersburg: Sirius, 1911).

—, 'Novyi talant' [A New Talent], *Russkie vedomosti*, 29 March 1915.

Van Gog, V. [Vincent van Gogh], *Pis'ma* [Letters] (Leningrad–Moscow: Iskusstvo, 1966).

Verkharn, Emil' [Émile Verhaeren], 'Moskovskie vospominaniia' [Moscow Memories], *Russkie vedomosti*, nos 3, 5, 1914.

Vinogradov, S. A., *Prezhniaia Moskva: Vospominaniia* [Bygone Moscow: Memories], ed. N. I. Lapidus (Riga: MultiCentrs, 2001).

Voloshin, M. A., *Surikov* (Leningrad: Khudozhnik RSFSR, 1985).

—, *Liki tvorchestva* [Aspects of Creativity], eds V. A. Manuilov et al. (Leningrad: Nauka, 1988).

# ACKNOWLEDGEMENTS

I have always wanted to dedicate one of my books to the artist Vladimir Domogatsky. The conversations I had with him remain among the most enduring memories of my life.

Alexandra Demskaya, the first person to take on the task of reconstructing the lives of Moscow's wonderful art collectors, and with whom I collaborated for many years, is invariably at the top of my list of acknowledgements.

I have been given invaluable help while working on the biography of the art-collecting Morozovs by my colleagues, the art historians Vladimir Polyakov and Yakov Brooke. Without the wise counsel of Tanya Chebotarev, who has read the manuscript more than once in faraway New York, of director Tanya Rakhmanova in Paris, who suggested some interesting compositional adjustments, and of Elena Lavanant, also in Paris, who checked the French texts quoted in the book, I could never have coped with the challenge I was facing.

I thank Mikhail Zolotarev, the historian of photography, who self-lessly shared his treasures with me; as well as historians Galina Ulyanova,

Souria Sadekova and Alla Listsyna, whose tweaks have enhanced the text; my editor Elena Mirskaya; and my agent, Alexander Klimin.

Without the aid of Tatiana and Sergei Razdobudko in Zurich, I would never have been able to find documents crucial for recreating the history of Ivan Morozov's studies in Switzerland.

The assistance of André-Marc Delocque-Fourcaud, Sergei Shchukin's grandson, and his wife Cristine, has been invaluable. The support of the Shchukin Foundation helped me to work in the Vollard and Durand-Ruel archives in Paris, where Flavie and Paul-Louis Durand-Ruel were most helpful.

I owe a debt of gratitude to the staff of the research library of the Tretyakov Gallery and of the Pushkin Museum, and to the archive staff of these institutions. Especial thanks to Natalya Alexandrova, a specialist working in the Pushkin Museum Manuscript Department, who responded obligingly to all requests and invariably helped in the quest for documents. It was in that archive, where I worked in my younger years, that Alexandra Demskaya passed on to me the enthusiasm which, forty years later, has resulted in this book.

Thank you to my dear friends, Lyuba and Richard Wallis, Olga and Ivor Mazure, and Masha and Andrei Ulyanov, who all these years have given me the support of their friendship.

I take this opportunity to express my endless gratitude to Arch Tait, who has brilliantly translated this book into English, and to the amazing team at Yale University Press, especially to my editor Julian Loose, and to Katie Urquhart for her work on coordinating the images.

The fact that I have been able to devote so many years to researching the history of the collections and the fate of the Morozov brothers is a debt I owe to my family and friends, to my sister, Elena Sigareva, who created the environment needed for the work, and to my son, Mitya Raev.

# INDEX

# INDEX

# INDEX

# INDEX

# INDEX

Moreau, Gustave 92, 140, 142
Moret, Henry 127
Morgan, J. P. 174
Morozov, Abram Abramovich 7, 9, 10–12,
  16–21, 24, 27, 51, 178, 229n17, n18
  (Ch. II), 231n15 (Ch. IV)
Morozov, Abram Savvich 10, 12, 229n12
  (Ch. I)
Morozov, Alexei Vikulovich 58, 114, 120,
  121, 178–80, 192, 242n6 (Ch. XV),
  244n11 (Ch. XVII)
Morozov, Arseny Abramovich 7, 20, 30, 69,
  72, 87, 126, 146–51, 178–80, 231n15
  (Ch. IV), 240n2, n4 (Ch. XII)
Morozov, David Abramovich 10, 12, 73, 74,
  229n15 (Ch. I)
Morozov, Elisei Savvich 10, 229n12 (Ch. I),
  231n14 (Ch. IV)
Morozov, Gleb 27, 118
Morozov, Ivan Abramovich xi–xiii, 1, 2, 6, 7,
  10–12, 15, 16, 20, 22, 23, 27, 29, 30, 35,
  40, 42, 52, 54, 57, 61, 69, 70–85, 87, 88,
  91–8, 101–9, 113, 114, 116–23, 126–8,
  132–4, 137–41, 144–6, 152, 158, 161,
  166–70, 172–9, 181–4, 186, 189, 191–3,
  196–200, 202–14, 216, 218, 219, 223,
  225, 227, 230n10 (Ch. III), 231n15, n21,
  33 (Ch. IV), 232n1 (Ch. V), 235n15
  (Ch. VII), 235n2, n5, n9 (Ch. VIII),
  236n2 (Ch. IX), 237n13, 238 n28, n32
  (Ch. XI), 238n1; 239n12, n14, n15, n19,
  n21, n23, n24, n29 (Ch. X), 240n4, n6
  (Ch. XII), 241n3, n5, n6, 242n11 (Ch.
  XIII), 244n3 (Ch. XVII)
Morozov, Ivan Savvich 229n12 (Ch. I)
Morozov, Ivan Vikulovich 121
Morozov, Ivan Zakharovich 9
Morozov, Mikhail Abramovich xii, 5, 7, 17,
  20, 29–31, 33–59, 61–71, 73, 75–80, 84,
  87, 88, 94, 95, 104, 16, 110, 121, 122,
  127, 129, 132, 141, 146, 151, 152, 154,
  156, 158, 159, 162, 168, 178, 203, 204,
  228n10 (Ch. I), 230n6, n7, n10 (Ch. III),
  231n13, n15, n17, n27, n33, n38 (Ch.
  IV), 235n4 (Ch. VIII)
Morozov, Mikhail (Mika) Mikhailovich 39,
  40, 67, 152, 204
Morozov, Savva Timofeevich (Savva the
  Second) xii, 6, 23, 91, 114, 229n14
  (Ch. I)
Morozov, Savva Vasilevich (Savva the First)
  7–10, 15, 51, 229n12, n15, n16 (Ch. I)
Morozov, Sergei Timofeevich 229n17
  (Ch. II)

Morozov, Timofei Savvich 9, 10, 12, 91,
  229n16 (Ch. I)
Morozov, Vasily 7
Morozov, Vikula Eliseevich 9, 178
Morozov, Yury 67
Morozov, Zakhar Savvich 10, 229n12, n14
  (Ch. I)
Morozova, Dariya 12, 12
Morozova, Elena 67
Morozova, Evdokiya Ivanovna (Little Dosya)
  110, 117, 118, 139, 152, 195, 196,
  239n14 (Ch. IX)
Morozova, Evdokiya Sergeevna (Dosya) (née
  Kladovshchikova) 82, 110, 116–19, 121–3,
  137, 139, 152, 173, 198, 237n12 (Ch. IX)
Morozova, Margarita (née Mamontova)
  (Margarita the Younger) 28, 30, 31,
  33–40, 42, 43, 47, 52, 54, 56, 57, 59, 63,
  65–8, 70, 71, 75, 91, 122, 127, 152–6,
  158, 159, 172, 180, 191, 203, 204,
  240n10, n22 (Ch. XII)
Morozova, Maria (née Simonova) 91
Morozova, Natalya 230n7 (Ch. III)
Morozova, Ulyana 8, 229n12 (Ch. I)
Morozova, Vavara (née Khludova) 7, 11–15,
  17–28, 30, 32, 35, 38–43, 50, 51, 53, 57,
  59, 63, 72, 73, 80, 89, 91, 118, 121, 122,
  125, 127, 131, 149, 152, 154, 158, 172,
  177, 178, 229n1, n22 (Ch. II)
Morozova, Vera (née Fedotova) 147, 151,
  240n4 (Ch. XII)
Morozova-Fidler, Maria (Marusya) 204
Morozova-Fiedler, Tatiana 42
Morrice, James 76, 174
Mozart, Wolfgang Amadeus 203
Mukhina, Vera 189, 243n21 (Ch. XV)
Munch, Edward 62, 206, 234n4 (Ch.VII)

Nemirovich-Danchenko Vladimir 26, 46
  231n4 (Ch. IV)
Nesterov, Mikhail 57
Nietzsche, Friedrich 153
Nosov, Vasily 120

O'Conor, Roderic 76
Orbeli, Iosif (Joseph) 224, 225
Osthaus, Karl Ernst 160
Ostroukhov, Ilya 10, 38, 50, 75, 64, 105,
  106, 128, 141, 158, 162, 166, 172, 173,
  178, 192, 206, 207, 213, 233n5 (Ch. V),
  234n7 (Ch. VII), 235n3 (Ch. VIII),
  237n10 (Ch. X), 240n18 (Ch. XII),
  241n1 (Ch. XIII), 242n3 (Ch. XIV),
  245n7 (Ch. XVII)

257

# INDEX

# INDEX